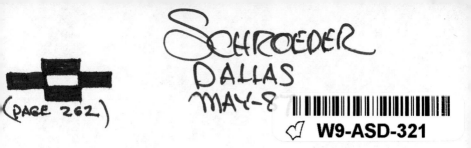

"WHAT IS MAN WITHOUT THE BEASTS?
IF ALL THE BEASTS WERE GONE, MEN
WOULD ALSO DIE - FROM GREAT
LONELINESS OF SPIRIT, FOR WHATEVER
HAPPENS TO THE BEAST ALSO HAPPENS
TO MAN. ALL THINGS ARE CONNECTED."
CHIEF SEATTLE

"IF YOU PUT A COYOTE ON A TENNIS
COURT WITH NOTHING IN THERE, HE
COULD HIDE BEHIND THE BALL!" A TRAPPER

A NOTE ABOUT THE AUTHOR

J. FRANK DOBIE was born on a ranch in Live Oak County, Texas, in 1888, and educated at Southwestern University (A.B., 1910) and Columbia University (M.A., 1914). Most of his teaching years were spent at the University of Texas: his first decade there was interrupted by service in World War I, and by two years at Oklahoma A & M College where he was head of the Department of English; he rejoined the Texas faculty in 1925, and was Professor of English there until 1947. During these years he also held a Guggenheim Fellowship and was Visiting Professor of American History at Cambridge University (England) where he was granted an honorary M. A. in 1944. Among his books are *A Vaquero of the Brush Country, Coronado's Children, On the Open Range, Tongues of the Monte, The Flavor of Texas, Apache Gold and Yaqui Silver, The Longhorns, The Mustangs, A Texan in England, Tales of Old-Time Texas, The Ben Lilly Legend, Guide to Life and Literature of the Southwest,* and *I'll Tell You a Tale.*

THE VOICE OF THE COYOTE

THE VOICE OF THE COYOTE

by J. FRANK DOBIE

Illustrated by
Olaus J. Murie

A Bison Book
University of Nebraska Press
Lincoln and London

Material from *Sierra Outpost* by Lila Lofberg and David Malcolmson is reprinted by permission of the publishers, Duell, Sloan and Pearce, Inc. Copyright 1941 by Lila Lofberg and David Malcolmson.

Material from *Zuñi Folk Tales* by Frank Hamilton Cushing is reprinted by permission of Alfred A. Knopf, Inc. Copyright 1931 by Alfred A. Knopf, Inc.

Material from *Talking to the Moon* by John Joseph Mathews is reprinted by permission of the University of Chicago Press.

First Bison Book printing, February 1961

Most recent printing shown by first digit below:

9   10

Bison Book edition, reproduced from the Sixth Printing, published by arrangement with Little, Brown and Company.

TO

BERTHA McKEE DOBIE

Through the years I have derived as much from her habit of clear thinking as from her particular criticisms. She is the most incisive and the most concretely constructive critic I have ever known. Her sense of form and fitness and her precision in details have gone into every book I have written. Her cultivated sympathy for nature has enriched this one especially.

INTRODUCTION: COYOTE AND MAN

ORIGINALLY I INTENDED to make this book only a modest collection of coyote tales which their tellers had delighted me in telling, and which I delight in telling in my own way. Treatment of the animal's characteristics was to serve as a kind of preface. Gradually natural history took dominance over tale. In the year 1921 I began setting down some things I heard about Señor Coyote and making notes on his record in print, but a full quarter of a century before that, while I was listening to the crickets behind the baseboards against the rock walls of our ranch home in Live Oak County, Texas, and to my mother's sweet voice, the coyote was talking to me. I did not at the time know that he was talking to me, but he was. As I have gone along with the tales and the natural history, I have come to the conclusion that nobody can understand either without some knowledge of the other.

Sympathy is equally requisite. Not even the most scientific mammalogist can comprehend the whole animal without hospitality towards the stuff of dreams that this more than mere mammal has influenced human minds to weave around him. Hospitality is not to be expected from those individuals who hear in the rhythms of nature only what Tennyson's Northern Farmer heard in the hoofbeats of his horse:

Proputty, proputty, proputty — that's what I 'ears 'em saäy.

Sympathy for wild animals, sympathy that is intellectual as much as emotional, has not been a strong element in the traditional American way of life. "I was wrathy to kill a bear," David Crockett said, and that is essentially all one learns about bears from the mightiest of frontier bear-hunters — except that he killed a hundred and five in one season and immediately thereafter got elected to the Tennessee legislature on his reputation. How familiar the iterated remark: "I thought I might see something and so took [or taken] along my gun" — as if no enjoyment or other good could come from seeing a wild animal without killing it. Buffalo Bill derived his name from the fact that he excelled in killing buffaloes, not from knowing anything about them except as targets or from conveying any interest in them as a part of nature. While Zebulon Pike and two of his explorers were lying in the grass on the plains of Kansas, November 1, 1806, a band of "cabrie" (antelopes), he records, "came up among our horses to satisfy their curiosity. We could not resist the temptation of killing two, although we had plenty of meat." Any restraint put upon killing was from motives other than sympathy. On one occasion Pike prevented his men from shooting at game "not merely because of the scarcity of ammunition but, as I conceived, the law of morality forbade it also." During the whole of a rainy day shortly after this moral act, "we employed ourselves," Pike says, "in reading the Bible, Pope's Essays, and in pricking on our arms with India ink some characters."

[x]

In *The Texan Ranger,* published in London, 1866, Captain Flack, fresh from the sporting fields of the Southwest, describes the game of slaughtering thus: The men of one community lined up against those of another to see which group could kill the most game during a day's shooting. A squirrel and a rabbit counted one point each, a wild turkey five points, a deer ten points. The number of points scored in the particular contest described by Captain Flack totaled 3470.

These are not instances of eccentricity but of the representative American way, until only yesterday, of looking at wild animals. Often while reading the chronicles of frontiersmen one does come upon an interesting observation concerning wildlife, but it is likely to be prefaced by some such statement as, "I didn't have a gun, and so I thought I might as well see what happened." The majority of country-dwellers in western America today would consider it necessary to apologize for not killing a coyote they happened to see doing something unusual. This traditional killer attitude is a part of the traditional exploitation of the land. A few early farmers conserved the soil — George Washington was one — but they were stray oddities. A few pioneers had naturalistic interests, but any revelation of such interests branded the holder of them as being peculiar or even undemocratic. The mass rule then, as now, was: Conform and be dull.

In 1846 a young Englishman named George Frederick Ruxton landed at Vera Cruz, equipped himself with pack mules, rode to Mexico City, then up through "the Republic" to El Paso, across New Mexico into Colorado, where he spent the winter, and thence back to "civilization," which seemed to him "flat and stale," on the Missouri River. He carried home a chronicle that remains one of the most delightful and illuminating books of travel that North America has occasioned — *Adventures in Mexico and the Rocky Mountains.*

In Colorado, as Ruxton tells in the book, he made acquaintance with a large gray wolf. He had just shot two antelopes. Why more than one was necessary for a meal for him and his half-breed guide, he does not say. Anyhow, the bounty left for the wolf attached him to the provider. For days he followed Ruxton. At camp every evening, he would "squat down quietly at a little distance." Sometimes Ruxton saw his eyes gleaming in the light of the campfire. After the men had rolled up in their blankets, the lobo would "help himself to anything lying about." In the morning, as soon as the men broke camp, the lobo, in Ruxton's words, "took possession and quickly ate up the remnants of supper and some little extras I always took care to leave him. Then he would trot after us, and if we halted for a short time to adjust the mule-packs or water the animals, he sat down quietly until we resumed our march. But when I killed an antelope and was in the act of butchering it, he gravely looked on, or loped round and round, licking his jaws in a state of evident self-gratulation. I had him twenty times a day within reach of my rifle, but we became such old friends that I never dreamed of molesting him."

No American contemporary of Ruxton's on the frontier would have resisted killing that wolf. He would have said that he was killing it because the wolf killed; he would have said that the wolf was cruel, sneaking, cowardly. Actually, he would have killed it because he was "wrathy to kill." It did not strike Ruxton that the wolf was cruel — at least not more cruel than man. It struck Ruxton that the wolf was interesting; he had towards it the sympathy that comes from civilized perspective.

This sympathy is found in the two extremes of society — savages and people with cultivated minds and sensibilities. A subsequent chapter treats of Indian harmony with nature, the feeling of brotherhood towards the coyote and other animals. "We be of one blood, ye and I," is the call of the jungle folk. "And what is man that he should not run with his brothers?" asked Mowgli of *The Jungle Book*. "Surely the wolves are my brothers." The

American Indian's sympathy for fellow animals was not sentiment or superstition; nor was it an expression of intellectual curiosity; it was a part of his harmony with nature.

Mary Austin, who perhaps more than any other interpreter of the Southwest has sensed the spiritual values in nature, said: "No man has ever really entered into the heart of a country until he has adopted or made up myths about its familiar objects." A reading of *The Land of Little Rain, The Land of Journeys' Ending* and other books of hers leads one to conclude that by "myths" she meant sympathy derived from knowledge and understanding. "The best thing we get out of any study of animal life is the feel of it." This feel, this sympathy, reaches its climax among the civilized in such diverse natures as tart Thoreau of Walden, sweet Saint Francis of Assisi, patrician Grey of Fallodon, penetrating and wistful Hudson of Far Away and Long Ago, scientific Jefferson, and plain William Wright of the bears, who, watching a great grizzly looking out for long whiles from the top of a snowy mountain, concluded that he was "enjoying the scenery." Among the wise, this civilized sympathy infuses knowledge. It is a kind of cultivated gentleness. It is foreign to harsh and boisterous frontiers and comes after many of the wild creatures to which it is directed have been destroyed.

I confess to a sympathy for the coyote that has grown until it lives in the deepest part of my nature. Yet sympathy is not enough for any study of natural history, any more than good intentions are enough for the executive of a powerful nation. I am not a naturalist or a biologist, but I have, I think, examined about all the scientific knowledge in print concerning the coyote. Seeking to make the observations of out-of-doors men my own, I have found a few such men who seem to me to know more about coyotes than most scientific writers. The garnered experiences, always freely given, of many men in the field have, in a way, offset the limitations of my own experiences. One of my minuses is not having met coyote men in Canada and Alaska, as I have met and gained from them in Mexico and through the Western states — but the coyote is a coyote anywhere you find him.

Some parts of what I have written may not be respectfully received by academic biologists who leave out the most real of all realities — imagination. History, it has been said, is the prolonged shadows of a few individuals. Tales and other lore that make up whole chapters towards the end of this book are the shadows that the slight creature called coyote has projected through the imaginations of people living with him for centuries.

I write of a species; many individual coyotes over long periods of time, scattered over continental vastness, play their parts in the record. They and the species of which they are "specimens" have somehow amalgamated for me into a single character of protean characteristics, living without aging through dateless generations — a character neither moral nor immoral; utterly devoid of a Karamazov conscience abridging the tragedy of the whole human race, though capable of voicing poignant tragedy; never noble, though often as fantastical as noble Cyrano de Bergerac. I do not suppose that Brother Coyote will mount into such an identity for my readers, but for me the record has developed into a kind of biography.

The biography of any individual, unless of an absolute recluse, is full of the interplay between him and other persons. The coyote was never a recluse. The impact upon him by wandering tribes, by civilizations that built pyramids in the Valley of Teotihuacán and perished, and then by inheritors of European cultures exploiting and adapting themselves to pristine lands, has been marked. The life history of the coyote consists not only of objective facts about the animal as an animal but of the picturesque and emphatic reality of his own impact on human beings. It has been my purpose to realize a being of nature with all of that being's meanings to associated humanity. Like the dog, the horse and the fox of Europe, the coyote cannot be disassociated from man and remain whole.

"A naturalist cannot exaggerate consciously," W. H. Hudson wrote; "if he is capable of unconscious exaggeration, then he is no naturalist." If in reading this life of a species, some adult confuses proven coyote cunning with impossible ruses attributed to the coyote tribe, I shall question his perceptive abilities; even though not a naturalist, I have tried to make the distinctions clear at all times.

The important debates are not concerning animal behavior but concerning the animal's proper ecological and economic place in man's world. Most of the land in which the coyote is most at home never will be thickly settled or intensively cultivated. Nature has said so. One can drive fifteen hundred miles from Brownsville at the mouth of the Rio Grande to San Diego, California, and be out of sight of range country only for short distances. One can drive two thousand miles from Oklahoma City to Seattle and with only minor skips be in grazing lands and mountains all the way. All these spaces of plains, brush, hills, mountains and woods are favorable to and are favored by native wildlife. To what extent should the coyote be allowed to continue here, also in Canada, Alaska and on south into Central America?

Biologists within the United States Fish and Wildlife Service (formerly the Biological Survey) and biologists outside are generally not in agreement. On one hand, there is the relentless indictment by the late E. A. Goldman, Senior Biologist in the United States Department of Agriculture, of the coyote as "the archpredator of our times," deserving of no quarter. On the other hand, there are moderators exemplified by E. Raymond Hall, whose *Mammals of Nevada*, published in 1947, summarizes arguments for the coyote's place in his own country.

The American Society of Mammalogists is on record opposing wholesale poisoning of coyotes. State game departments, ranchmen and farmers have generally co-operated with federal "control," though their opinions vary on how severe or how limited this control should be. Nobody is against protecting human interests from brute destruction. Many people are against wholesale destruction. The interrelations between one form of life and multitudinous other forms of life are so complex that annihilation of the coyote will not settle matters for the rest of us any more than annihilating the people of one nation will bring peace, plenty and freedom to the peoples of the other nations. In the chapter on "Adaptation" I have gone more specifically into coyote ecology.

Human values, intellectual and spiritual, are not invariably coincident with economic values. Every national park, zoological garden and natural history museum in the land attests to this truth as respects wildlife. Tourists do not go west primarily to lodge in hotels and tourist courts. If chambers of commerce in Western states that strive for tourist money had imagination, they would arrange hearing places for those who would like to hear coyote voices, just as the national parks provide visible bears; and they would both lure and educate tourists by publishing a truth thus finely expressed by H. E. Anthony of the American Museum of Natural History:

"To many who have heard the ecstatic little prairie wolf greet their camp-fire from out of the dusk, or have arisen at break of dawn and heard his frenzied hymn to the sun, a West without the coyote seems colorless and flat."

As Tolstoy said, there are questions "put only in order that they may remain forever questions." Putting on the spectacles of science in expectation of finding the answer to everything looked at signifies inner blindness. All of the ecological, biological and other logical studies that public bureaus and private enterprise may forward still will not bring those "authentic tidings of invisible things" that the lifted voice of the coyote brings in the early evening while lightning bugs soften the darkness under the trees, or that the voice of some other belonger to the rhythms of the earth brings in a simple tale of Brother Coyote.

CONTENTS

[xix]

THE VOICE OF THE COYOTE

I · "THE FATHER OF SONG–MAKING"

IT IS LATE AFTERNOON on a small ranch down in the Brush Country of Texas. The center of activities is between a quadrangle of rail corrals and a wooden windmill over a hand-dug, rock-curbed well. The main doer in the activities is the owner of the ranch; four or five Mexican men help him. Before daylight tomorrow morning they will be riding. They have just butchered a beef — which to them never meant a calf or a year-ling, but a grown steer. Dark of hue and strong with a gamelike aroma, quarters of the beef hang from crossbeams of the wind-mill tower. A tightly stretched rope is hung with strips of meat which two or three days of sunshine and dry wind will cure into jerky. The hide, hair side down, is laid across the corral fence. The big paunch and the guts — but not the ones the Mexicans will cook into *menudo* — have been dragged out into mesquite

[3]

bushes not far away. One — two — three — six buzzards are already circling overhead, very slowly, and more are sweeping in. Darkness will come before they and their gathering fellows can feast; and within a short time after dark there will be nothing left for them to feast upon.

Off from the corrals maybe four hundred yards are two Mexican houses. The women from these houses are already stewing meat and grinding corn to make tamales. In a fine grove of live oaks, up the hill in the opposite direction, is the rock house in which the rancher and his family live. About dark as they sit at a supper of fried steak with hot biscuits and brown gravy, the rancher says, "Well, we'll have singing tonight."

The speaker was my father. The particular beef-killing day I am remembering was forty-odd years ago. Fresh meat and singing went together in the same place forty or fifty years before that; they still go together. After a group of vaqueros — as Mexican cowboys in the border country are called — fill up on fresh beef in the evening, they are going to sing, and if they have been freshly brought together for a cow hunt, they will sing more. When coyotes smell meat after dark, they also are going to sing.

"Well, we'll have singing tonight." We did not have to wait. High-wailing and long-drawn-out, the notes of native *versos* came over the night air. Perhaps they were about Gregorio Cortez on his little brown horse, perhaps about the young vaquero who did not come back with his comrades from the trail to Kansas, perhaps about the mulberry-blue bull with the goring horns. Whatever the theme, the wild notes seemed to go up to the stars. And as they reached their highest pitch, a chorus of coyote voices joined them. When, at the end of the first ballad, the human voices dimmed into silence, the coyote voices grew higher; then all but one howler ceased. We heard a laugh, and one lusty vaquero yelled out, *"Cantad, amigos!"* — "Sing, friends!" The friends responded with renewed gusto.

For a time the antiphonies challenged and cheered each other,

now converging, now alternately lapsing. The vaquero singing, on high notes especially, could hardly be distinguished from the coyote singing. Mexican vaqueros are Indian in blood, inheritance and instinct. Anybody who has listened long and intimately to the cries of coyotes seeming to express remembrance of something lost before time began must recognize those identical cries in the chants of Plains Indians and the homemade songs of Mexicans.* English-speakers living with the coyote seldom refer to his voicing as "singing"; to them it is "yelping," "howling," "barking"; but to the vaquero people it is nearly always *cantando*.

Back in the golden days, Adelina Patti went to San Francisco, sang, captured the world, and at a reception met courtly old General Vallejo. After gracious compliment, he added, "But, Señorita, you must hear our own California soprano."

"Who can this be?"

"*Señorita, el coyote.*"

One summer night, standing by my dead campfire, I listened to a Mexican riding along a trail that passed about a hundred yards away. He was alternately singing and whistling while two or three far-scattered coyotes, first one and then another, responded. They sounded as if they were traveling with him. I heard him a mile away at first; he passed, and as long as he was within hearing he and the coyotes kept on sending up their voices. Between the poles of the earth there seemed to be nothing but those notes of lone man and lone brush wolf.

* "The slow rhythm of the drums began and from each little fire came Apaches, singly and in groups, to gather in a great circle. Then came an Apache voice in song rising above the sound of the drums. As the voice rose and fell, it was not unlike that of the singer's brother, the coyote." — Ross Santee, *Apache Land*, Charles Scribner's Sons, New York, 1947, 26.

"Gradually, as the late evening drew on, the group of twelve dancers [Taos Indians] accelerated their tempo and cried out in sharp, wild '*Ayis*,' like coyotes barking." — Malvina Hoffman, *Heads and Tales*, Garden City, New York, 1943, 393.

"I often heard this song of lament in night journeys in Mexico. It must be of Indian origin. On first hearing it, I fancied it, at a distance, to be the howling of [coyotes]." — Julius Froebel, *Seven Years' Travel in Central America*, etc., London, 1859, 244-245.

The sound belongs to night characteristically, but not exclusively. A daytime bark is likely to be more sporadic; often, also, the nighttime bark is sporadic. One misty January afternoon my wife and I listened to three coyotes on the Texas coast for at least an hour. At first they were disembodied voices, and I thought that the leading voice was coming from some bushes near by until Mrs. Dobie discovered the coyote about half a mile away, across a dry laguna. He sat on his haunches and with nose pointed skyward wailed and wailed; at intervals between the wailings, two other coyotes yipped, now together, now separately. When we located them, they were a hundred or more yards from the wailer, but before long all three were idling near each other. The yippers did not sit on their haunches to bark, and their voices were finer. The mating season was approaching; whether these two responders were females nobody could assert. It is generally thought that the long, hoarse howls come from males only.

Coyotes do not at all confine their voicings to the mating season. They are heard all the year round, but perhaps more in the fall and early winter. They are comparatively quiet at pupping time. Hunger no more than sex urge seems to motivate their music. I am positive that they sing for pleasure and out of sociable feelings as well as, sometimes, from feelings of loneliness.

"Prairie tenor," some call *Canis latrans*. He does not bark like a dog, but he barks. He yelps as well as wails. Often his falsetto yips, coming fast like machine-gun fire, make him comical and familiar. Then he is the Laughing Philosopher of the Plains, cheering the bored and amusing the witty. Where he is unhounded by man — civilized man filled with lust to kill and with morbid righteousness against any other animal that kills * — he

* This holier-than-thou attitude of hunters towards other preyers on game is probably more pronounced in the United States than in any other country. It is a part of the self-righteous American attitude towards other countries. Combination of the attitudes is exemplified in a letter signed by H. G. Stell

goes about delighting in all the plays along his Broadway. As the Zuñi Indians tell it, when he sees the blackbirds dancing, he is beside himself with joy; when he hears the ravens laugh, he sticks his tail straight up and laughs out of sheer sympathy. Sometimes his voice is as idle as the cricket's chirp; now it fills a valley like mist,* carrying whoever listens to "old, unhappy, far-off things" and to the elemental tragedy of life.

According to Comanche legend, certain tribesmen long ago learned the coyote language through a boy who, while little and lost, was adopted by a family of coyotes. He learned to talk with them before hunters saw him run into a den, smoked him out and brought him back to his family. A few Comanches can still understand what coyotes say.[1]

John Gould, who lives at Wichita Falls, near the Texas-Oklahoma line, tells this story. "Oliver Poemoceah was my good friend for many years. He was a leader among the Comanches of Oklahoma, especially active in affairs of the American Native Church, which uses peyote † in some of its rites. In February, 1946, a heart attack took him to a hospital in Lawton. Before long his friend Ernest Mihecoby visited him and said, 'Last night two coyotes came close to my house and howled. They told me that you will get better.'

"Soon afterward, Oliver showed decided improvement. On March 15, Mihecoby made him a second visit. 'The coyotes have

that was published on the editorial page of the *Dallas Morning News*, November 1, 1947. In part the letter reads: "The white-headed eagle, called 'bald eagle' by early ornithologists, was chosen as our national bird because it gains an honest living. It is a fish-eater. The golden eagle, on the contrary, is a bird of prey [as if fish were not prey also, despite the fish-on-Friday superstition]. The founders of our republic wanted no predator eagle as an American emblem, though many European nations took it as a device."

* Dear reader, can you decide which is preferable here: *fills a valley like mist*, or "overflows the vale profound"? Vales and coyotes do not precisely go together, and not many people who associate with coyotes carry Wordsworth in their hearts, but what a richness his figure brings to the spirit!

† Peyote grows in restricted areas along the Texas border and in Mexico. The dried peyote buttons are now eaten by Indians clear into Canada. The eaters have visions characterized by bizarre colors.

come to my house again and spoken,' he said. 'This time I could not interpret their message.'

" 'I know what that means,' said Oliver Poemoceah. 'It means I am going to die.'

"He died that night."

The coyote, it seems, cannot speak English. He speaks many Indian languages fluently — for he is fluent beyond all other four-footed creatures of the Western Hemisphere. He also speaks Mexican-Spanish; pure Castilian, not at all, and only now and then a word of what some call the American language. The English-American speakers have never taught him any language but that of lead, steel and strychnine.

"Nothing so predisposes men to understand as to know that they are understood." Grey of Fallodon might have extended the philosophy to coyotes — and other creatures. The coyote people must have sensed long ago that the human aborigines of their ranges understood them. The chief celebration of the Yuma Indians is a wail for the death of their god Kukumat: "Midnight star is rising in the east and gives its light. Night-Hawk and Coyote wail." When the ceremony was first held, according to Yuman tradition, "a strange noise was heard in the air just as the midnight star appeared. It was the Night-Hawk, who knew the time and began to sing. Coyote heard the song and tried to imitate it. The mourners caught the melody and have sung it ever since." [2]

For centuries the coyotes have been telling the Navajo Indians something glad. The Yebichi dance that they chant in the fall is the "dawn child's" song of happiness: "Just when morning is coming on, I give my call. . . . Right out of my mouth I call. By means of darkness I call. I call when it is quite dark. With the aid of my tail I call. At dawn, you know also, I call. At sunrise I call." [3]

The Seri Indians, whom Coyote in the time of beginnings taught to brush the thorns off cactus pears and eat them, sing:

The coyote is happy in the moonlight.
He sings a song to the moon —
While he dances.
And he jumps far away —
While he dances.[4]

At the day's ending when all children should go to sleep, a Mexican mother of the border country, sitting at the door of her *jacal* of wattled walls daubed with adobe and roofed with thatched bear grass, relates to her little one a *cuento* of the coyote song.

"Listen with attention," she will say. "Can you not hear the plaint of some lone coyote in the distance? Listen."

It may be that the child hears a coyote; it may be that none is calling. Anyhow, the mother continues. "At night, my little one, the coyotes come out into the open and seek their food. Always at the coming, you will hear the leader calling for his mate. She answers. Soon afterwards, you hear many quick, short yelps. The other coyotes have gathered about the leader and are playing a game. They form a circle, and as they run around and around, they try to catch each other's tails. They go *yip, yip, yip, yip-ee*.

"Then the leader says, 'Let's go to the blue corn.'

" 'What for?' says the mate.

" 'To make *atole* (corn mush),' says the leader.

" 'With what will you stir it?' says the mate.

" 'With my tail, with my tail,' says the leader.

" 'It is not of bone, it is not of bone,' says the mate.

" 'Yes, it is of bone, yes, it is of bone,' says the leader.

"Now the other coyotes sing in a chorus, all together: 'It is not of bone — yes, it is of bone; it is not of bone — yes, it is of bone; no-yes, no-yes.' And around and around they run, trying to catch each other by the tail."

By now the little one has let the "no" and the "yes" of its own chant die into sleep.[5]

Through senses, particularly the sense of smell, far more apprehensive than man's, coyotes receive sensations that man cannot detect — and they report. Being closer to them in sharpness of the senses than civilized man, primitive man understands the report better — or thinks he does. Anywhere between the Gulf of Mexico and the Pacific Ocean where coyotes talk, people of the soil listen for their forecastings of the weather. Many listeners are without faith, but believers and unbelievers alike will regard a voice of hope, a promise of benefits. In time of drouth the coyote is a prodigal promiser of rain.

After the First World War, while I was managing Los Olmos Ranch on the Nueces River — in the Brush Country — I came to know well an old Mexican *pastor* (goatherder) named Toribio. He wandered alone with two dogs and about seven hundred Mexican goats out in the big pastures and camped in bleak solitude by a treeless tank. All he knew was goats, goat dogs, thorned brush, medicinal teas from native plants, coyotes, rattlesnakes, paisanos and other things belonging to the soil. He had been born in peonage in Mexico and had been brought up with goats. He was lithe and high-strung. The spur-ringing vaqueros considered him crazy. When, once every six months, kidding time brought Toribio and his flock to ranch headquarters, the commissary (with not more than a hundred dollars' worth of goods), the houses and a half-dozen half-active people excited him as traveling to Washington to visit the Great White Father used to excite Indian chiefs. Periodically, I carried provisions to his camp.

One summer evening towards sundown, I drove my car up to it with a bucket of sorghum molasses for Don Toribio's sweet tooth. The goats of many colors were already in their brush pen, excepting two or three pet nannies that he milked. Eager as always for any break in monotony, the *pastor* was voluble. With antique respect, combined with natural dignity and devoid of fawning deference, he always called me *Amo* — Master. It was terribly dry that year, and, of course, I lamented the drouth.

"Have no fear, Master," he chirruped. "Without doubt, it is going to rain, and how soon! The coyotes are singing now every morning after sunrise, and they are singing on the hills. Do not deceive yourself, Master. When the coyotes sing in this manner, it will rain without fail. They speak clearly."

He went on to explain, as I have heard a hundred times, that the usual howling after sunset and before daylight is no sign. The coyotes must howl after the sun is up — the higher up, the better the sign. Moreover, they must howl from the hills and not down in the swales. Another Mexican, whose fountain of hope had been drained dry by many drouths, said, "The coyotes sing when even the prickly pear is shriveled, and they sing when the frogs are thanking God for the water they swim in. All coyotes are liars."

"What," asked wise Don Alberto Guajardo from below the border, "does the coyote announce to his kind by those notes distinctly different from the accustomed ones of early morning?" For many listeners, the quality and not the timing of the singing expresses coyote wisdom. He yips for good weather. He has the bull voice, deep and lonely, to announce bad weather. There is a saying, "*Cuando llora el coyote, se va á llover; cuando grita, se seca.*" (When the coyote wails, it is going to rain; when he shouts, it will be dry.) What he likes best is clear, cool nights. Then it's "Whoopee, boys, we're going twenty miles tonight."

On the plains of Nebraska far to the north, people listen to the little announcer. "Presently," wrote Willa Cather in the prose-song of her own prairies, *My Ántonia*, "in one of those sobbing intervals between the blasts, the coyotes tuned up with their whining howl; one, two, three, then all together — to tell us that winter was coming."

Jim Bridger, Bill Williams, Old Rube, Sol Silver, Black Harris, Broken-Hand Fitzpatrick, Uncle Dick Wootten, Grizzly Hugh

Glass, Blackfoot Smith and the other Mountain Men lifted hair, danced their own scalp dances, lived for months at a time on nothing but meat, sometimes eating liver for bread, and were, in fact, "the white savages of the West." They absorbed Indian beliefs as well as knowledge. Most of them had strong faith in "medicine wolves," called also "medicine dogs." Some early travelers reported these animals to be "supernatural," "phantom wolves"; others described them as a special species of feist-like size resembling the jack rabbit. The medicine wolf was nothing else than the coyote.

The Indians, wrote Father De Smet, regard it "as a sort of Manitou. They watch its yelpings during the night, and the superstitious conjurers pretend to understand and interpret them. According to the loudness, frequency and other modifications of these yelpings, they interpret that either friends or foes approach." [6] Osborne Russell, a trapper who lived among the Snakes (Shoshonies) for nine years and became as familiar with their tongue as he was with the classical poets who solaced him in solitudes, had "often seen this prophecy tolerably accurately fulfilled and again as often fail, but a superstitious Indian will always account for the failure." [7]

The attention paid to the howling was not necessarily superstitious at all. In the wilderness, one species is warned by the actions of another. The dull-eyed buffalo utilized as sentinel the nimble and sensitive antelope. The antelope doe heeded the cry of the curlew in flight near her fawn hidden in the grass; the curlew's cry might mean the approach of a coyote. The piñon jay, called by Mexicans *amigo del venado* (friend of the deer), by its sharp cries alerts the buck against stalkers with guns. The wild turkey takes note of every squirrel bark, every rustle of leaves made by the armadillo, every caw of the crow. Camped at night where any movement meant a possible enemy, frontiersmen had all their senses startled when they heard a mule snort or a horse suddenly stop grazing. Mules especially could smell Indians far off. The cry in the night of the killdeer, that bird which never lights on bush or tree, and which always cries out its shrill note when disturbed on the ground, was a sentinel's warning. It might mean that only a skunk was about; it could mean Comanches.

No wonder that the Mountain Men as well as the tribesmen regarded the cry of the medicine wolf. "Watch all signs and be especially on guard when you don't see or hear any sign" was the maxim. It was not the mere presence of prairie wolves that indicated Indians; on the contrary, Jim Bridger and others persisted, "Indians were rarely near when many wolves were present." [8] It would be according to nature for coyotes to howl in a particular way upon the approach of Indians. I have ridden with hunters who swore they could tell by the bark whether their hounds were trailing a wildcat or a panther. The bark of a dog at the approach of his master differs from his bark at the approach of a stranger. So, to Mountain Man as well as Indian, the coyote was a kind of watch dog. "Round the camp, during the night, the cayeute [sic] keeps unremitting watch," wrote George Frederick Ruxton.

The familiarity that existed between Indians and wolves before the lethal white man made all animals afeared can now hardly be realized. In his noble books on the Blackfoot and Cheyenne Indians, George Bird Grinnell emphasizes the easy relationship. If Indians "pass close to some wolves," he says, "these will bark at the people, talking to them. Some man will call out to them, 'No, I will not give you my body to eat, but I will give you the body of some one else if you will go along with us.' " [9] While James Willard Schultz, as he tells, was living with the Blackfeet, he and his young wife rode out on the plain one fall day to hunt. She was so happy that she kept singing. "Out of a coulee rushed a small band of buffalo, loping westward; a lone coyote also appeared, sat down on his haunches, and stared at us. 'Hai-ya, little brother,' said Nat-ah-ki, 'are you also happy?'

Then she continued, 'Of course, he is happy. His fur is so thick and warm that he does not fear the coming cold, and he has plenty, oh, always plenty, of food.' " [10]

For all his littleness and for all the abuse heaped upon him — abuse that long ago became a convention among English-speaking people — the coyote has aroused the imaginations of people associated with him more than the biggest and most powerful bulls of the biggest herds ever have. "My first memories," says a grandmother, "are of the times when we lived on the ranch and my mother would say, 'Drink your milk or the old coyote will get it.' I have heard other mothers say to children, do so and so or the kitty or the dog or something else will get it, but coyotes were more real to us than anything else alive."

And it is the voice of the coyote, more than all else, that has had this effect. It arrests the attention of even the lethargic, and for others revives the dews of forgotten mornings. Down in Guatemala the *gente* say that the coyote talks to the fences and they let him through. When barbed wire came, the coyote could not at first make himself understood, but before long the barbed wire fences understood also and let him through.

Speculative out-of-doors livers in many places have arrived at fantastical credences about this voice. A stolid hunter tells about a coyote he sighted from horseback one day and chased across open country into high grass, where it disappeared, not far ahead. Keeping his eye on the spot, he galloped to it, but upon arriving could see nothing of the animal. Then he heard "a hollow-sounding, far-away bark." He could not figure out how the coyote had gone any distance in so short a time, nor why it would be barking anyway. He kept on looking and soon spied the coyote belly-crawling through the grass, not far off. It had tried to outwit him, he said, by "barking into a badger hole," thus making that faraway, hollow sound. No, he never actually saw a coyote barking into a hole, but he "knew" about the trick. He also "knew" that the coyote produces a "very queer kind of bark" by placing his lower jaw against the ground and putting his foot into his mouth while he exercises his lungs. No less fantastic are folk theories that in order to "break up" his voice the coyote vibrates his lower jaw from side to side while barking, and that he makes his chest shiver by stamping the ground with rigid forelegs.

An Arizona rancher solemnly told me — and his belief is a common absurdity — that when a single coyote sounds as if he were three or five, he is yapping with his nose poked into a little hole he has dug in the earth. Who does know what precise arrangement in the coyote's laryngotracheal mechanism enables him to scatter, shatter, multiply and "place" his voice so deftly? Among the aboriginal dialects one name for this supreme ventriloquist might well be I-Am-Many. Here may be a basis for research by acousticians and phoneticians.

For five years Ross Graves, trapper at Fort Davis, Texas, had a pet coyote named Ike. Ross Graves loves to play the fiddle. Many a night, alone in camp, he would play it while Ike howled. "High C on the fiddle would really make Ike cut loose. Low notes did not seem to appeal to him. The chopped-up notes of his barking were not all in the same key; some were in a higher pitch, some in a lower. He seemed to control them in his throat altogether.* Ike did not have to have a fiddle to set him going. When the weather was going to change, he would let out a long, lonesome howl followed by a few yips."

I used to think that there could be nothing to the ancient belief, probably of Indian origin, that coyotes bark into each other's tails. I still don't know. Louis Martin, an old trapper located in the Big Bend of Texas, is expert at calling coyotes up

* "I have seen the coyote bark and howl quite often when in a trap. They always stood on all four legs, sticking the nose up towards the sky at about a 45 degree angle or better, with the mouth partly open. As they do not move the jaws while barking or howling, I believe the different notes originate altogether in the throat." — Arthur Meile, trapper, Valentine, Nebraska, in a letter, April 1947, to Fred Dille of Nogales, Arizona.

by imitating their voices. One time, well hidden, he called up three not yet fully grown. When he saw them coming, as he describes, they were strung out in a line that did not keep regular, each of the two behind the leader snapping on the tail of the coyote in front, "whining and laughing." They were playing and would go round and round. Anyone who has watched frolicsome pups tagging each other by the tail or snapping at their own tails can get an idea of coyote antics. Joe Hill says that many a time he has through glasses watched two coyotes "spinning round like a top," maybe clockwise for a while, then counterclockwise, throwing their heads up this way and that way, barking. In their song of the Coyote Dance the Seri Indians describe another posture:

> When the coyote is very hungry
> He sings his song —
> With the nose on the ground
> Running round and round.[11]

While chasing their prey, coyotes do not characteristically bark, but just as some dogs are silent on a hot trail, some coyotes give mouth. When he was a young man chousing cattle out of the canyons of the Devil's River country, Ray Brotherton saw two coyotes barking while chasing a jack rabbit. Years later, standing on a bluff overlooking the Rio Grande, Ray Brotherton's son heard coyote barking across the river and presently saw a jack rabbit come into view with two coyotes not far behind. They kept on barking and cutting across circles until they passed out of sight. The running bark is uncommon and is yippy.

Many a coyote sends up a victory song at night after killing meat. The reply from far away seems to express a wish rather than jubilation. Coyotes belonging to the same group or pair often range miles apart. Weather and lay of the land favoring, a man can hear one five miles away. There is no telling how far one of them can hear another. Moreover, they seem at times to relay signals.

It is claimed that coyotes have regular "choir lofts," particular spots on elevated places, where they go for vespers. Perhaps they have. Many animals are as habitual in conduct as human beings: you can set your watch by the regularity with which a road-runner on summer days comes to water; a buck, before the running season starts, has a very definite range and lying-up place; a sparrow hawk will day after day perch on a wire between two certain telephone poles; elk prefer a certain plot of ground on which to shed their horns; undisturbed bears use the same den year after year, generation after generation.

To locate precisely an unseen barking coyote is often very difficult. An ear that can aim directly to a dog barking in woods or to a doe whistle-snorting in a thicket may be vague or entirely off on any coyote sound. Here is Hamlet's "old mole" shifting, *hic et ubique,* in the earth so fast. The barker is the elusive light of the friar's lantern translated into sound, the will-o'-the-wisp prestidigitated into voice. The superstition that a howling coyote turns at night into a ghost that no bullet can harm is but a manner of saying that the howler makes a target as insubstantial as Macbeth's air-drawn daggers.

Sometimes just before daylight a coyote will bark very near a camper; as light comes, he retreats, his voice receding. Every morning J. W. Montgomery was hearing "laughing" out from his solitary camp in the brush. One dawn while he was drinking coffee — and the peace of his mesquite fire — he heard such an unusual laughter that he decided to investigate. He judged the laughers to be about three hundred yards off. After he had walked fully half a mile, the wind favoring him, he came upon a strange scene.

He could see clearly across a prickly pear flat. There ten or twelve coyotes were moving away from him, abreast of each other. Each was *waw-waw-wawing* in a different voice at the big rat nests in the pear, though no coyote stopped to dig, and apparently no coyote was catching anything. After a while the whole pack, evidently one large family led by their mother, disappeared in tall grass. Another time Montgomery came upon a big lone coyote, a male, digging into a rat's nest. He would dig a while, then look up and *waw-waw*.

Many listeners have expressed themselves on coyote voicings; more precisely than anyone else almost, Archer B. Gilfillan has observed technique. "The peculiar thing about the coyote song," he says, "is that when two coyotes are singing a duet, as they are very fond of doing, they do not bark haphazardly or in unison, but they catch each other up with lightning-like quickness, so that two coyotes will produce such a torrent of barks that the uninitiated would swear there was a large pack of them. On a cold winter's night you will hear this two-piece orchestra tuning up on some distant butte, and then miles away in another direction you will hear an answering chorus; then the cry will be picked up in still other directions, until it seems as if the whole landscape were tossing this weird melody up towards the cold and unappreciative stars." [12]

But there are many ways of singing the tribal lay. Often it is made up of only a few solitary yips — and ends. Sometimes, without preliminary tuning up, the "polyglot serenade" will open from all sides at once, as instantaneously as a herd of three thousand sleeping steers can jump to their feet and break into headlong stampede. Describing camp experiences on the Plains about 1870, W. E. Webb wrote:

"The coyotes will steal in from all directions and sit quietly down on their haunches in a circle of investment. Not a sound or sign of their coming do they make. A man on guard may imagine that every foot of the country immediately surrounding is visible and utterly devoid of any animate object. All at once, as if their tails were connected with a telegraph wire and the coyotes had all been set going by electricity, the whole ring gives voice. The initial note is the only one agreed upon. After striking that note, each particular coyote goes it on his own account." [13]

Another description purporting to be realistic is from the point of a view of a tree overlooking a gathering of about twenty coyotes. "Their leader let out one low, sad note, as if to command attention, very much as the leader of an orchestra raises his baton and looks around at the musicians under his authority. Then the other coyotes gathered around him in a circle, all facing him. Then one coyote opened with a tenor howl of most piercing quality, and was joined in succession by the basso, contralto, soprano, alto, baritone, and so on until the whole pack was in full cry, all keeping time by jumping up and down on their four feet with their noses lifted high in the air." [14]

All my life nearly I have been hearing that the voice of a coyote will not echo. Indians used to imitate coyotes, lobos and owls to signal each other at night. Frontiersmen claimed that human imitations echo whereas voices of the animals do not. The claim must have originated in prairie country, where there are no echoes. The baying of a hound, the music of a hunter's horn, the bellowing of a bull, the chopping of an axe, a woodpecker's pecking, and a poorwill's incessant pouring forth after dark, all make brave and beautiful echoes in a canyon, and so do the midnight *who-who-oo* of the owl, the hoarse bass of the lobo and the sharp yelp of the coyote.

Jack Potter, who used to manage a big range in Billy the Kid's territory, told me this anecdote of mimic signaling. One spring night in 1881, Paco Anaya and his parents were talking about "Beely el Chivo." Their ranch was twelve miles from Fort Sumner, where the Kid had a sweetheart. He was now, as everybody in New Mexico knew, in jail at Lincoln awaiting execution of the sentence of death. The family went to bed, but Paco could not sleep. After a while he heard a coyote-yip, then a second yip. Eagerly he waited for the third yip. It came. He aroused his parents. "Get up," he said, "and dress, but do not light the candle. Beely has come."

"Be still, my son," the elder Anaya said. "Go lay yourself down again. It is certain that that is not the voice of el Chivo."

But Paco knew that it was the voice of the Kid. He stole out, answered with three coyote yips, and el Chivo was before him.

One night in 1851, while camped with a train of emigrants whom he and Jim Bridger were piloting across the Plains, Captain William F. Drannan gave two or three yelps just to hear "my coyote friends" respond. The wild and instant response out in the brush, not more than two hundred yards away, alarmed some of the Easterners against an Indian attack. Jim Bridger suggested that he and Drannan give "the double howl." The response this time made the women fearful of an attack of "the dreadful beasts themselves." A few evenings later Drannan suggested a dance. At least twenty-five people were eager for the diversion, but there wasn't a fiddler in the crowd. A buffalo had just been killed, and the scouts knew what the effect of the smell of fresh blood on the night air would be. "We've got a band engaged to play," Jim Bridger said. He gave the coyote howl. The "band" struck up, and until midnight the music did not stop.[15] Some of the people wanted peace. Captain Drannan said that he could quiet the band in a minute if he were sure no Indians were in the country. How? By firing his rifle a time or two. A shot in the direction of howling coyotes will certainly disperse them.

The way turkeys gobble back at the beating of a hammer or nearly any other noise is one of the comicalities of nature. Coyotes are at times equally responsive to odd sounds. Some individual may be moved to mock-answer the braying of a burro. The six o'clock whistle at a little town amid a wilderness of brush is answered daily by an irregular encirclement of coyote voices. Any ranch dog that barks after dark to get a come-back will get it if a coyote is within hearing.

The silent smell of mortality will have its answer, prolonged and profound. "We used to say," Agnes Morley Cleaveland remembers in *No Life for a Lady*, "that coyotes detected the presence of death with some macabre instinct. This night they sat close to the buckboard, with the dead horse lying in the harness and the dead child in the mother's lap, and howled the night through."

In 1905, Dr. Urling C. Coe went out into the Oregon range country. The narrative that follows is abridged from his *Frontier Doctor*.[16]

"The young buckaroo left his jaded horse in my stable and got into the buggy to guide me. It was not long after dark when we set out to drive thirty miles to the camp where Sid Powers' outfit was rounding up horses. His wife and another woman were cooking for it. Mrs. Powers was at an advanced stage of pregnancy. On the preceding day she had decided to take a little jaunt on her husband's horse. This horse was not used to skirts. A hard fall and the nervous shock from it had evidently brought on labor.

" 'A hoss camp ain't no place fer having kids,' the buckaroo remarked.

"For about twenty miles we followed a wagon road to the southeast, making good time. Then we turned off at almost a right angle to go northeast without any road at all and only the direction to follow. The going was slow and rough through the sage brush, but the North Star in a clear sky made coursing easy. When we had gone what I judged to be a good ten miles, I stopped the team and asked the silent buckaroo where camp was. He suggested that either he or it was lost. We decided that we had been bearing too far north and veered eastward. Another mile or two, and still there was no sign of camp. We felt sure that a fire would be kept burning as a signal. But camp was in a basin beside a waterhole, the buckaroo said, and one would have to get on the rim overlooking the basin in order to see the light.

"I stopped the team again to consider the situation. It was now that darkest hour which comes just before the dawn. Although the urgency of the woman's case was uppermost in my mind, I was caught in the spell of the desert night and sat for a minute listening to the profound stillness. Then just ahead of us and to the right, a violent burst of howls suddenly shattered it. The coyotes sounded as if they were strung along a crest. They howled in unison, and in their cries I sensed, or thought I sensed, a note I had never before heard.

" 'That's a different song from the one coyotes usually sing,' I said.

" 'I was thinking the same thing,' the buckaroo replied.

"I drove a short distance and stopped again to listen. Then a sound like the faint echo of a woman's scream floated to us from a point far ahead. It was immediately answered by a chorus of long-drawn coyote howls. I drove on for a few minutes and stopped again to listen. Another scream sounded, a little plainer than the first. The coyotes wailed their response. Driving on, we were soon between the wailers and the screamer, her cries growing more distinct. There were both pain and terror in those screams, and the pain and the terror were echoed in the howls.

"We came in sight of the campfire. When we reached it, some of the squatting men got up and took the team. I found the patient lying on a camp cot in a tent attended by Sid Powers and the other woman. She had intended to go home in a few days for her confinement, but the accident had changed her program.

"She was frightened to the point of hysteria. She attributed the pains to some internal injury. After I had examined her and assured her that she had no serious injury, her fright and nervousness subsided and she quit screaming. After that we heard nothing more from the coyote chorus."

Although reckoned as a desert animal and sometimes ranging far from water, the coyote does not inhabit those absolutely waterless wastes that the word *desert* has come to connote. He may, however, know about water that nobody else bigger than a wasp knows about. One time while I was traveling with a pack mule and a Mexican guide across a barren part of the state of Durango, we made camp after dark beside a very small *pozo* on the edge of a dry arroyo. I asked the guide how he came to know about this little hole of water. He said that a long time ago a coyote told a man it was there. One had to dip the water out with a cup. It had hairs in it and smelled so strong of coyotes that I could not drink it except in the form of boiled coffee. In the *playa* country — low coastal sands — of Sonora against the Gulf of California, coyotes dig down two or three, maybe four feet — not perpendicular, but sloping holes — to the brackish water; any occasional human penetrator into that barren country drinks after the coyotes.

During the Sierra Mojada silver boom of the '70s in northern Mexico, a party of prospectors ran out of water on a stretch of desert a hundred miles wide. They wanted to turn back. Their Mexican guide told them that it was farther to water behind than to water ahead. Their horses were exhausted. They did not think they could endure. While they paused undecided, the guide said, "Listen!" There was only silence, but the guide was sure he had heard a single coyote-yip just beyond a ridge. The men following him, he walked to the ridge. There below was a coyote. He had some mud on his tail. One of the Americans raised his gun to shoot. "No!" the Mexican exclaimed. "He has shown us water. We are debtors to him. We cannot kill him. Look down to the left. Behind those *hoja sen* bushes is the little mud hole he has been drinking from." The muddy water sustained them.

It was such experiences as this that gave rise to the old saying, "He has heard the coyote bark" — synonymous to having "heard the owl and seen the elephant" — to having been beyond the rim of ordinary human encounters.

Among the cynical seamen under the command of Commodore Stockton in California during the Mexican War was one who wrote: "In the night at Temple's Ranche, an alarm was given. The enemy was approaching with yells and shouts. The long-roll sounded, and the men sprang to their arms. They were thrown into position to repel a charge, and momentarily expected General Castro's army to appear. The cries and yells continued, but no attack was made; they remained under arms for about two hours, and would probably have kept so until daylight, had it not been for an old Indian. He informed us that our alarm proceeded from a couple of coyotes. . . . The hideous noise coyotes keep up resembles [in combination] the howling and yelling of various animals, the shrieks of women, the crying of children, and the barking of dogs. . . . While these two insignificant animals were keeping over three hundred men under arms for two hours, General Castro fled from Los Angeles." [17]

To young and loving Susan Magoffin on the Santa Fe Trail in 1846, her first coyote serenade was "a mixture of cat, dog, sheep, wolf, and the dear knows what else. It was enough to frighten off sleep and everything else."

One traveler found the serenade "terrible"; another, "intolerable." To the excellent Ruxton the howl seemed "mournful and unearthly"; to perspicacious McGillycuddy Agent, "dismal." Riding up to a ranch one day just at meal time, Charles M. Russell, who painted "Nature's Cattle" * with many variations, said, "Boys, there are three things I love to hear: the old dishpan banging for chow, a coyote barking, and a wolf howling." To Enos Mills, the "shoutings and far off cries" expressed "pure gladness and wildness." Those people who describe them as "blood-curdling" use journalese.

There are many pleasing sounds in nature. I know of but one truly painful — that of too many cicadas in hot weather. The song of the canyon wren, tripping down, down, down the scale,

* The title of one of his pictures.

fills one with lightsomeness. It is *lovely* — and may Hollywood barkers be sextuply and duodecimally damned for debasing that word! The rising howl of the coyote is not lovely and cultivated like the voice of Bugle Ann, but many a time the wild and dark and elemental beauty of it has taken me far away and filled me with a sense of the mysteries. Weird, too, I have called it, because it often evokes the Anglo-Saxon personification of Destiny — "For Wyrd has swept them, all my line, to the land of doom." As Lotchi of the Zuñis put it, "So, too, when a hunter coming home late at night meets in his trail a coyote howling, he bethinks himself of the time when he must say farewell to the living, and go his way to the Lake of the Dead." [18]

There are those, I know, who interpret this form of the coyote's howl as maniacal. The unprecise ignorant call anything they do not comprehend "crazy." When I was a youth and my thoughts were long, long thoughts, I heard nightly the howl of the coyote, and this Voice of Away-and-Away-Out-Beyond always made them longer. Now that the years have added themselves upon my head, when I listen to it in the stillness of night, my thoughts are still long, long thoughts. For me, only the fluting cry of low-flying sandhill cranes in the misty dusk of a winter evening so expresses the wild, the free and the limitless. If I could, I would go to bed every night with coyote voices in my ears and with them greet the gray light of every dawn. When I remember their derision of campfires, their salutes to the rising moon, their kinship cries to stars and silences, I am ten thousand times more grateful to them than I am to the makers of the blaring radios and ringing telephones that index the high standard of American living.

Very often, the song is anything but weird or sad. Genius is vitality; vitality is of the morning, and thus Audubon remembered the coyote: "If [the camper], aroused from his slumbers by the howling of this animal, raises his blanket and turns his head toward the east, he can see the red glow, perchance, that fringes the misty morning vapours, giving the promise of a clear and calm sunrise in the mild climate of Texas, even in the depth of winter." Gladsome the song often rises, joyous, insouciant, positively hilarious, as gay as a prairie of bright phlox under the April sun, as tonic as the redbird's matins. In its variousness, it runs all the gamuts. "Spirit of the West," Ernest Thompson Seton rhapsodized, "I wish I could do justice to your meaning. . . . Like the prophets and saga-singers, you voice your spirit's thrill in a song, a shouting, that is the very same in nature with the love-mad song of the nightingale, only louder, stronger, farther-reaching, as becomes the nobler, singing thing that you are." [19]

The poet, if there be one, always says the thing better than anyone else can say it. If the coyote survives and if, in the realms of the beautiful and the spiritual, America ever catches up with her patent office, the song of the coyote will be besung as richly and repeatedly as the song of nightingale or skylark has been in English poetry. George Sterling, of California, has in "Father Coyote" [20] done better on the subject perhaps than any other poet so far.

> At twilight time, when the lamps are lit,
> Father Coyote comes to sit
> At the chaparral's edge, on the mountain side —
> Comes to listen and to deride
> The rancher's hound and the rancher's son,
> The passer-by and everyone.
> And we pause at milking-time to hear
> His reckless carolling, shrill and clear —
> His terse and swift and valorous troll,
> Ribald, rollicking, scornful, droll.

II · ADAPTATION

IT TAKES MORE POWER of thought to meet change than to make it. Eli Whitney's invention of the cotton gin made the Civil War inevitable. Compared with the amplitude and no-bility of Lincoln in mastering the Civil War, Eli Whitney's genius measures no higher than a tinker's. No mechanical pro-peller of society into a higher standard of physical living — George Stephenson, Thomas Edison, Henry Ford, and so on — has evidenced any power of intellect towards the conduct of society amid resulting changes. The haters of Franklin D. Roosevelt have never comprehended that he did not so much make change as meet it. To make machines, money, wealth and war successfully entails a trivial exercise of the intellect com-pared with the wisdom required to meet the problems that ma-chines, money, wealth and war bring to society.

It would be silly to consider the coyote as an "intellectual being." But no other wild animal of historic times has shown itself so adaptable to change. The popular manner of calling some men "foxy" or "as smart as a coyote" is just. The coyote-smart people may have intellectual potentialities, but they are

[31]

not intellectual; they are merely cunning in an animal way, taking advantage of situations and often overcoming the noble in intellect and spirit.

Under wilderness conditions, the multitudinous forms of nature find a balance, everything from grass to grizzly bears living on something else and giving back something. The balance constantly shifts; among the living, the normal is change. Left to themselves, undisturbed by man, animal populations rise and fall, biological and other physical influences constantly fluctuating. There is now no way of computing what were the relative numbers of coyotes to numbers of rabbits, deer, antelopes, grouse and other accompanying species in North America before the advent of civilized man. We do know that where the coyote was most abundant, game animals he is now supposed to check were also most abundant.

The coyote was familiar to Spaniards in Mexico almost three centuries before English-speakers knew of the animal's existence. The first report of the animal to receive attention in the Old World — a very limited attention — was by Clavijero in 1780.* The *coyotl*, he wrote, is "one of the most common quadrupeds of Mexico, in form like the dog, voracious like the lobo, astute like the fox, in some qualities resembling the jackal." But knowledge of the animal hardly existed among English-speaking people when President Thomas Jefferson in 1804 sent the Lewis and Clark expedition out to explore the unknown expanse of plains and mountains called the Louisiana Territory which he had just

* For a detailed account of early conceptions of the coyote, see Chapter XIV. Francisco Javier Clavijero (1731–1787) published his *History of Mexico*, in Italian, in 1780; seven years later it appeared in an English translation made by Charles Cullen. Before this, Buffon's *Natural History of the World* was making a profound impression on Western civilization. The first of forty-four volumes comprising the work appeared in 1749, the last in 1804, sixteen years after his death. For a long time this work was the chief source of information on American fauna. In it there is no mention of the coyote. Clavijero seems to have been more eager to subtract from the great French naturalist, especially for not having made use of an obscure Latin work by Francisco Hernández, than to give scientific facts about the coyote.

annexed to the nation. The explorers had instructions to report "especially on those animals not known in the United States." They were not scientific naturalists, but they were intelligent observers. For a time after first sighting the prairie wolf they mistook it for a fox. They called it "burrowing dog" and "wolf of the plains" as well as "prairie wolf." They had traveled two thousand miles across the virgin continent and had been away from the last white man's cabin for a whole year, when in May 1805 the following description was entered in the Lewis and Clark journals (published in 1814):

"The wolves are very abundant, and are of two species. First, the small wolf or burrowing-dog of the prairies which is found in almost all the open plains. It is of an intermediate size between the fox and dog, very delicately formed, fleet and active. The ears are large, erect and pointed; the head is long and pointed, like that of the fox; the tail long and bushy; the hair and fur are of a pale reddish-brown color, though much coarser than that of the fox; the eye is of a deep sea-green color, small and piercing; the talons are rather longer than those of the wolf of the Atlantic States. . . . These wolves generally associate in bands of ten or twelve, and are rarely if ever seen alone, not being able singly to attack a deer or antelope. They live and rear their young in burrows, which they fix near some pass or spot much frequented by game, and sally out in a body against any animal which they think they can overpower; but on the slightest alarm retreat to their burrows, making a noise exactly like that of a small dog." [1]

Lewis and Clark were more accurate on their other main discovery in the animal world, the grizzly bear, than on the coyote, which they may have confused at times with the swift fox. It is curious how their "burrowing dog" conception has persisted.* Nature follows art, whether the art be false or true to life, and people see what they are expected to see; hence undiminished

* See opening paragraphs of Chapter VIII for facts concerning coyote dens.

reports of generations of little vipers running into the mouths of their parents. Perhaps the best early review of Western animal life is *Sporting Adventures in the Far West*, by John Mortimer Murphy (London, 1879). "I have," he says, "seen a small pack of seventeen or eighteen couples of coyotes rise out of burrows in the ground, apparently at once, and scud about in every direction to escape dogs." The 1944 edition of the *Encyclopaedia Britannica* repeats the absurdity, saying that coyotes "live in burrows in the plains and hunt in packs at night."

The fact is that many men who have lived on the Plains all their lives and have seen thousands of coyotes have never seen one come out of a burrow except occasionally at pupping time. However, on shadeless prairies on hot summer days, some coyotes go into the earth for shade and coolness. One July day in North Dakota R. E. Bateman saw an animal's head in the opening of a burrow a short distance off. At first he thought the animal was a badger, but upon digging it out discovered it to be a male coyote. Then he noticed that whereas, in the same territory at this time, coyotes were frequently visible during early morning and at evening, none was seen in the heat of day. He deduced that other prairie coyotes seek underground shade. Joe E. Hill has shot many coyotes rushing out of prairie dens during hot weather, but, as he says, the coyote prefers to shade himself, if possible, above ground so as to have a view. "During summer heat, coyotes dig out holes a foot or so deep under heavy clumps of salt grass. In the forenoon they lie in shallow beds scratched out under the west side of bushes, in the middle of the day shift to the north side, and then in the afternoon move to the east side."

The greater part of valid knowledge concerning coyotes has come during the past quarter of century, largely through the United States Biological Survey and its successor, the Fish and Wildlife Service. Scientific designation of the coyote as *Canis latrans* came in 1823 from Thomas Say. As biologist, he accompanied the Long Expedition from Pittsburgh to the Rocky Mountains, 1819–1820, and encountered the type specimen near Council Bluffs, Iowa. He commented on the "wonderful intelligence" of the species and detailed its manner of eluding traps. "Prairie wolves," he wrote, "are by far the most numerous of our wolves, and often unite in packs for the purpose of chasing deer." [2] . . .

Prairie wolf * was, at this time, an accurate name; its habitat was mostly prairie country, while the so-called timber wolf ranged over the great prairies as well as through mighty forests east and north. In Mexico, however, Clavijero had noted that "the Cojote loves the woods" and generally ranges alone. [3] At the opening of the nineteenth century, vast areas of land in the Southwest now covered with cactus and thorned brush that hide the coyote were open prairies over which he trotted openly. Like the buffalo and the antelope, the animal originally preferred the open.

The statements by Say and by Lewis and Clark on the pack unit are corroborated by several other early observers. In 1846–1847, George Frederick Ruxton, whose youthful death I consider more of a loss to literature than that of "the marvelous boy" Chatterton, saw "cayeutes" in "bands of from three to thirty" along the runs of deer and antelopes, "extending their line for many miles." Lieutenant J. W. Abert, who was in the same years on a military reconnaissance across the Plains, observed that the big buffalo wolves did not "congregate in large packs like the prairie wolf," which "hang on the heels of the buffalo, to pick up the infirm and those the hunters have wounded, as well as to prey on what is left of the slaughtered." The French naturalist Houzeau records bands of from twenty to thirty chasing a

* "Cased wolf" became the trade name for the animal, from the fact that the pelt was cased — peeled off without slitting the body — and dried over a frame, like that of a muskrat or possum, whereas the pelt of the gray wolf was slit down the belly and stretched flat to dry. "Barking wolf" was another not uncommon name.

buffalo separated from the herd. They generally hunt "in small bands," says one of the naturalists who contributed to Emory's meaty report on the United States-Mexican Boundary Survey. In the journal he kept of his expedition up the Missouri River in 1843, Audubon mentions gray wolves frequently and prairie wolves several times. Once he saw two prairie wolves amid a compact group of eighteen gray wolves. The other prairie wolves he mentions seem to have appeared singly. Yet in *Quadrupeds of America* (prepared in collaboration with Bachman), Audubon says that "they hunt in packs of six or eight, which are seen to most advantage in the evening in pursuit of deer. . . . They associate in greater numbers than the larger wolves." An English sportsman named Vivian, hunting in the West in 1877, observed that "the timber wolf is generally either alone or in company with only one or two others, whereas the coyotes are often in small packs." [4]

Beginning in 1812, Ross Cox was for six years an employee of the Northwest Fur Company, making numerous expeditions far up the Columbia River and to the east. In relating personal adventures, he was perhaps more Munchausenesque than any other early chronicler of the Far West, not even excepting Jim Beckwourth. It is difficult to evaluate some of his observations. "The prairie wolves," he wrote, "generally travel together in numbers, and a solitary one is seldom met with. Two or three of us have often pursued from fifty to one hundred, driving them before us as quickly as our horses could charge." [5]

The Prince of Wied, on the northern Plains in 1833–1834, and various other early travelers, say nothing of coyotes in bands but note their appearance singly or in pairs. Rudolph Friederich Kurz is explicit: "Isolated wolves [evidently prairie wolves and also gray wolves] are frequently seen on the prairie or in the dense forests but never in gangs except when they smell blood and come together in mob fashion in pursuit of a wounded animal or to devour the carcass of one just slain." [6] Despite all that has been quoted, I doubt if coyotes hunted in bands as extensively as reported. Josiah Gregg, the most intimate and authentic of all early historians of the Plains, found the coyote pretty much as he is today, "living upon the remains of buffaloes killed by hunters and the large wolves, added to such small game as hares, prairie dogs, etc., even reptiles and insects." [7]

However characteristic pack-units may have been of *Canis latrans* under aboriginal conditions, the animal became increasingly solitary after man broke into "Nature's social union." Two or three coyotes co-operating to run down a jack rabbit, or a dozen congregating to feed on discarded fish washed ashore from the boats of commercial fishermen, do not compose a pack. Many mature men who have spent their lives among coyotes have never seen more than eight running together, and that many only a very few times. At dawn one October day in Mexico I saw eight together, and one November morning in Montana I saw seven. Presumably in each instance the group was a family. Seeing two or three in company is not uncommon, but more often they appear singly. Coyotes delight in coming together,* especially at night, before separating for the hunt. They are essentially social. Had they, bison-like, persisted in following an inherited instinct for gregariousness, they would by now have been eliminated from most of their territory. The passenger pigeon perished because it could not modify its habit of extreme gregariousness.

Banded into big packs or alone, in the early days prairie

* "On meeting, two coyotes may trot towards each other, may even touch noses, and, after hunting about near each other, move apart. Almer Nelson, in charge of the Federal Elk Refuge on the outskirts of Jackson, Wyoming, looked out his window at daybreak, in the middle of winter, and saw six coyotes scattered over the fields hunting for mice. While he watched, the coyotes in their hunting gradually moved towards a center until they were all assembled. Here they sat in an irregular circle and howled in chorus. The clamor soon came to an end and the coyotes dispersed over the fields, each going on its way, to return again in the evening." — Adolph Murie, *Ecology of the Coyote in the Yellowstone*, 36–37.

wolves were numerous beyond modern conception. Making observations in California in 1843, Lansford Warren Hastings noted that prairie wolves were much more numerous than gray wolves. "In traveling through valleys," he said, "you will pass many hundreds during the day; . . . they pass within a very few rods of you." [8] A trapper told George Bird Grinnell that about 1860 he and his sons caught in one night eighty-three big wolves and coyotes in a stockade baited with dead buffalo.[9] Coyotes seem to have been more plentiful, relatively, on the southern Plains than northward. Mrs. John B. Kendrick of Wyoming remembers seeing, long ago, about a hundred and fifty wolves collected on a hill in front of the Senator Kendrick ranch in the Big Horns. Perhaps they were in the process of making one of their episodic migrations. At that time coyotes were scarce in the region. Competition between the two species was not marked; but, like the panther, the timber wolf occasionally destroys a coyote. Annihilation of the timber wolf in the United States has probably favored the coyote.

Prodigal slaughterers of buffaloes and other big game naturally saw concentrations of wolves — and nearly every party of men fresh upon the Plains slaughtered with a prodigality that might revolt a prize boar in a hog pen.* The civilized Francis Parkman and his friends were no exception. Returning in the fall of 1846 to the Missouri River from the Wyoming country, Parkman

* Why did they slaughter in such a senseless wholesale manner, often no more sportsmanlike than a butcher cutting the throats of huddled sheep? In his noble interpretation of the Osage Indians, *Wah' Kon-Tah* (University of Oklahoma Press, Norman, Oklahoma, 1932, page 57), John Joseph Mathews wrote:

"The ubiquitous white man, in his inscrutable desire to proclaim his presence, slaughtered wild life. The great stretches of prairie and the wild blackjack hills seemed to inspire in him consciousness of his inferiority, and he shouted his presence and his worth to the silent world that seemed to ignore him. Where the Indian passed in dignity, disturbing nothing and leaving Nature as he had found her, with nothing to record his passage except a footprint or a broken twig, the white man plundered and wasted and shouted; frightening the silences with his great, braying laughter and his cursing. He was the atom of steam that had escaped from the pressure of the European social system, and he expanded in this manner under the torch of Liberty."

traveled the Santa Fe Trail down the Arkansas River. About the refuse of a great buffalo slaughter made by Arapahoe Indians, he saw and heard "hundreds" of wolves, both prairie and timber. After his own party had camped four days, shooting buffalo bulls for sport as they came in to water and curing only the choice meat of buffalo cows, they left the waste they had made. A mile away, Quincy Adams Shaw missed a knife and went back to look for it. He found, says Parkman, "literally dozens of wolves prowling about the smouldering fires, while multitudes were roaming over the prairie around; they all fled as he approached, some running over the sand-beds and some over the grassy plains. The vultures in great clouds were soaring overhead, and the dead bull near the camp was completely blackened by the flock that alighted upon it; they flapped their broad wings and stretched upward their crested heads and long, skinny necks, fearing to remain, yet reluctant to leave their disgusting feast. As Shaw searched about the fires, he saw the wolves seated on the distant hills, waiting for his departure." [10]

The "infinite variety" cultivated by the coyote while adapting himself to changes in environment has probably been characteristic of the species from remotest times. Then as now, the coyote was flexible in hunting habits, killing for himself, accepting refuse from bigger killers; diurnal as well as nocturnal, taking his chance at wood rats out by night, at prairie dogs out only in daylight, at jack rabbits stirring mainly in the evening; sleeping by day on a full belly, hunting by day on an empty belly; in the desert digging for prickly pear roots, on the edge of a swamp slipping up on frogs as skillfully as a coon; no more fixed to one spot of ground, like a wild mare bent on foaling at the same spot annually, than fixed to one habit of eating; careless by nature, careful under necessity.

Long before white men appeared, the coyote had become well accommodated to the human species of his habitat. The aborigines owned nothing that he bothered, and their religious regard for him was a protection against molestation. About 1870 Stephen Powers found coyotes "thick about every mountain rancheria" of the California Indians; "they often chased the dogs into the village itself." An old hunter told him that he had seen "Indian dogs more than once turn on a coyote and drive it off a few rods, when it would fall on its back, turn up its legs, and commence playing with them." [11] By the time the great orientalist Richard F. Burton reached Utah, in 1860, the coyote was rapidly learning to observe civilized man from the highest bluff, "troops of them" keeping open watch from hill crest or other elevation.[12] A present-day hunter with hounds observes that the coyote no longer lingers to stare at a man in curiosity as he once lingered. He is "satisfied with a brief glance over the shoulder." He tries to see without being seen. He has learned to lie down in water so as to appear a half-sunken log, to hide in a straw stack in an open field, to camouflage himself in immobility in the scantiest vegetation, rising up "out of nowhere" to break away when man comes threateningly near.[13] During my own time, coyotes in the brush of southern Texas have learned to expose themselves much less while satisfying curiosity.

The common belief that coyotes note at a glance whether a man has or has not a gun and conduct themselves accordingly is a gross exaggeration. The most sagacious coyotes do not usually take time to make the distinction. However, Ed Snyder of Billings, Montana, gave me an instance that knocks such generalizations into a cocked hat. A sheepherder with a short-range .22 rifle found himself helpless against a coyote that quickly learned the range of his bullets. While the herder was on one side of the flock and was actually shooting, this coyote would dash in and kill a sheep on the other side — out of range. The herder would rush across in time to prevent the coyote from eating but could not get close enough to shoot it. This happened several times. Finally, Ed Snyder's greyhounds caught and killed the molester.

The prairie wolf's range, at the time Lewis and Clark penetrated it, extended roughly from the Pacific to the Mississippi River and over into some prairie land east of the Mississippi,* and from British Columbia to southern Mexico. As this domain was appropriated by the white man and as the white man's chickens, sheep and other live property took the places of native fowl and quadrupeds, the coyote accepted the substitute flesh with alacrity and gusto. He himself was anything but accepted. In addition to being poisoned and otherwise destroyed as a menace, he was, especially in colder zones, trapped for his fur, hounded for sport, shot at by everybody on general principles. In recent years he has been fenced out of ceaselessly patrolled sheep and goat pastures containing tens of millions of acres. But, "Life is very sweet, brother; who would wish to die?" The coyote has extended his life by extending his range.

"Brush wolf," the trappers of northern Alberta and Saskatchewan were calling the new penetrator into their grounds early in this century.[14] In the Pecos River country of Texas, Joe Hill began trapping when the first herds of sheep came in, and he has watched the lupine lovers of life in the open, as they were hunted down, take refuge in the dense, hot salt-cedar flats along the river, where mosquitoes are so bad that the young ones have their ears crimped from the biting. In New Mexico, J. Stokley Ligon has seen the coyote while being cleared from the sheep-grazed plains resort to the Truchas Peaks, even above timber line, where he was formerly altogether unknown. Coyote mates now den far up in the Big Horns, coming down only for a quick meal. Once established in mountain roughs and coverage, the little wolves are more difficult to dislodge than from the prairies.

Before the Klondike gold rush of 1898, the coyote did not occur in Alaska. Individuals of the species seem to have followed the pack trains of prospectors, drawn first by the abundant camp

* Prairie du Chien, in southern Wisconsin, settled around 1765, was named for the prairie wolves in the region.

refuse at the southern end of the trail and then, on north, by the hundreds of dead and dying horses. Over and over the animal's freedom from provincial restrictions has been demonstrated. In the '70s, when stock cattle were being trailed northward out of southern Texas to ranges taken over from the buffaloes and the Indians, the trail drivers made a habit of killing every morning calves that had been dropped on the bed grounds during the night (for newborn calves cannot travel). Coyotes followed the herds for the pickings. This was about the only way they could take a Longhorn cow's calf. Likewise, they have been known to follow a herd of sheep for hundreds of miles. "R. E. Dunlap left the Pecos River a few miles north of Roswell with a band of sheep and traveled across the sand hills to Portales, a distance of seventy-five miles. Cockleburs were very plentiful along the Pecos, but occurred nowhere else in the whole country. The second night after the arrival of the sheep at Portales, a trapper caught a coyote that had great numbers of cockleburs in its hair. This coyote had evidently trailed the sheep from the river." [15]

Today the coyote's howl is as familiar on the Yukon as it was a hundred years ago on the upper Arkansas. The species now ranges clear to Point Barrow, the northernmost tip of Alaskan land, and at the same time it has progressed southward from Mexico to Costa Rica in the tropics. [16] During the last quarter century, coyotes have been found in every state of the Union excepting Delaware, breeding in Indiana, Ohio, Alabama and other states formerly unknown to them. Most of the occurrences east of the Mississippi have been traceable to escapes from zoos and private owners. Where the escapees have not been able to find their own kind to breed with, they have frequently crossbred with half-wild dogs. [17] The animal does not like too much dampness; it has never, for instance, occupied the eastern coastal prairies of Texas. Its power to come back on its original range, unless constant guard is kept, is more remarkable than power to occupy territory that it did not enter before civilized man over-turned the original balance of nature.

The spread into Eastern states has been largely sporadic and local; in most places it has been severely checked. Economic consequences prevent the coyote from receiving the toleration that the fast-spreading starling receives in the same territory. In 1905 the Biological Survey was of the opinion that coyotes were as

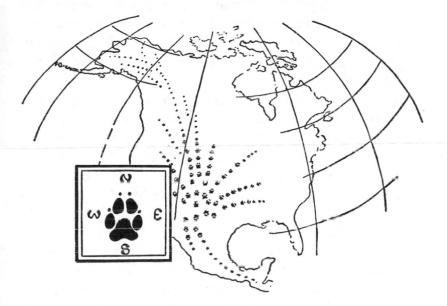

numerous in the United States as they had ever been.[18] Today, they are far less numerous.

Coyotes are the arch-predators upon sheep. Sheep are the arch-predators upon the soil of arid and semi-arid ranges. Wherever they are concentrated on ranges without sufficient moisture to maintain a turf under their deep-biting teeth and cutting hoofs, they destroy the plant life. Quail, which require cover, cannot survive too close cropping. Unless long-term public good wins over short-term private gain and ignorance, vast ranges, already greatly depleted, will at no distant date be as barren as the sheep-created deserts of Spain. Metaphorically, the sheep of the West eat up not only all animals that prey upon them — coyotes, wildcats and eagles especially — but badgers, skunks, foxes, ringtails and others. On some sheep ranges, wholesale poisoning and trapping have destroyed nearly all of them. The surface of the earth does not offer a more sterile-appearing sight than some dry-land pastures of America with nothing but sheep trails across their grassless grounds. The free-enterprisers of these ranges, many of them public-owned, want no government interference; they ask only that the government maintain trappers, subsidies on mutton and wool, and tariffs against any competitive importations.

In 1915, the federal government began systematic destruction of predatory animals. Between July 1 of that year and June 30, 1947, constantly expanding federally controlled operations, which include co-operation with states and with owners of livestock, accounted for the destruction of 1,884,897 coyotes — in Texas about a third of a million, and in Idaho, Wyoming, Oregon, Utah, Nevada, California and Colorado by descending numbers. The national destruction for the year ending June 30, 1947, was 103,982. Coyotes destroyed but not found by the poisoners and trappers would add many tens of thousands to the total. There is no available record of hundreds of thousands killed during the same years by individuals not in government pay; the bounties paid by counties in Western states would reach high totals, California, for instance, paying a bounty on 75,000 scalps in one year early in the century. The total number of coyotes killed in the United States during the year 1946, by bounty hunters and state trappers as well as by federal employees, is said to have totaled 294,000. Pelt records are only fragmentary, for in southern Texas, even during winter months, and in all states over the summer months, coyote pelts are worthless and the dead animals are not skinned.

To say, as is sometimes said, that the coyote has held his own in the ranching country is not correct. While he has been extending his range eastward, northward, southward and (in Oregon) westward, the extensions being in many places only along thin lines and in spots, he has been extirpated from large centers of his native home. The record for one of these centers is characteristic of many others. "When I went to work for the Biological Survey in southern Colorado, in November, 1914," John W. Crook told me, "I shot coyotes nearly every day while riding between camp and trap lines. Repeatedly I shot two, three and four a day. They were visible wherever a man rode. About the middle of December that year I saw eighteen in one pack near Russell Springs; several times I saw ten and twelve together. I caught six and seven a day in traps. Sheep losses to coyotes amounted to 15 or 20 per cent annually. They were killing some calves for a rancher named Neal Jones. He had a dump ground near headquarters. One evening I put out fifty poison baits at these dump grounds, where coyotes came every night; the next morning I skinned thirteen coyotes right there. The next winter, 1915, I saw twenty-six coyotes scattered over a meadow.

"Within two or three years such gatherings were no longer visible. About 1935 the coyote showed a distinct slipping. About 1942 he showed that he was whipped. During the whole winter of 1946–1947 I saw one solitary coyote — just one. In southern Colorado at least, the animal is doomed to go the same way that the lobo went."

If the economic returns were high enough, the coyote could be exterminated from the United States as the gray wolf and the fever tick have been exterminated. The cost would be exceedingly high, and extermination is not desirable. The desires of the sheepman are no more accepted by all landholders than his desires for tariffs are accepted by all wearers of wool clothes.

What thorough destruction of the coyote would mean to nature is suggested by the following account. Coyotes had been very destructive on a sheep range in the Big Horn Mountains of Wyoming. Denning high up in the rimrocks, they multiplied despite rifles, traps, strychnine and cyanide guns. They killed and buffaloed the sheep dogs. Then, in 1945, "the Federal pest control service came to the rescue with a magic powder called thallium. White, odorless and tasteless, thallium is so deadly that handlers must wear masks when they inoculate bait. So far, Mr. Coyote has been unable to detect thallium. It leaves no occasional survivor to learn. Hawks, crows and even the noisy magpies disappeared after the thallium campaign" [19] — also, no doubt, other birds, along with skunks, foxes, badgers and additional carnivores.

Occasionally a coyote learns to climb a sheep fence, usually by being pushed into it. Manufacturers call their product sheep- and coyote-proof fences, but there are no coyote-proof fences. A coyote does not have to excavate much to get under the bottom wire, which is against the ground. A smart coyote flattens out and works under the wire on his side instead of on his belly. A man near Fort Stockton, Texas, had a small pasture which coyotes kept entering, killing the sheep. He built a fence eight feet high, all net wire, with an apron on the ground. One coyote persisted in entering, no one could tell how or where. He could not squeeze through the wire; he did not go under the apron; his only way of entering had to be by climbing, and he climbed out as well as in. A fence-climbing coyote almost never gets hung in the wire as heavy dogs frequently get hung. One coyote climbed a six-foot picket fence four times, killed his sheep each time, and got away.

A coyote that climbs runs less risk of traps than one that digs under. A digger usually selects places that a trapper can anticipate. For hundreds of miles along the tortuous Rio Grande, American sheep pastures are constantly guarded against coyotes that steal across from Mexico for a fill and then steal back, though the unwise often decide to linger in the land of plenty.

A biologist saw one swim the Rio Grande where it was a hundred yards wide and canyon-swift.[20]

While federally controlled operations — since 1915 — accounted for nearly 2,000,000 coyotes, they accounted for over 30,000 gray wolves (including the lesser red wolves). By 1880, at which time most of the buffaloes had been slaughtered and range cattle were rapidly taking their place, professional wolfers were poisoning and otherwise killing gray wolves — along with coyotes — in enormous numbers. To see a gray wolf on his own range now, a citizen of the United States must go to Mexico or far into Canada, perhaps clear to Alaska. The size and habits of the gray wolf prevent its hiding itself; its power and predatory nature make it intolerable to owners of livestock. The lone lobo, noble in isolation, was as unadapted as the pack.

The increasing money value of game to landholders is intensifying destruction of coyotes far away from sheep, goats and chicken farms. This value is made by people who want to shoot and have money to pay for shooting. The majority of them would rather stalk in a pasture where there are, say, seven targets and no coyotes than in a pasture where there are only five deer and seven coyotes. Only a fraction of them would prefer to flush seventeen bobwhites under a sky made more delightful by a hawk rather than to shoot twenty-one bobwhites that have never dodged the shadow of a hawk or heard its thrilling cry. There are many exceptions, but game hunters in general are more at home exhibiting their kill in town than they are out among wild creatures. They pay for licenses; the Game Commissions of states in which they pay are under compulsion to join in the destruction of coyotes.

In October 1946, A. B. Bynum, in charge of government trapping in the Uvalde, Texas, district, turned in the scalps of 522 coyotes slaughtered in one month by the cyanide trap-gun. He set the guns daily himself, his wife helping him run the lines. Perhaps 50 coyotes that died got away in the brush, he says, so that they could not be counted. This number broke all records of coyote destruction by individual trappers in America. The record could not have been made except in the Brush Country of southern Texas, which contains the main concentration of coyotes left on the continent. It could not have been made except by use of the cyanide gun, called the "coyote getter."

An explosive cartridge, attachable to the upper end of a steel peg, contains a charge of sodium cyanide and is hooded by a soft absorbent, usually wool or rabbit fur. At the place where the gun is to be set, the peg is driven into the ground and the hood is smeared with a fetid scent alluring to canines, also to a lesser degree to other species, including skunks and occasional sheep and cattle. The cartridge explodes only when an upward pull on the small bulb-shaped covering releases a spring. Upon exploding, it shoots the cyanide through the soft covering directly into the mouth of the pulling coyote. Instantly almost, the poison ruins all the vitals of the animal, and in less than five minutes it is dead, usually not more than seventy-five steps from the machine. Cyanide is the "soon-speeding gear" that so many Nazis cunningly used to free themselves from enemy retribution.

Every agent for the destruction, or "control," of animals capable of learning from experience has its high day and then loses the maximum of effectiveness. Today is high day for the "coyote getter"; its use is just becoming common above the forks of the creek. The man power required to use a large number of the instruments over an extensive area is much less than that required to set and watch an equal number of steel traps. Some coyotes will doubtless learn — indeed, some have already learned — about the device, as their forebears learned about strychnine and steel traps. The swift action of both gun and cyanide will, however, keep the proportion of escapers low. Deadly as it is, the cyanide gun will in the long run prove another supplement to, rather than a complete substitute for, steel trap and poisoned bait.*

The coyote's continuing efforts to survive against man have not increased his capacity for recognizing cause and effect — any more than mankind's intellectual capacity in the Age of Hollywood shows increase over that of the Age of Socrates. There is no record of a coyote that could not be caught. "There never was a cowboy that couldn't be throwed, and there never was a horse that couldn't be rode." The coyote far enough advanced to put two and two together can seldom add two more and arrive at six. Oren L. Robinson, of the Jackson Hole country, was once following a trapped coyote dragging a trap chain with a three-pronged grapple hook on the free end of it. The hook kept catching in small bushes, jerking the coyote back. Finally, the coyote picked it up in his mouth and carried it some distance. This behavior may be unduplicated in trapping history; it is certainly unusual. Before long the coyote stepped on the chain, thus jerking a prong of the hook into his mouth. Right there he stopped, absolutely baffled, and gave up.

Roughly, the Brush Country † of Texas lies south of a line running west from San Antonio to about Del Rio on the Rio Grande. Except at the western tip of this line, there are almost

* It is not so deadly as sodium fluoroacetate, popularly known as Compound 1080, which three Polish scientists discovered early in World War II and which the Wildlife Research Laboratory of the U. S. Fish and Wildlife Service, at Denver, Colorado, has tried out in the field. It is particularly toxic to the cat and dog families. A pound of the poison would, it is computed, kill a million pounds of susceptible animal life. A coyote that eats a rat or ground squirrel killed by a particle of Compound 1080 dies. It could probably be used to annihilate most of the coyotes of America; if it were so used, many birds and other useful animals would also be killed. The Fish and Wildlife Service people are exceedingly chary of its use. They hope that it will continue to be sold only to governmental agencies.

† In character the Brush Country is as extraordinary as the Everglades or the Painted Desert. Having described it in two books already, *A Vaquero of the Brush Country* and *The Longhorns*, I shall not here duplicate the description.

no sheep in the Brush Country. The few flocks of Spanish goats are protected by shepherds and dogs. The Brush Country runs down into the lower valley of the Rio Grande, irrigated and thickly populated, where coyotes refresh themselves on orange juice. It includes the million-acre King Ranch and other estates of feudal latitudes. It includes also many small ranches, many cultivated fields bordered by brush pasture, many oil fields with derricks and pumps pricking the brush. Sweeping northeast up the coast of the Gulf of Mexico, it takes in the sand-bar islands, on which coyotes follow the tides to pick up the wash of the sea. Amid an infinitude of mesquites bearing succulent beans, thorned bushes furnishing berries, prickly pear purple in season with tunas, and an abundance of jack rabbits, cottontails, wood rats, armadillos, ground squirrels and other flesh, no coyote of the Brush Country need ever starve — except when the terrible drouth comes. Even then, there are mesquite beans for a long season. When the *chapotes* (Mexican persimmons) ripen, some fall to the ground; others remain in easy reach on the soft-leaved, thornless bushes; coons, hustling for themselves high up, knock many down — and the coyotes gormandize upon them with as little effort as Elijah exerted to take the bread and flesh brought by ravens. In the opinion of some range men, coyote depredation on deer in the Brush Country is increasing; that is what men in the business of trapping want them to think. The trapping of them here is certainly on the increase.

Cattle people are generally conservative in the manner of the old-time English squire. The King Ranch may import bull snakes to swallow rattlesnakes and hire a biologist to ration the diet between skunks and armadillos, but lots of the ranchers — including some of the oil millionaires who sink their excess profits in land and live in Houston with their income tax lawyers — tend towards the George West point of view. On his big ranch in Live Oak County, Mr. George West always had big steers and plenty of deer, and he never arranged hunting parties in order to influence politicians. One time an eager young man met him in San Antonio.

"Mr. West," he said, "you wouldn't mind if I went down to your ranch for a little deer hunt, would you?"

"Oh," Mr. West said, "you can't see any deer down there nowadays for the brush. People shoot at deer in the brush and scare my steers, and the steers run all the tallow off themselves. No, I can't let you hunt deer."

"But Mr. West," the eager young man went on, "I just want to get out on your famous ranch. I won't shoot at the deer. I'll shoot the coyotes."

"No," said Mr. West, "I've got to protect the coyotes to keep the jack rabbits down. If those jack rabbits were left alone to breed, they'd eat up all the grass."

"Well," the eager young man brightened, "I'll just shoot jack rabbits. That would be fine sport and useful too."

"No," Mr. West replied gravely, "we've got to have the jack rabbits to feed the coyotes."

The young man by now had lost his eager look.

"Maybe you've heard of the balance of nature," Mr. George West concluded.

To consider going back to the primal balance of nature is as futile as to expect mass manufacturing to revert to master-and-servant handicrafts. More knowledge of many factors in nature, a nicer weighing of values, and a flexible adjustment of procedure to fit diverse regions are necessary in making up the balance on the coyote. The principal charges [21] against the coyote are that on his native ranges throughout the West he destroys sheep, goats, chickens, turkeys, an occasional small calf — usually sick — deer, a limited amount of other game animals, and too many game birds; and that in extending his range northward and eastward he destroys, in addition to domestic animals, foxes and their natural food and preys upon the breeding grounds of ducks, geese and shore birds. In accommodating themselves to high mountains, coyotes are said to increase in size and activity, preying more on domestic stock, wild turkeys and deer than they do lower down where rabbits and other rodents abound. An investigator of Merriam's wild turkey, which belongs to high altitudes, sums up by saying: "The coyote is out of place in forested mountains, and is there far more detrimental than beneficial." [22]

The principal defenses of the coyote are that he is an enormous benefiter in keeping down rabbits, rats, prairie dogs, ground squirrels and other rodents, that he is valuable as a fur-bearer, and that he is a tonic to desirable species on which he preys, eliminating the unfit, killing off the diseased, and otherwise promoting the survival of the fittest. Opponents of intensive poisoning say that the poisoners and trappers destroy a vast number of skunks, badgers, foxes and other animals valuable not only for fur but in the eternal and ever-fluctuating process of balancing nature. The *Journal of Mammalogy*, now in its twenty-ninth year, is a storehouse of data and conflicting opinion.

Thorough ecological investigation has not been carried on long enough or widely enough to warrant all the answers. Two biologists, after studying for a season the relationship between coyotes and bobwhite quail on one ranch in southern Texas, concluded that the predators are taking two out of every three nests. In California, investigators found that the killing off of all flesh-eating predators on a certain area resulted in increased disease and death rate among quail.[23] California ranchmen in another area poisoned off all the coyotes and then had most of their grass eaten out by kangaroo rats, which in addition sowed the land with noxious dock. If all the coyotes in the world were dead and all the quail on the continent were concentrated in California and Texas and the hunting season on them were closed, they would be reduced to subnormal numbers by the first prolonged drouth. Nature's diastole and systole operates

[52]

through all forms of life; it operates with melodramatic swiftness among birds and the smaller mammals.

Biologist William H. Burt (Michigan, 1946) says: "According to recent studies, the coyote as scavenger and mouser probably does more good than harm." Victor H. Cahalane (Chief Biologist of the United States National Parks) says, 1947: "Throughout the ages the coyote has helped to weed out the unfit and keep survivors alert. Largely due to it and other predators, the deer, the antelope and other hoofed mammals have evolved into swift, graceful, efficient animals. Were it not for the coyote, they would not only over-populate and over-eat their ranges, but would doubtless become lazy and have cirrhosis of the liver." [24]

No tendency among human beings is more common than to blame others for what the blamers themselves do. Uncritical blame by groups of men is extended to wild animals as well as to foreign nations. Some years ago people in the sheep- and goat-populated hills northwest of San Antonio decided that the disappearance of quail in their territory was due to armadillos. They began killing the armadillos. Then they discovered that the destruction of cover by their own sheep and goats was the essential cause of the dearth of quail. Men, often illegally, shoot the deer out of a district, and then blame the coyote.

When a particularly vicious dog appears in a neighborhood, not all dogs are destroyed, but only the vicious. The popular idea is that all coyotes are chicken-catchers, sheep-killers, fawn-devourers, bobbers of calf tails, and so on. Paul Gilbert, Secretary of the Nebraska Game, Forestation and Parks Commission, has computed that about 20 per cent of all coyotes on the plains are guilty of destroying property. A vice of the species is the habit of only some individuals. Observant chicken-growers in the midst of a coyote population have found that their enemies are not coyotes in general but particular animals and that if the

[53]

particular thief is destroyed, predations on the chickens cease — until another particular thief shows up. When trappers move into an area, they usually destroy non-predators first; they are easier to get. Wily predators hold out longer than their innocent kin. Some students of predatory control think that it would be cheaper and more sensible to destroy only the destroyers, but nearly all trapping and poisoning are promiscuous.

The master studies of the relationships of the coyote to other animals of its environment have been made within the past ten years by Adolph Murie, biologist and naturalist, a pioneer in the field. His yet unpublished study of *Cattle Losses and the Coyote on a Southwestern Range* (Arizona) leaves the coyote generally guiltless of predation on cattle, though exceedingly active on carrion. However, Emerson's Law of Compensation always works. As cows are bred up for sow-like weight and form they lose their protective instincts. The Fish and Wildlife Service reported 376 coyote attacks on calves over the United States in 1947. Cow people who side against the coyote seem to be on the increase. In the summer of 1948 *The Cattleman*, published by the Texas and Southwestern Cattle Raisers Association, ran a series of eyewitness accounts of coyote attacks on calves. I still think that a range cow should have enough elemental life in her to keep coyotes off her offspring. Unless she has, the meat from her kind will descend to the level of hothouse chicken so far as invigorating qualities are concerned.

Murie's *Ecology of the Coyote in the Yellowstone* finds coyote destruction of game birds, elk, deer, antelopes and bighorns too limited to be harmful. "The problem of big game species in the Yellowstone is not one of predation, but of inadequate winter range, a problem shared by many districts throughout the Western states. . . . The coyote has been suspected of limiting the increase of trumpeter swans — a species threatened by extinction. No evidence was found that the coyote preys upon the swans. Positive evidence points to lead poisoning and starvation. . . . Apparently the Yellowstone coyote does not increase indefinitely. The population level is kept down by disease, possibly in some cases by starvation. The species is subject to natural controls. Artificial control is not advisable. A desirable member of the assembly of animals, the coyote contributes to the interest and variety of Yellowstone National Park fauna." [25]

III · TAKING ADVANTAGE OF THE SITUATION

THE COYOTE'S REACTIONS to many circumstances are inherited. His feet are pointed by nature to runways between hill and hill that ancestors followed ages ago; a trapper who sees sign of a coyote intruder in a sheep pasture long cleared of predators sets his traps where preceding coyotes traveled. But readiness to break custom and turn aside for some unaccustomed benefit is also a part of coyote inheritance. He is an opportunist, taking advantage of realities around him, new as well as old, machine-made as well as natural.

There is, I am positive, a relationship between the coyote and the badger not sensible to civilized man. Perhaps the aborigines understood it better. The most prized artifact among my possessions is a small *olla* from Casas Grandes, Chihuahua, that Tom Lea, Sr., of El Paso, presented to me. A thousand years ago this pot of clay was fashioned by the skilled hands of some artist among a people whose culture became extinct before America was discovered. Beautifully proportioned, it has the head of a coyote modeled in bas-relief on one side and the head of a badger

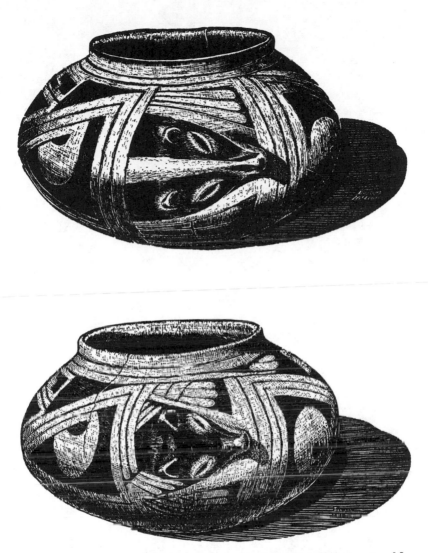

Casas Grandes pot showing coyote head in bas-relief on one side and badger head on the other. It was fashioned perhaps a thousand years ago; the tribe to which the artist belonged, living in the region of Casas Grandes, Chihuahua, Mexico, had vanished before the discovery of America. Casas Grandes pottery is distinguished for sculpturing of animals, but this is the only known representation of the coyote.

on the other. *Tlalcoyote* is the Mexican name for badger, which comes from the Aztec *tlal-coyotl* (*tlalli* meaning *earth*); hence, coyote of the earth — the coyote that lives, or digs, in the ground.

In the tales of the Navajo, Coyote and Badger go around with each other, hunting together and calling each other cousin. This did not keep Coyote from carrying on scandalously with Badger's wife — but that story belongs somewhere else. One day while they were sitting down on the mesa, Coyote said, "Let us sing for snow." Badger said, "No, it's you who are always wanting to sing. Go ahead and sing."

Coyote started singing. He sang, "Snow, snow, snow, snow as high as the grass. With that much snow we can kill rabbits." Then Coyote told Badger to sing. Badger sang the same song, only he asked for snow as high as the groundwort. Coyote has longer legs than Badger, and that is why Badger sang for only half an inch of snow.

The badger is the original digger and trapper of the western world. The American badger is of another genus from the European, and does not dig dens of the astounding proportions that Brock — as the badger is familiarly called in England — digs and, with families and friends, lives in for generations. One of Brock's ancient communal strongholds on the Berkshire Downs — tons of excavated earth piled in front of the entrance to a subterranean maze of tunnels on different levels — remains to me in its way as memorable as Stonehenge. But the American badger digs with extreme rapidity and ease, digs deep and digs often, dispersing rather than concentrating his excavations. A Mexican digging a posthole in hard ground will say, "Oh, that I had a *tlalcoyote!*" A man after a burrowing badger with spade and grubbing hoe will hardly overtake him. A sheepherder in the Pecos country sitting in front of his dugout on a hillside about dusk was surprised by a badger running past him and through the door into his earthen cavern. He followed to investigate. By the time he had struck a match and lit his kerosene lantern, the

[59]

badger had already disappeared into the back wall of the dugout.[1] In one night's time this digger will sink a number of holes five or six feet deep after ground squirrels. One winter morning Al Stephenson of Montana, trailing a badger in the snow for about twelve miles, found that during the preceding night's travel it had sunk twenty holes after pocket gophers. Once the badger starts down after meat, he is sure to reach it.

Usually, the badger does not range far. He often brings food home to eat or to store in his cellar, even when there are no young to provide for. When food is scarce he ranges out, "sinking a house in the earth wherever sleeping time overtakes him." [2] It is doubtful if he digs holes for the express purpose of using them as traps — as the trap spider does; but holes he has made after rodents serve as refuges for rabbits, skunks, snakes and other creatures, and he often makes a round to see what they have caught. Cottontail rabbits make badger holes their homes, and occasionally jack rabbits lie in them during daytime. The coyote, out more in daylight than the badger and much more mobile, can be seen sniffing at every badger burrow he passes. Sometimes he picks up a bone or a bit of meat left by a badger.

One December day in 1933 while I was deer-hunting on the Olmos Ranch in La Salle County, Texas, I tied my horse on a hill and began walking down a draw not too brushy for noiseless stepping. Before long I saw, about twenty steps ahead of me and to my left, a coyote haunched down and intently looking at something that brush and prickly pear prevented my seeing. I froze in my tracks. The coyote seemed very patient and also very eager. His ears twitched with expectation, his rump wagged. He was so intent on watching that for two minutes or so he did not notice me. Then he seemed to feel my presence; he turned his head slightly, and in two jumps disappeared.

I walked directly to the spot he had occupied and looked where he had been looking. There, only a few feet away, a badger was burrowing into a wood rat's nest in a clump of

prickly pear. He made little noise as he tore up the mound of sticks and thorns and truffled into the ground. He appeared to be unaware of my presence. All rat dens in prickly pear have more than one runway. At this one, the coyote had sagaciously taken a position against a runway opposite the badger. Presently, out popped a large fat wood rat. It scooted right by my feet. Had I been the coyote, I should have nabbed the juicy morsel. Within a minute or so, the badger evidently discovered that his game had escaped. Nose to the ground, he came almost to my feet before he smelled me. Then he looked up, without apparent interest, and moved leisurely on into the brush. His behavior corroborated the fact that the badger's senses are nothing like so acute as the coyote's. That night, my good friend Santos Cortez told me that he had seen as many as three coyotes camped around a badger digging into a wood rat's fortification. As goat herder in the chaparral and as a hunter who supplied an outfit of men with venison and javelina meat, Santos had had many opportunities to slip up on creatures in the brush. He liked to linger and watch.

This coyote did not, I feel sure, smell me; the air was still. He certainly did not hear me; he had not noticed my approach, and from the instant I saw him I had remained motionless. He saw me only when he turned his head, without excitement. He turned his head only when he sensed me. Through what sense did he become aware of the presence of something strange? A hunter slipping up on a moose, Gray Owl said, will make the animal uneasy by "concentrating" his mind upon the animal. "Those who would catch a woodsman of the old school asleep do well to come carelessly. A stealthy approach seems to establish some telepathic communication with the subconscious mind of one who lives with nature. This faculty is borrowed from the animals, and is common amongst Indians." [3] While Malvina Hoffman, whose daring genius combines science and art, was modeling savages in order to people the Hall of Man in the Field

Museum at Chicago with bronze representations of racial types from around the globe, she had to win the confidence of the most primitive human beings. "These people, generally called savages," she wrote, "are far more intuitive and psychic than we are." The coyote at the rat's den sensed me, I think, through that sense called intuition. Neither rationalism nor biology can comprehend it.

Sometimes the not swift badger makes use of the coyote to run game into a hole. One was observed following a coyote that chased a cottontail into a burrow. Of course, he was not going to dig it out for the benefit of the coyote. The coyote can dig well enough in soft earth and habitually gets out his own small ground-dwellers, but he cannot go deep like the badger and he cannot dig in hard places and among rocks and thorns like his tough-pawed associate.

Joe E. Hill has twice seen dust rising from a prairie dog town some distance away and then, through binoculars, watched a badger digging while two waiting coyotes flanked him. In each instance the badger got meat, but a prairie dog or two came out by him into the mouths of the coyotes. Again, Joe Hill has seen a badger traveling in apparent high spirits, tail and long front toes turned upward, abreast of two or three coyotes.

A. L. Inman, of Cliff, New Mexico, told me that once while he was watching a badger dig "like a steam shovel" after a prairie dog, a waiting coyote ran up to the badger and gave him a hard bite on the rump. The badger whirled and chased the coyote off a short distance and then returned to digging. Again the coyote nipped him and again, growling and grumbling, the badger chased him away. The action was repeated several times. When I told J. J. Dent, game-watcher and warden, about this badger-nipping coyote, he asked, "You don't know the rest of the story?"

"No."

"Well, I did not see this myself," Dent went on, "but another reliable man did. The coyote kept badgering the badger. I guess he was impatient and wanted the badger to bring something out quick. Pretty soon the badger got the hole he was digging big enough to turn around in. He went out of sight, and the coyote poked his nose in. The badger grabbed it. When that coyote finally got loose, he didn't act like he was on the hunt for another badger."

"When I was a kid," Con Price says in his reminiscences of the Dakota and Montana ranges, "an old Indian told me a story about a coyote and a badger and said they hunt together as partners. I have watched them travel together all right. I have seen a coyote watching a badger dig after a ground squirrel or a prairie dog. When the badger brought his game out of the hole, the coyote grabbed it and ran, and, being so much faster, got away with the spoils." [4]

Edward Royal Warren, Colorado naturalist, was driving in a prairie dog country when he saw two coyotes trot over a rise, one behind the other, followed by a badger. They ran off, the badger taking their tracks. A hundred yards or so away, the coyotes stopped, then turned and trotted on, the badger still following. Mr. Warren quotes a report, in *Yellowstone Nature Notes*, of a badger and a coyote playing together with "the intimacy and freedom of two bear cubs." In June of 1946, Weldon B. Robinson and Maynard B. Cummings, of the Wildlife Laboratory at Denver, watched a coyote and a badger "hunt together" for half an hour. The coyote kept the lead but frequently stopped to wait for the badger to catch up. Finally the coyote lay down while the badger hunted near by; then, apparently tired of such slow business, it ran off, leaving the badger hopelessly behind. This was in the Yellowstone National Park. That same day the observers while driving on a highway "frightened a coyote and a badger from behind a large rock at the edge of the road." [5]

Human beings err in trying to assign utilitarian motives to all behavior of other animals. A ranchman will sit in the shade looking out over the landscape and twirling a spur rowel by the hour. Why does he twirl the spur rowel? Why, just to be doing, to occupy time, to work off nervous energy of which he is not conscious. Much animal behavior is just as motiveless. Driving over the pass between the South Platte and Trout Creek in Colorado, my wife and I on an August afternoon saw a doe, followed closely by a buck, trotting after a badger. The deer turned back at seeing the car, while the badger crossed the road and went on up a draw — tending to his own business. The sprightly deer were no doubt just whiling away time on the grave badger — a very large, very gray and, it seemed to me, an especially serious individual. I ran up an embankment and watched him through glasses until he disappeared beyond a pine in a gully. A coyote may at times follow a badger as unpurposefully as this doe and her buck were following one.

The very flowers of the field seem to enjoy "dancing in the breeze." One sunny winter morning thirty-odd years ago a forest ranger in Arizona riding across Wild Horse Prairie in the Holbrook country saw an aggregation of coyotes ahead, stopped his horse and for a long while watched them. He counted fifteen, most of them sitting on their haunches. Now and then one would take after another, and the chase would cover maybe a half mile; then both would come back to the sitters in the sun. "They seemed to be enjoying themselves," the forester said, "but I've puzzled lots of times over their purpose."

Many odd friendships have occurred between individuals of divergent species — a cow and a rabbit, a mountain lion and a mule deer, a crow and a sheep, a bear and an antelope. It is not at all improbable that occasionally a particular coyote and a particular badger become comrades. Some coyotes no doubt delight in teasing badgers, apart from any idea of getting food, and occasionally the phlegmatic badger may enjoy sparring back. It is certain that coyotes relish badger meat. Coyote remains have

been found in badger stomachs also. Out of 14,829 coyote stomachs examined by Sperry, 47 contained badger remains; 12 of the 47 occurrences were identified as carrion.[6] It may be that once in a while co-operating coyotes master the difficult technique of killing a badger; it is doubtful if any lone coyote could kill a grown badger in sound health. The dog that can whip a badger is exceedingly rare.

Sentiment or no sentiment, there seems to be a kind of mutual attraction, an obscure rapport, a secret behind the impalpable curtains of nature, between coyote and *tlalcoyote*. The Casas Grandes pot with sculptured face of coyote opposite sculptured face of *tlalcoyote* will spin on its rounded and perfectly balanced bottom. The eared features are not upright, but horizontal. Twirl the pot, counterclockwise, and coyote follows badger and badger follows coyote — each "winning near the goal," forever associated and forever separated.

"Every ignorant person will kill a badger." Most of the badgers killed are killed — not ignorantly — by government trappers after coyotes. Badgers come readily to scents, poisons, traps placed for coyotes. Their holes are a nuisance to range riders, but a benefit to the soil. Badgers control rodents. Their fur is an economic asset. Their existence delights all people cultivated enough to know that the pursuit of happiness is not limited to killing out of doors and to making money indoors.

There are rat dens impregnable to any squat badger, much more to any coyote. In a single cave within the lava-rock mountains of western Sonora I have seen enough cholla joints, heaped there by generations of pack rats, to fill a box car. Cholla cactus has a thornier defense than prickly pear. Yet any of the numerous species of wood rats inhabiting cactus country can run across or through the spines without injury to their delicate little feet. They are out mostly at night, feeding a great deal upon cactus, and it is then that coyotes catch them. The intimate studies of coyote habits have all been northward. Some day an ecological study of the south country of big prickly pear will reveal many interesting relationships between coyote and wood rat.

In the land of big prickly pear, rat dens dome up from a foot to five feet and stretch two or three yards across. The contents include dried pads of nopal, thorned stems of tasajillo (a cactus), thorny sticks of mesquite, catclaw and other spined brush. cow chips, horse chips, bones, pieces of deer antlers, rocks, tin, rags and other discards from man — any form of matter that the rat can find and carry. Rattlesnakes, bull snakes, chicken snakes and coachwhip snakes can get into the fortress easily, but there are

no blind ends to the tunnels, and unless a rat is surprised, it can retreat outwards. The chances of finding a rattlesnake in an unused den are good. The wood rat is a cleanly animal, not to be confused with wharf rats and other species that follow man. Some civilized men and many Indians have found its flesh succulent.

To enjoy roast meat, the coyote makes use of man's machinery. In the Brush Country nearly every winter and always in drouthy times, ranchmen burn pear for cattle. The pear-burner is a portable cylinder for holding gasoline, an attached air pump, and a short, flexible rubber hose running to a perforated metal coil. Compressed air forces the gasoline out of the coil in a fine spray. Ignited, the spray singes the thorns off pear leaves almost instantaneously, and sets afire the dry tinder composing rat dens.

Probably as many rats are roasted as are run out. The flame-thrower makes a roaring noise that can be heard by cattle and human beings hundreds of yards away. A coyote can hear it much farther. To him it is a dinner bell. Several coyotes will hang around a pear-burner. They like rat meat roasted as well as raw. Burn a rat's den one day, return the next, and you will likely find that a coyote has investigated the ash-covered tunnels.

One species of rat common over large areas that sportsmen should be grateful to the coyote for destroying is the cotton rat, a very active enemy of quail. Its nests are usually more vulnerable than those of wood rats, and it comes out more in daytime, when hawks hunt it with success, especially the marsh hawk — another unacknowledged friend of bipedal preyers on quail. The bipeds turn loose their house cats, more deadly all the year round on game birds than shotguns in the hunting season and more destructive of song birds than all the air guns — and then, while complaining of the quail shortage, gloat over shooting a coyote, which, according to the great biologist and naturalist Vernon Bailey, takes "special delight" in killing cats.* But, rats!

In the fall of 1946 I spent several days on a border ranch where a crew of men with bulldozer and other machinery were constructing a tank. The bulldozer was tearing down a thicket of pear and brush on earth to be scooped out and piled into a dam. One day at this tank I saw a coyote standing in a fringe of brush. The tanker said that the coyote was a regular attendant, catching rats routed out by the bulldozer and looking for mashed ones.

---

* "During long years of trapping and trying to read all the signs, I have found a large number of house cats killed by coyotes. My belief is that most coyotes will kill any cat that does not beat them to a tree. Some coyotes will certainly eat a cat as readily as they eat a rabbit. One captive coyote I had would kill and eat every cat that came within the length of its chain. Many times tracks in mud have shown me where coyotes had run a cat up a fence post, no trees being available, and then somehow managed to dislodge it and devour it. Most of the cats they put up trees can probably outwait them." — Joe E. Hill. A woman in Montana told me that her pet coyote, a two-year-old female, made friends with every animal about the place — dogs, hogs, a pet deer, horse — except the cats. It had killed several cats.

One coolish morning on this same ranch I set a big rat den afire to loiter by while I rested from deer-hunting. The crackle of sticks had barely started when I heard a faint sound in thick brush bordering the little opening in which I stood. A shutter flash of movement caught my eye the briefest instant before a large wildcat jumped out. He stopped as suddenly as he had come, not ten steps away. For maybe two minutes, without moving an eyelash, he gazed past my immobile form. Then, with one effortless spring, he flashed back into the brush and was gone. My conclusion is that coyotes are not the only people of the *monte* who make deductions about the effect of fire on rat fortifications. Of course, the wildcat may have just happened along.

In winter many range cattle are fed a ration of cottonseed cake, scattered in small pieces over the ground. It is very nourishing and is not unpalatable to human taste. Coyotes probably learned about it soon after it was manufactured. They find fragments of the cake overlooked by lumbersome bovines; often they eat with the cattle, coming to the caking grounds at the sound of the feed truck. In the winter of 1947–1948, a boy of the Brush Country calling his cattle to cottonseed cake saw a coyote approaching through the brush; every day after that he watched for coyotes while he called and often saw three or four coming for their share. Joe Hill, who feeds cottonseed cake to his dogs and captive coyotes, once counted nineteen coyotes foraging over a feed ground in a dry lake.

Range cattle like to bed in open places, especially along a fence or road. A country pup breaking his neck to plunge his nose into a pool of warm calf dung explains why coyotes habitually visit bed grounds. Calf dung is permeated with milk not fully digested. Old hounds well fed on canned dog food eagerly lap up the droppings of young calves. Nine hundred and ninety-nine times out of a thousand, a coyote following cows and calves is not planning to kill but is only expecting a calf's deposit. Coyotes investigate, too, the bed grounds of big steers. There might be something in their droppings. Like blackbirds, they pick undigested grain out of horse droppings.

In the running season, buck deer fight each other, antlers clashing against antlers. The sound attracts other eager bucks. Every battle of the bucks is doe-inspired. Hunters, more in the Brush Country of south Texas than anywhere else, station themselves in coverts and rattle horns to lure bucks into range. Many deer are wounded and left to the coyotes. The coyotes know what horn-rattling means as well as they know what a shot in hunting season means. One horn-rattler told me that while he was up in a tree trying to entice a buck, he saw a coyote circle the place four times. Finally a buck came into view; the hunter wounded it, and as it ran off, the coyote fell in behind, yipping for help. In the bird-shooting season, coyotes no doubt stalk hunters, gleaning the dead and wounded quail and doves they have been unable to find, just as foxes in England glean behind pheasant-shooters. A duck-hunter told me of seeing a coyote, notified by shots, find a wounded duck in marsh grass.

From the Rio Grande to Canada, coyotes long ago learned that cars on highways provide food. They are not so constantly visible as patrolling magpies, crows, ravens and buzzards, but at night and in early morning, they hunt up and down the roads for dead rabbits, possums, birds and other victims of blinding headlights. Occasionally, but only occasionally, is a coyote run over by a car, either in daylight or in darkness. Before dashing across the road, he is likely to look both ways.

In the snow of Yellowstone National Park, Adolph Murie found coyotes traveling up and down roadsides in the wake of a snowplow and following buffaloes that partly cleared meadow ground by pawing for grass.* The coyotes were finding exposed

* It is in this manner that cattle sometimes follow horses to graze where the stronger uncloven hoofs have pawed and broken through crusts of ice. In the Big Bend country of Texas, deer follow cattle to eat the yucca stalks, which

[73]

field mice.[7] Resistant by nature to bitter cold, field mice do not hibernate, but harbor in dry grass and make their living beneath the snow.

Out of the cold Northwest comes this sympathetic picture. "The big bull elk began pawing down through fourteen inches of snow for the bunch grass beneath. Two hundred yards farther up the mountain, a gray coyote stepped into view. After looking down the slope for a minute at the elk, he trotted into the meadow. There he poked his nose through tufts of grass sticking up out of the elk's tracks, looking for mice. Although I watched him carefully, I did not see him catch a mouse. Slowly he investigated each of the pawed-out places, until he came up within a few yards of the bull. There he stood for a few moments sizing up the situation. Then he trotted casually around the bull, until he was directly in front of him. Stopping again, he looked up into the elk's face from a range of only a few feet.

"If the old bull saw him, he did not show it. To say he ignored the saucy coyote would be an under-statement. He was the royal rajah suddenly confronted by one of the untouchables. He didn't look at the little wolf — he looked right through him, and went on feeding as though he didn't exist. As for the coyote, he seemed to regard this lack of recognition as just what he wanted. After a moment or two of close study, he dodged around to one side of the bull and stood almost in his shadow. The elk still ignoring him, he moved even closer.

"Then as the bull lifted his forefoot to paw away the snow from the grass, the coyote stood poised to pounce on any mouse that might be kicked out of cover. I watched that smart little wolf use the proud old bull for a mouse-digger for the better part of half an hour. Several times I saw him duck right under the elk's belly and snatch a mouse from under his feet. Finally, the old bull lay down, and the coyote went happily on his way." [8]

_____

are very succulent but which the deer do not have the power to break down from amidst the dagger-pointed leaves protecting them.

Adolph Murie concludes that a good part of the evidence against coyotes as destroyers of grouse simmers down to the fact that they pick up grouse that have killed themselves by flying into wire fences — a frequent accident among these precipitous birds.[9] On the plains of the Pecos, coyotes patrol fences regularly to pick up quail killed by flying into wire. Joe Hill, who gave me this fact, says that foxes and cats catch more quail and other birds than coyotes. Something in coyote nature seems to make the animal enjoy getting food by indirect methods. It is not at all unlikely that coyotes flush grouse and quail for the purpose of trying to make them dash into wire. One coyote [10] jumped against net wire enclosing domestic turkeys, thus scaring them into flying over, and then wantonly killed thirty of them.

John W. Crook watched two coyotes for a full hour "fooling around" some ducks in a creek. Finally one coyote crawled on its belly to the edge of the water and dived. At seeing the movement, the ducks dived also. Whether the coyotes could distinguish under-swimmers from other ducks, Mr. Crook did not say. The ducks dived, stayed under a short time, surfaced, and flew away. The coyote came up with a duck in his mouth, swam ashore, and started off, the other coyote joining him. Crook then shot and killed the diving coyote. He examined the dead duck. It had been bit in the head.

In the San Joaquin Valley a farmer observed a coyote making a habit of following irrigation water and picking up pocket gophers flooded out of their holes. This coyote became friendly with the man and went about with him like a dog. The man placed a high value on the coyote's services and was extremely angry when a "sportsman" shot it. A coyote that means loss on a poultry farm may be a positive gain in an alfalfa field where gophers are working. "The economic status of a coyote may be a question of locality." [11] In whatever locality he rustles, the coyote looks for the main chance. This bent is not, of course, confined to any one species. An orange peel dropped where pill bugs have never sensed citrus fruit will attract scores in one night's time; a prairie fire that puts grasshoppers to flight will, in northwest Texas, attract Mississippi kites many miles from all directions to hunt the air ahead of the flames.

The provider of meat that the coyote positively fears is the panther, or mountain lion. After killing a deer or some other animal and eating what it wants, the panther loosely covers the carcass with leaves, sticks, grass, and such. Its choice of flesh is the kidneys and the leaf fat of the entrails, and in getting to these parts it guts the carcass. Thus the panther may leave a fat buck cleaned against soon spoiling but otherwise almost untouched to tempt the meat-eating world. I have helped eat a fresh ham from a panther-killed buck. Any coyote in the country is sure to sense the blood — also the individual that drew it. The coyote knows that the keen-scented, stealthy panther may be near the carcass, or that if gone far away, it is due to come back in the softest and quickest of ways. The coyote fears to take chances with this provider. The provider habitually eats only fresh meat, disdaining all tainted flesh. A trapper who is a kind of coyote himself told me that he once kept an eye on two lion-killed bucks for six days before coyotes touched either. The lion did not return to his kills, but his odor had to evaporate and the carcasses turn to carrion before the coyotes dared eat. J. W. Montgomery, a trapper at Langtry, Texas, unusually careful of facts, thinks that coyotes hardly ever bother a lion's kill before it has lain four days. He watched one deer carcass that coyotes padded a trail around for ten nights before they began devouring it. The greenest coyote, Montgomery claims, will run from a trap scented with panther urine.

By reading plain tracks, Guy Skiles saw where a panther had leaped from a bluff upon a coyote that was eating from a dead calf bogged in a mud hole. The panther ate the coyote up.[12] Now and then a panther coming upon a trapped coyote kills it and eats it.

One day years ago a cowboy loped up to a roundup near ranch quarters in the Davis Mountains (Texas) and reported that he had just sighted a panther eating on a deer it had killed while three coyotes, keeping their distance, were circling the panther and barking at him. The ranchman took his dogs and two cowboys and went straight to the kill. The coyotes were still near, but they were leaving untouched the deer carcass, which the panther had covered up, after finishing his meal, and had left. It is said that buzzards do not molest a panther's kill until it begins to decay.

In the hot countries of Mexico, the coyote has the jaguar to fear even more than the panther. A ranchero in Sinaloa who was losing stock to a *tigre* took a young goat out to an open hillside one evening, cut its throat, smeared the blood about, put strychnine into the carcass, and then, armed with rifle, pistol and machete, climbed a tree to await the enemy. The moon rose full, and in the clear light he saw a coyote trot up, gorge on the goat and writhe to death. The ranchero made no move. After a long while, when the moon was high, he heard a *tigre* rumbling. The beast was coming out of the barranca — a deep canyon. The ranchero waited. Suddenly he saw the white spots on the *tigre* almost at the dead goat. It stood there, opened its mouth, and let out a bloodcurdling rumble. Then it leaped clear over the goat, seized the dead coyote in its jaws, and trotted away into the woods. The ranchero had forgotten about his weapons.[10]

The coyote divides all animal life into three categories: animals to be eaten; animals to aid him in capturing food; animals that will eat him. Bears and men, along with panthers, belong in the third category.

"Tracks in the sky," Indians call buzzards.* The Indians of

---

* "The Gaucho pointed to the sky and said, 'See! There is a lion!' I started from my reverie and strained my eyes, but to no purpose, until he showed me at last, very high in the air, a number of large vultures. They were up there, he said, watching a lion devour some carcass." — Captain F. B. Head, *Rough Notes Taken . . . across the Pampas*, Boston, 1827, 220.

[79]

Baja California and elsewhere would not in the old days kill a panther or a buzzard, because the first brought down meat difficult for them to kill, and the second showed them where it was waiting.[14] "Tracks in the sky" tell trappers where to set traps — at carrion — and to locate dens, to which the parent coyotes have brought meat. Mexicans claim that buzzards will not eat a dead coyote, *"porque son amigos"* (because they are friends). The Deer Dance of the Yaqui Indians pantomimes two coyotes and two buzzards trailing down a deer together. Buzzards will eat dead coyotes, at times at least, but if the coyote regards anybody with feelings of friendly sentiment, it should be the buzzard. The coyote can smell far, but he can't smell nearly so far as the buzzard sees. Sitting at his ease or trotting along, he watches the buzzards sweeping the skies; the buzzards always watch each other; and when the coyote sees them circling together high up and then spiraling downward, he knows they have located meat — for him. The buzzards sail around a coyote; he kills for them. Maybe he won't leave much, but something; maybe he will kill a skunk merely to wallow on it; they devour it. *Son amigos.*

"And never a coyote comes out of his lair for killing, in the country of the carrion crows," says Mary Austin in her wise and beautiful book *The Land of Little Rain*, "but he looks up first to see where they are gathering." After he arrives at their gathering, or as they gather at his meal-taking, the crow people continue to be useful. Flying or perched on a tree, they caw out notice of any approaching intruder. He looks and judges for himself whether to leave or keep on eating.

After spending many hours watching coyotes and ravens in conjunction, Adolph Murie wrote: "On the morning of January 15, 1938, I saw a coyote trotting along the base of Mount Everts on the margin of a wide flat. Across the flat a raven was standing on a snow-drift. When the coyote had trotted to a point opposite the raven, about 200 yards away, it turned its course directly toward the bird. By that time, a second raven had alighted beside the first one to feed on a tiny food morsel it had been carrying. When the coyote was somewhat less than ten yards from the feeding raven, it made a quick dash. The raven easily escaped and lit again a few yards to one side. The coyote sniffed the spot where the raven had been feeding and then made another dash for it. These tactics were repeated six or seven times before the bird flew off about 250 yards. After peering at the departing bird, and seeming to hesitate whether or not to follow, the coyote trotted after it. When the coyote had covered half the distance, the raven circled back, wheeling fifteen or twenty feet over the coyote, which looked up.

"The raven lit on the snow again to feed on its morsel, and the coyote trotted along as if to pass it, but suddenly turned to make another quick charge. These rushes, as before, were repeated five or six times. Once the coyote leaped high in the air toward the raven and rolled over twice when it hit the snow. The raven finally flew away along the river and the coyote disappeared in a draw. It appeared that both animals were enjoying the fun, for the raven could easily have flown away to escape if it were annoyed, and it would seem that the coyote, which was probably well fed by the abundant carrion, would not have been so persistent unless he were enjoying the play." [15]

Another time Adolph Murie watched two coyotes interrupt tugging at a carcass to rush repeatedly at ravens and magpies hopping just beyond reach. The sallies were evidently not attempts to catch the birds but to drive them away. Then, going separate ways, the two coyotes, each followed by circling ravens, carried off pieces of the carcass to bury. A lady in Bozeman, Montana, reports having seen a crow fly down and pick hair out of a coyote's tail.

In the Rocky Mountains country, magpies indirectly get the coyote blamed for destroying life taken by a far inferior predator. Magpies catch wood ticks (which give spotted fever to people) off horses, deer, elk and cattle. A magpie lighted on the hock of an animal and picking ticks from its belly or from between its legs makes a pleasing sight. Wood ticks concentrate on the neck behind the ears. They paralyze colts and fawns. Watching magpies, the coyote is led to the paralyzed animal, and in finishing it off is useful rather than harmful.

A hawk will occasionally swoop low after a coyote carrying a rabbit, but it must be seldom that he gets what he is after. An adult marsh hawk was seen swooping down persistently on two moving coyotes, very much as a mockingbird dives peckingly at a dog or cat. Range men have told me of seeing coyotes run along under a hawk that had seized a rabbit. The animal is wary of eagles, which catch half-grown pups.

The caracara, called prairie eagle in the border country and named "bone-breaker" by the Mexicans, in habits both raptorial and carrion, preys particularly on jack rabbits. Caracaras often hunt in pairs. If the jack rabbit gets into brush before they overtake him, they will fly as close down as they can, trying to drive him out. Whenever a rabbit is hooked by claws, it makes a distressing cry that can be heard by a coyote several hundred yards away. Any coyote is interested in any hunt from the air. He can follow the caracaras by the cackling talk they make as well as by sight. He can get under any brush that a jack rabbit can get under, and thus he sometimes takes what the caracaras have cornered. Sometimes he snatches a rabbit before the caracara can eat it or get away with it.[16]

The sound that seems to lure a coyote more quickly than any other into unwariness is the cry of a distressed jack rabbit. "Coyote-callers," as simple in construction as mechanical turkey-callers, are now manufactured. Imitation by human mouth of a mouse squeak is not much of a feat; imitating a rabbit's squeal of distress is more difficult; simulating a coyote howl well enough to make real coyotes respond is a rare accomplishment. The one convincing man-howler to whom I have listened is famous hundreds of miles away. There is nothing new about calling up coyotes by imitating a rabbit squeal,* but the practice seems to be spreading. Some men consider calling up coyotes and shooting them sport.

J. R. Alcorn of Nevada, whose exposition on the subject [17] indicates that he is an artist at giving all three kinds of calls, recommends howling — especially in fall, winter and early spring — in order to locate coyotes by their responses. The imitator can then go to the vicinity of some responder and give the "distress call," the high-pitched cry of a rabbit. In one day, Mr. Alcorn decoyed twenty-four coyotes and two lynx cats into visibility and shot seven of the coyotes. On another day, fourteen magpies and one marsh hawk came to the distress call. Magpies frequently precede the approach of a coyote to the call, he says. While hidden among boulders, Mr. Alcorn watched one coyote approach within six feet before she discovered him, by a movement of his shotgun. Some coyotes came running to the caller, others trotting. All ages and both sexes come. When the wind is blowing, coyotes are likely to scent the human deceiver before getting in sight; when they do scent him, they turn and go the other way at once.

Grazing sheep stir up insects that are eaten by cowbirds; cowbirds pick bloodsuckers off the sheep. In favoring the other, neither species is motivated by altruism. The coyote no more recognizes debt to his benefactors than the usual recipient of wealth from an unearned increment recognizes his debt to the society responsible for that increment. Nor are the receivers of benefits from the coyote any more grateful.

Very likely there are more receivers than we know about. The

* "If any one imitate the voice of the hare, in order to attract wolves, a number of magpies immediately come and settle in the neighborhood." — Maximilian, Prince of Wied, *Travels* (1832–1833) in Thwaites, *Early Western Travels*, Vol. 24, 44.

In 1847 a nine-year-old German boy who had emigrated to Texas with his parents and was living on a farm near San Antonio used to "lie down in the tall grass and bleat like a calf until the wolves came up to within five or six feet, and then he would jump up and throw rocks at them." — *Life and Memoirs* of Emil Frederick Wurzbach, San Antonio, Texas, 1937, 14.

interdependences of the particles, from lice to men, making up the living world are intricate beyond comprehension. In Lower California an ornithologist found a nest of the northern ash-throated flycatcher in a woodpecker hole in a giant cactus. The birds had filled about 200 cubic inches with hair from rabbits, kangaroo rats, ground squirrels and other animals. How and where, the ornithologist asked himself, could the birds have secured so much and such a variety of hair? He went to picking apart the hairs in the nest. He found two small pieces of coyote dung that had not been completely shredded out. Here was the source of the flycatcher's hair nest.

It is possible to overemphasize coyote intelligence. What science calls symbiosis is nothing more than the instinctive use that one form of life makes of another; much of it entails no more intelligence than ball moss exercises in attaching itself to a live oak tree. Without apparent exercise of intelligence, the shark-sucker fish adheres to the surface of the shark's body, is transported to wherever the shark catches food, and eats pieces not devoured by its host. But there are degrees in everything, from the leech of the genus Hirundo to the leech of Homo sapiens.

IV · CO-OPERATION

THE HIGHER THE INTELLIGENCE of any species, the more variations in behavior among its individuals. The degree of their uniformity is in ratio to their stupidity. Sheeplike people fear any divergence from the walled trails in which they walk up and down. They come to believe, often passionately, that the walls are sacred and that anybody who jumps over or points out a new trail is anti-social, subversive, at best "a crackpot." Coyotes probably are not so intelligent as the most sheeplike human beings, but on their own level of intelligence they often exhibit extraordinarily individualistic conduct.

Lieutenant Wise of the U. S. Army, in California during the Mexican War, relates that one day while hunting in the hills near Monterey, he saw three coyotes. "I blazed away," he says, "with the carbine, which brought one of them tumbling down the steep slope, but, much to my surprise, his two friends followed and actually bolstered up their wounded comrade and assisted him out of sight before I could send another bullet." [1]

Not many trappers put credence in the often repeated assertion that coyotes bring food to one of their tribe held in a trap.

However, John W. Crook asserts that he has several times seen where a rabbit was brought to and eaten by a coyote dragging a trap. Accused in his lifetime of nature-faking, Enos Mills, nevertheless, made many acute observations acceptable to naturalists. After commenting on the commonly known efforts of parent coyotes to divert human beings from a den, he says: "I have also seen one or more coyotes stay near a crippled coyote as though taking care of him, and attempt to lure away any hunter who approached." [2]

Such conduct would not be contrary to nature. The fang and claw conception of life in the wild has been overemphasized by a society devoted to propagating the philosophy of greed under the guise of free enterprise. In that book of revolutionary thought, *Mutual Aid*, first published in 1890, Prince Kropotkin adduces many instances of social consciousness among animals.[3] A weasel picked up and carried away an injured comrade; a wounded badger was likewise rescued; a blind pelican in Utah was well fed by other pelicans on fish they had to carry thirty miles; two crows brought food to a wounded crow in a hollow tree. When I was a boy, I and my brothers and older sister rescued a half dozen or more young grackles that had been dislodged from their nests by wind and rain, placed them in a keg filled with straw, set the keg on the roof of a shed near the trees in which the grackles nested, and watched adults feed them until they flew away. The feeding seemed to be communal. Now and then, a fresh cow on the range permits an orphan calf to suck and finally claims it.

It is in catching game that coyote co-operation seems most cunning, at times taking the form of carefully prearranged strategy. In the fall of 1896, Bob Beverly * was riding for the Quien

* Bob Beverly, now of Lovington, New Mexico, is an old cowboy of open range days who meditates on experiences. In his privately printed *Hobo of the Range Land* (Lovington, New Mexico, 1940), he wrote: "The cowboy of the old West worked in a land that seemed to be grieving over something — a kind of sadness, loneliness in a deathly quiet. One not acquainted with the plains

Sabe cow outfit on the plains in the vicinity of Midland, Texas. One day, as he writes in a letter, he and another hand named Barnes Tillous were passing near some dry lakes. The salt grass in them had been burned during the summer and now, after a rain, it was fresh and green. At this time of year sand-hill cranes migrated south by the tens of thousands.

"As Barnes Tillous and I rode along," Bob Beverly says, "we spotted a large bunch of the cranes in the grass about a mile off. They were gathered close together and were standing with their necks stretched up as high as they could stretch them. They seemed to be intent on watching something. Then I noticed a coyote in the grass, off three or four hundred yards, turning somersaults and running round and round, keeping all the cranes intent on him.

" 'You see that coyote?' I asked Tillous.

" 'Yes,' he replied, 'but over there is the one they had better be watching,' and he pointed to grass back behind the cranes.

"I looked and saw another coyote slipping along, nearly crawling on the ground, keeping a bunch of sagebrush between him and the cranes. We stopped and sat there on our horses to watch the show. As the crawling coyote got nearer and nearer, the one that was doing the acting jumped higher and cut more capers. He was working faster and faster to hold the attention of the cranes.

"In a little while the coyote slipping up got within about thirty yards of the cranes. He made a jump and ran full speed for them. Sand-hill cranes require some time to take off, and the coyote caught one before it left the ground. The actor-coyote had farther to run, and by the time he got to the spot all the cranes were gone except the one held by his *compadre*. He grabbed it, and right there they tore the crane in two and ate it." [4]

M. P. Skinner has been field naturalist with the Roosevelt Wild

---

could not understand what effect it had on the mind. It produced a heartache and a sense of exile."

Life Experiment Station at Syracuse, New York, since 1924; before that he was naturalist in the Yellowstone National Park. His credentials are acceptable anywhere. In *The Yellowstone Nature Book* he details an instance of coyote ingenuity that just about takes the prize for planned economy in the animal world.[5]

One summer afternoon while walking along the shore of Yellowstone Lake, he saw a few pelicans fishing in water beyond a large boulder on the beach. Between the shore and not distant woods stretched a grassy meadow. Presently he noticed two coyotes sneaking up through the grass to the boulder, one full grown and the other smaller — probably a female and one of her pups. To get to the pelicans, any animal of prey would have to expose himself, and exposure would certainly alarm them. The coyotes, hidden from the pelicans, waited behind the boulder for five minutes or so; then the grown coyote waved her tail so that the pelicans could see the tip. Their curiosity was evident, and they began to wade, haltingly, shoreward. Still, they were too cautious to come all the way. After some more waiting, the grown coyote dashed out on the beach; the birds were safe against a surprise catch — and they knew it.

The half-grown coyote was still hidden from them. The other one, after sitting still for a short while and watching the big birds, began running up and down on the beach, "catching up bits of wood and throwing them into the air, chasing her tail, crouching and making sudden springs into the air." Then she trotted off up the meadow without a glance backward. The pelicans were still curious. Perhaps they were remembering the waving object they had seen at the boulder. They began nearing it, where the little coyote waited. At this juncture, a big elk crashed out of the forest with a snort and scared the young coyote away. He went trotting up the meadow, the way the old coyote had gone, the elk after him.

Sure now that they were safe, the pelicans came ashore. A swift dash from an unexpected quarter showed that they were wrong. A third coyote, hitherto unseen by the watching naturalist, sprang out of the grass and caught a pelican, which he threw "across his shoulder" and carried up the meadow after the others.

A teacher in a school for boys near Colorado Springs told me that one morning he observed two coyotes sneaking along the margin of a lake in which ducks were feeding. The ducks were out of reach, but to make themselves doubly safe flew to the other side and after a while went to diving for food among reed stalks. The next morning the teacher saw the ducks at the same place they had been the morning before and saw a coyote — only one — come along and scare them across the lake. They kept out in the open a considerable time before they went to feeding against the reeds. Finally one got in close to the bank lining, and a coyote, presumably a confederate of the first one, grabbed it.

Summer and winter, day and night, all the year round, buffalo wolves dogged the great buffalo herds of the plains, as persistently as cowbirds stayed with them in temperate weather. They pulled the drags and stragglers down at will. While the little prairie wolves sometimes got a buffalo, their portion of that wonderfully nutritive meat was as a rule only what poor relations usually get from the powerful. Coyotes sometimes gang up in packs like gray wolves, overcoming prey by sheer numbers, but generally they show more variety and spontaneity in their co-operative ruses. By nature they largely depend for meat upon juicy prairie dogs, rabbits and other "small deer" that call for cunning, rather than power, in the capture.

Under the aboriginal balance of nature, prairie dogs were in some seasons a primary source. Because prairie dogs eat grass, in drouthy times even the roots, competing with property in the form of livestock, they have been poisoned out until now comparatively few exist. They were once incredibly numerous — perhaps as numerous as the extinct passenger pigeon. On a ride across the Staked Plains in 1852, R. B. Marcy traversed one prairie dog town covering about 1,000,000 acres that contained, according to his estimate, 50,000,000 animals. In 1853, John R. Bartlett traveled for three days, at the rate of twenty miles per day, across a prairie dog town along Brady Creek, a branch of the Colorado River of Texas. He noted the prairie dog habitations to be on the average about ten yards apart. He estimated that if the town were 50 miles long and only 10 miles wide and if the holes were 30 feet apart and averaged only 2 animals to the hole, the 500 square miles within the town limits would contain 30,000,000 prairie dogs. In 1900 the careful biologist Hart

Merriam roughly surveyed a dog town 100 miles wide that extended for 250 miles north of San Angelo, Texas. Estimating 25 prairie dogs to the acre, he arrived at 400,000,000 animals on the 16,000,000-acre expanse. As late as 1931, Vernon Bailey, always conservative with figures, estimated that there were 6,400,000 prairie dogs in Grant County, New Mexico, alone.[6]

A typical prairie dog hole goes down almost perpendicularly from ten to twenty feet, extends out horizontally an equal length, and has side chambers. It is protected against surface water by a funnel-shaped mound from six inches to a foot high. The inhabitants keep their grounds cleared of weeds that enemies can lurk behind; they refuse to burrow against brush and trees. They are strictly diurnal in habits. They are always on the lookout and warn each other of danger by incessant barking and chattering. Their enemies are varied: snakes that glide, hawks and eagles that fly, and all the carnivores — wolves, coyotes, skunks, foxes, badgers, wildcats, and even hungry panthers. As General R. I. Dodge said, the prairie dog "has no more dog about him than the grey squirrel." Had the animal been given another name, carnivorous white men would probably have joined Pueblo Indians in eating it.* The Indians snare it; coyotes have to be more artful.

In some ways Don Alberto Guajardo of Coahuila, Mexico, was the most interesting man of the *campo* — the whole outdoors — that I have ever known. He knew more about native medicinal plants than a dozen *curanderas* — herb women — and used to export bales of them, dried, to Czechoslovakia and Italy. He employed weavers to make blankets — and I wouldn't trade two that I cover myself with every winter for anything that the U. S. Army issues to its soldiers. He knew how to bleat up both deer and jaguars; he claimed to have had a bullet wound cleaned properly, after one of his revolutionary episodes, by lying in shallow water of the Rio Grande and letting minnows exercise their surgical powers on it. In youth he had taught himself to read Latin, French and English; in old age he compiled history from masses of Spanish documents that revolution brought — in Alexandre Dumas style — to his hands. Always he asserted that the main contributor to his education had been an old Lipan Indian.

One time during his boyhood, he told me, he went out deer-

* "It is not easy, says Doctor Johnson, to fix the principles upon which mankind have agreed to eat some animals and reject others; and as the principle is not evident, it is not uniform." Richard Burton, who quotes this Johnsonian deduction in *The City of the Saints*, says that the Mountain Men tried "wolf mutton," coyote meat, in hard times and found it "by no means bad." Frontiersmen, however, did not resort to it so frequently as to panther meat, which is excellent. According to George Bird Grinnell (*The Fighting Cheyennes*, page 72), the Cheyennes looked upon coyote pups as a delicacy. When times get hard enough, any meat is good — "Hoover hogs," for example, as armadillos came to be called in some localities about 1932. But the meat of a grown dog-coyote is as rank as that of the rankest old billy goat.

hunting with this Lipan. They were skulking in scattered brush on a mountainside overlooking a valley populated by prairie dogs. The sky was threatening rain. While they were looking, listening, lingering, the sound of a great barking of prairie dogs came up to them. Then Don Alberto noticed a coyote on the edge of the prairie dog town, close to the base of the mountain. The coyote went to scratching at a dog hole into which his approach had sent the owner.

"Surely," said Don Alberto to the old Lipan, "that coyote is not crazy enough to think he can dig down to the bottom of a prairie dog hole."

"No, no," replied the old hunter, waving his finger back and forth to accent the negation. "The coyote knows what he is doing. Wait with patience and you shall see."

By now thunder was rolling up. Even people without coyote prescience on weather matters could tell that it was going to rain. The plan of the engineer at the prairie dog hole became apparent. He was pulling down the craterlike mounds around two or three holes and using the dirt to throw up a rough V-shaped dam, the flanges pointed uphill and enclosing one of the holes near the apex. Presently the heavens turned loose. The rain was a regular "gully-washer and fence-lifter." It rained pitchforks and bobtailed heifer yearlings. Water flowed down the mountainside in sheets. That caught by the coyote's dam poured into the hole. Meantime the coyote had placed himself in a waiting position just downward from the apex. The typical prairie dog hole has a roomy side tunnel, or station, not a great distance below the mouth, where the owner and his family can remain clear of water going on down to the bottom. Many a boy trying to drown out a prairie dog has learned that buckets of water are not enough. But here a stream was being diverted into the hole. As the rain slackened, the two watchers on the mountainside saw a prairie dog emerge for air, only to be nabbed by the ingenious coyote.

Some years ago I spent a night with H. C. (Pete) Gamison at his cabin overlooking Eagle Nest Lake in northern New Mexico. At that time Gamison had spent towards half a century on the trails of wild animals. His English training for a doctor's career contributed to his civilized perspective on nature. One time, he told me, he watched a pair of coyotes out to catch a prairie dog. They tracked leisurely along, one right behind the other, towards the edge of a prairie dog town. A great chattering arose. The prairie dog they were headed for could see only the lead coyote, the one behind keeping his head down and his body hidden by that of the first. When near the mound on which this prairie dog stood nervously scolding, the lead coyote made a rush, and of course the prairie dog ducked. The sun was shining from a clear sky, and the coyote's leap over the hole darkened it. He went on, other prairie dogs chattering and ducking, the noise growing dimmer as he passed.

But the second coyote had stopped when the first one leaped, flattening himself out behind the dog mound. There he waited until the prairie dog should come up. After a considerable while, it reappeared, looking intently towards the enemy that had passed but was still in sight. It is the nature of a prairie dog to look for what has scared him. He is so low on the ground that his vision across level terrain is very limited; he sits upon his tail to raise his vision — sits and barks. While this one was indulging its nature, expressing sharp displeasure at the same time, the coyote accomplice made a leap and caught it. Then there was a tussle over the morsel, the two coyotes soon tearing it to pieces and devouring it.

Three days after learning from Pete Gamison, I called on Ernest Thompson Seton at Seton Village, a few miles out from Santa Fe. He was past eighty then; for two hours he poured out talk on the wild white cattle of Chillingham, in England, and on coyotes. Tears came into his eyes as he described the agony of one he saw strychnined. He vividly delineated co-operative strategy on prairie dogs very much as Pete Gamison had delineated it. As I was leaving, I bought a copy of *Trail of an Artist-Naturalist*, the story of Seton's life. That night I followed in it the mapped maneuvers of Coyote No. 1 and Coyote No. 2 at a prairie dog town.

A trail-driver and old-time cowman named J. W. Maltsberger, of Cotulla, Texas, gave me this account. On the Plains, early one morning many years ago, he saw a coyote stopping up prairie dog holes with dirt. After stopping up a few holes, the coyote retired some distance and sat down to look. He did not have to wait a great while before prairie dogs, eager to get to their breakfast, began coming out. The coyote kept quiet until one of them moved out towards the holes he had just plugged. Then he made a dash for it. The prairie dog, cut off from retreating into its own burrow, made for a neighbor's. But the door was closed. For a second the prairie dog hesitated at the refuge so unexpectedly vanished. The hesitation cost him his life.*

Hay-makers on top of a loaded wagon at George Bird Grinnell's Wyoming ranch had a clear view of another way of stalking a prairie dog. They saw the coyote, though he seemed oblivious of them, forty or fifty yards off "standing absolutely still, his nose and tail straight out in a line, one forefoot lifted from the ground, . . . pointing a prairie dog that was feeding near its hole over a slight rise of ground. Every little while the prairie dog would sit up and look about, and when it did this, the coyote would freeze. When the dog dropped down on all four feet and began to feed, the coyote would very slowly and stealthily creep a few feet nearer. This action went on for some

---

* Some people have held that a prairie dog will not go into a hole other than its own. J. Stokley Ligon of Carlsbad, New Mexico, for many years with the United States Biological Survey and the Fish and Wildlife Service, answers this credence thus in a letter: "A hard-pressed prairie dog cut off from his home burrow will go into any old or new hole he can get to in order to save his hide. There are always an ample number of 'dodge holes' in any dog town for just such emergencies. However, a prairie dog does not seem to relish having to resort to an escape hole; he usually streaks for his own quarters if he thinks he can make it."

minutes." Even after the coyote got over the slight rise of ground, the prairie dog did not detect him. Whenever the prairie dog looked, the enemy was immobile. Finally, the little grass-gnawer dropped down from the last survey it was ever to make of this egg-shaped earth; the coyote shot across the twelve or fifteen feet of intervening ground, picked up his prize, and trotted on.[7]

Many animals with keen eyesight for anything in motion seem to see stationary objects as a part of the landscape. Time and again, taking advantage of the wind and of the tail-shaking which accurately predicts the raising and lowering of the heads of white-tailed deer, I have slowly moved up close enough to feeding does to distinguish the individual hairs in their eyebrows. The beast of prey has infinite time to wait and limitless powers of immobility. A coyote does not mind waiting an hour motionless, flattened out near a prairie dog hole, for the submerged inhabitant, who also waits, to reappear; he does not mind waiting hours for a jack rabbit he has spotted under a sagebrush to go to sleep.

"What is time to a burro?" The instinct of animals, both predators and preyed upon, for waiting in vegetative blankness is beyond the patience of all but a few human beings. The spider at its web and the fawn motionless all day long in its grassy bed, except when its mother comes to suckle it swiftly, are characteristic of the whole animal world. On tireless wings, sweeping the ground of whole townships with telescopic eye, the buzzard "awaits the will of God" with no more apparent restiveness than the bud awaits sap and sunshine to unfold it into leaf. Coyotes probably get most of their meat by still-hunting alone, guided by scent and hearing as well as by eyes, now lying in wait as patiently as a snake beside a mouse runaway, now slipping up as unobtrusively as the shadow of a tree projects itself across the sward.

There is no way of estimating what percentage of the rabbits

[95]

eaten by coyotes are waylaid and what percentage are caught on the run. Many too young to run are consumed. Charles C. Sperry, after examining the contents of nearly 15,000 coyote stomachs, taken from 17 states over a period of 5 years, found that rabbits comprised 33.25 per cent of the total food eaten. In some states during some months the percentage rose to 55.[8] Wherever jack rabbits are plentiful and coyotes exist, this prolific hare of the West affords their principal non-vegetable food supply. Time and again the killing off of coyotes has raised cries of wrath and despair from graziers and from growers of fruit, grain and vegetables. A dozen or so jack rabbits will eat as much vegetation as a sheep, a fifth of what a cow eats; a horde of them will in a few nights denude a green field with the thoroughness of grasshoppers.

Coyotes habitually relay each other in chasing the jack rabbit. While both are on a dead run, a coyote will, with an upward pitch of his nose, sometimes knock the jack high into the air and grab it with his mouth as it comes down. At the end of a chase by two coyotes that I once saw, the one that caught came so close to me, standing by a bush, that he got scared and dropped the rabbit. Going downhill, a coyote can gain, but uphill and on level ground the jack rabbit has the advantage. If it did not circle, it could probably run away from nearly any coyote, but pursued animals circle — like a lost man. Thus, two or three coyotes working together can take turns cutting across circles and making stands.

Jack rabbits wax and wane in numbers by cycles. The year 1898 was one of the drouthy years in southern Texas and jack rabbits seemed to be taking the country. Tom Coleman of the vast Callaghan Ranch, much of it prairie, engaged George Bigford to kill them at five cents a head. Camping over the range, Bigford and his wife rode out daily in an open-topped buggy and shot. Each used a .44 Winchester. They loaded their own shells every night, often sitting up late to load a day's supply.

Many a day they took over a hundred scalps. During the season they killed over 10,000 jack rabbits. When they began shooting in the morning, buzzards would immediately appear; the buzzards and the coyotes had a continuous feast.

It was about this time that George Bigford witnessed a coyote maneuver that I have never seen or heard reported by any other man. In 1865, when he was ten years old, two years before the great Chisholm Trail for Texas cattle was traced off, he helped his father drive a herd of 2000 cattle to Arkansas. As buffalo hunter, Texas ranger, ranch hand and hunter he had, when

I interviewed him at Carrizo Springs, Texas, in 1931, lived all his life next to the ground. He was one of the best factual observers and one of the most directly honest men I have ever known.

He said that one day he saw about eight coyotes rounding up a considerable number of jack rabbits, bringing them into a loose huddle from various directions. The coyotes had no pen to drive them into, as the rabbit-drivers of the West use. They simply got the rabbits into a concentration, approaching from all sides, in the way that Pueblo Indians of New Mexico round up rabbits. Then one coyote dashed in and caught, the others quickly following. They were so close in and the rabbits were so numerous and so confused in scattering every which way that every coyote appeared to make a catch.*

* In the Red Forest of the Caucasus, about 1882, a noted English sportsman named Clive Phillipps-Wolley, accompanied by an old Russian forester who

According to Joe Hill, coyotes co-operate in driving jack rabbits into fences of closely strung barbed wire or woven smooth wire, built to enclose sheep. They work both sides of a fence together so that if the chased rabbit gets through — and the wire generally checks and is likely to stun it — it is picked up by the chaser's partner. "I have seen fifty miles of outside fence worked on both sides by coyotes after jack rabbits," Joe Hill says. "I have seen where a racing coyote slid for ten feet coming to a halt at a fence."

If coyote antics can trap pelicans and sand-hill cranes, why not jack rabbits also? Years ago an engineer on the Southern Pacific Railroad named Billy Renehan told Sam Woolford of San Antonio this story. One morning while he was looking out over the prairie from his engine cab on a sidetrack, he noticed a coyote silently jumping up and around. Then he saw a second coyote off some distance slinking slowly and carefully forward. Between the two, a sitting jack rabbit appeared to be fascinated by the didos of the first coyote and to be unaware of the approach of the other, which, when it got close enough, made a leap and knocked the victim over. Both shared it.*

Asked for a bear story, the "Big Bear of Arkansas" replied, "It is told in two sentences. A bear is started, and he is killed." For coyotes in their chases, the end is not always inevitable. In Idaho, a rabbit hotly pursued by a coyote jumped into an

was expert at reading sign, came upon a snow-covered opening in which a small band of roe-deer had been lying down when they were attacked by wolves. According to tracks, the wolves had entirely surrounded the opening and then dashed upon the deer from all sides at once. The remains of four or five were still visible. — Clive Phillipps-Wolley, *Big Game Shooting*, in the Badminton Library of Sports and Pastimes, II, 34.

* "It was a bright moonlight night when the vixen went into a field in which many rabbits and hares were feeding. On first seeing her, some ran away a few yards, some sat up on their hind legs and gazed at her, and some squatted close to the ground. She at first trotted on gently, as if not observing them; then she lay down and rolled on her back, then got up and shook herself; and so she went on until the simple creatures, cheated by a show of simplicity, fell to feeding again, when she quietly leaped amongst them and carried off an easy prey." — Thomas Smith, Esq., *The Life of a Fox*, London, 1843, 14.

abandoned prospect hole about twelve feet deep. The intent coyote followed. When men who saw the chase looked down, the rabbit was hunkered on one side at the bottom and the coyote on the other, the rabbit apparently as unfearful of the coyote as the coyote was now unhungry for rabbit. In common distress there are no aliens. Watching two coyotes chasing a cottontail, Henry Fletcher of the Big Bend of Texas saw the rabbit dash into a hole just as the lead coyote was about to grab. The coyote's head went in, but the hole was too small to admit his body. "He seemed to spin around on his nose. He got up with utter disgust on his face and went off." Sometimes the rabbit gets away in a most unplanned-for manner. Any port in a storm. Lincoln Lang, who ranched with Roosevelt, saw a blood-stained jack rabbit fleeing a coyote stop under the horse he rode.

The antelope is noted for its headstrong instinct to go in a direct line. One that is headed straight across a road in front of a fast-running car will sometimes dash into it rather than swerve — provided the driver of the car is also as headstrong. But in the end a chased antelope will usually circle so that the chasers can relay each other, just as mustangers used to run down wild horses. One plainsman recounts having sat on his horse for two hours watching three coyotes chase an antelope while the circles grew smaller, the coyotes on the inside of it cutting across shorter and shorter distances until they finally downed the animal.[9]

The clearest and fullest description of the operation on antelopes that I know is by George Bird Grinnell.[10] One morning while looking afoot for horses that had strayed from his camp in Wyoming, he got to the top of a hill just as an antelope doe came into view, closely followed by a coyote. "Both seemed to be running as hard as they could, and both had their tongues hanging out as if they had come a long way. Suddenly, almost at the heels of the antelope, appeared a second coyote, which now took up the running, while the first one stopped, and sat down and watched. The antelope ran quite a long distance, always bearing a little to the left and gradually losing speed. As she kept turning, it was evident that she would either run around the hill on which I stood or come back near it.

"I had become so interested in watching her that I forgot to look at the coyote that had halted near me, downhill. When I looked for him, he was trotting over a little ridge, keeping in view the chase now far off. He could easily have run across the cord of the arc, but he knew too well what the antelope would do to give himself that trouble. After a little, it was evident that she would come back to the hill on the side opposite to where I saw her pass. The rested coyote now trotted out two or three hundred yards on the prairie and sat down, watching. The antelope was headed almost directly towards him, and soon I could see that there were two coyotes behind her, one close at her heels and the other a long way back.

"The waiting coyote became quite excited in action. He no longer sat up, but crouched close to the ground, every few moments raising his head very slowly to take a look at the doe, and then lowering it again, so that he would be out of sight. Sometimes he crawled on his belly a few feet, evidently trying to put himself directly in the path of the oncoming antelope, and he seemed to be judging accurately. As the doe drew near him, I could see that she was staggering, she was so tired. The coyote behind could at any moment have knocked her down if he had wanted to, but he seemed to be waiting for something. The third coyote was now running faster and catching up.

"When the antelope reached the place where the first coyote was lying hidden in the grass, he sprang up and in a jump or two caught her by the neck and threw her down. At the same moment the two coyotes came up from behind. There was a brief scuffle, in which yellow and white and gray waving tails were all mixed up. Then the three prairie wolves began tearing away at their breakfast."

There is hardly another story of an American animal so moving in its quietness as Mary Austin's "The Last Antelope," in *Lost Borders*. For seven summers Little Pete camped at Lone Tree Spring with his flock. He was akin to the big juniper, to the hills, to the stars, to his own sheep, and to a lone antelope that ranged the valley. Summer after summer the coyotes raced and relayed on this antelope; it came to be a kind of game between pursued and pursuers. But years leaden all gracility, and one day, hard pressed, the pronghorn took refuge in Little Pete's flock. After that, the Mexican shepherd many a time would not take the sheep down to muddy the water until he was sure that his silent and distant-keeping companion had drunk. In the end it was not the coyotes that got the Last Antelope. It was a homesteader with a rifle, a self-righteous indignation against coyotes as "killers," a contempt for Mexicans, and a patriotic fidelity to the American way of life.

The hounding of antelopes sometimes proves to be a dangerous business for coyotes and disproves the popular idea that this animal never takes risks on his game. Ray Williams, who was for several years employed by the Texas Game Commission to study the antelope, told me that one June he watched eight grown antelopes run a coyote for twelve miles. It finally took refuge in a thornless bush called *clepino*. There the antelopes went to jumping on him with their knived hoofs. A buck hooked him out — dead. Antelope defense, and even aggression, against coyotes is well established.[11]

The grown antelopes destroyed by coyotes are oftener than not, it seems, sick or disabled; the same is true of grown deer. However, if deer retreat, coyotes know how to drive them into disadvantageous positions. One trick is to get them into deep-crusted snow.[12] The sharp-hoofed ones break through it at every jump, while on padded feet the lightweights skim across it, to surround and finally bring down the least enduring. In soft snow, if it is not too deep, the slim-legged deer may have the advantage. Coyote depredations on deer and antelope are mainly confined to the young. To catch fawns, two or three of them habitually work together, one worrying the mother while the other kills. If the doe did not become intent on chasing off the threateners, thus leaving her young exposed, she could by staying beside the fawns protect them with her sharp hoofs.

Coyotes employ similar ruses on sows and peccaries with pigs, and occasionally on a domestic cow or an elk with calf. They work in pairs to catch ground squirrels, one skulking along a ridge while the other scurries them uphill from open ground below.[13]

Foxiness in eluding men and dogs is cited oftener as proof of wild animal intelligence than foxiness in getting a living. Most people see game animals only as game. For one sensitive revelation like B B's *Wild Lone* * — the whole story of the life of a fox in the woods, meeting the badger, listening to the owl and the thrush, scenting walnut leaves, investigating a beetle, enjoying hunger, love and secrecy — there are a thousand narratives of the hunt, replete with the visible dodges played by the quarry.

In being chased as well as in chasing, the coyote shows his instinct for co-operation. Instances of it that have come my way seem, however, not so well authenticated as those of the coyote as chaser. For a generation Pete Crawford was noted as guide and hunter on the Rio Grande border. It must be said, also, that Pete Crawford mastered the art of entertaining his guests.

In 1926, as he used to tell, he and two other men were driving in a car over miles-wide tobosa (grass) flats when they saw a coyote. They turned after it and soon overtook it, but its sharp and quick turns kept them going for seven miles. By this time the coyote was so exhausted that it had great difficulty in dodging away from the wheels. Then a second coyote suddenly ap-

---

* Adolph Murie, whose *The Wolves of Mount McKinley* is a classic of reporting by a scientific watcher, considers *Wild Lone* "about the best nature writing I have read." Published in England in 1938, it has had scant circulation in America. B B is Denys Watkins-Pitchford, superb illustrator of his own books.

peared and put itself right in front of the car. After running alongside the exhausted coyote for a bit, it gradually angled away, seemingly in an attempt to draw the car after it. "It acted like a bird trying to entice a person away from its nest. There could be no doubt that it was trying to help the winded coyote." Pete Crawford and his companions took the dare, just for the sake of sport, but about this time the played-out coyote got through a fence, and then both of them made away.

The speed of various coyotes has been — unofficially — measured. Like horses, some naturally run faster than others. A Montana coyote clocked by R. E. Bateman for 5 miles spurted up to 35 miles per hour and at the end of the chase was going 30 miles. Charlie Stone, of Fort Stockton, Texas, who has broken many springs and all but broken his own neck chasing coyotes over rough prairies, avers that one got up to 55 miles per hour and held that speed for about half a mile, in front of "a new Chevrolet." His neighbor Clayton Williams says that a coyote once ran down a straight smooth lane in front of his car for 2 miles at 45 miles per hour. Victor H. Cahalane records a top speed of 43 miles per hour in a straight line for several hundred yards. Failing to outrun the car, this sprinter began twisting and dodging, and held out for 47 minutes before being run down and killed.[14]

Leon V. Almirall, a constant hunter of coyotes in the Northwest, saw one of his dogs chase two coyotes, catch up with the laggard of the two and get the better of it in fighting until the second coyote, which had escaped, came back and dashed into battle. The two made the dog retreat.[15]

It is not uncommon for a coyote, the female especially, whose immature offspring is being chased by hounds to spring in behind the pup, zigzag back and forth across the trail, and linger until the hounds get close enough to follow her. If they follow — and only the best-trained hounds resist such a temptation to switch — she will strike out in a direction contrary to that taken by her young one. In the Frio County brush of south Texas, hunters came to know well a pair of coyotes that they named Jim Ferguson and Ma Ferguson. If the dogs started Jim Ferguson and got hot after him, he would circle into Ma Ferguson's vicinity, and before long the dogs would be after her. If they started Ma, sometimes with a half-grown pup, she would be relieved in time by Jim. They afforded sport to hunters for four or five years, and so far as is known, neither of this pair ever was hounded down. As among men, it is the exceptional coyotes who have biographies.

P.S. "I have been told that they will frequently drive deer into the lake and sit down behind the sand-hills, on shore, watching until the exhausted animals return, and fall an easy prey to their pursuers." — Letter, from Chicago, concerning prairie wolves in *American Turf Register*, September, 1830, II, 40.

V · CALL THOU NOTHING UNCLEAN

THE COYOTE'S FAVORITE FOOD is anything he can chew; it does not have to be digestible. If his family had a coat of arms, it would bear the classical words, *Nihil a me alienum puto*. His catholicity respecting comestibles is absolute; he calls nothing "unclean." His investigative nature demands not only seeing, hearing, smelling, but often also chewing.

It took years for English-speakers coming out of the East into the Southwest to learn from Mexicans to stake their horses with *cabestros* (ropes woven from horse mane and tail), instead of with rawhide *reatas*. Later they used fiber ropes. A coyote will hardly chew hair or fiber unless it is tinctured with blood or grease, but a rawhide *reata* is his meat. Tallow or neat's-foot oil rubbed into the *reata*, to limber it, makes it a delicacy. Many a camper on the prairie has walked out in the dawn to find his horse gone, cut loose by a coyote.

After gnawing off every shred of flesh and sinew from the carcass of an old bull that has died on the range, coyotes will come back to the dried-up remainder for years and chew on a patch of hide. One has been known to walk backwards dragging a flint hide, as stiff as a board, for a mile.[1] A cast-away leather strap, cracked and dark with age, is a find. Of course, there is a bit of nourishment in any hide substance. Starving men have cut up their buckskin leggings and shoe tops to boil into soup.

One of the first railroads on the Pacific slope was a short line connecting Walla Walla, Washington, and the port of Wallula. A company chartered in 1868 had a train running over it in 1873. The first ten miles of the road had wooden rails, long stringers of fir laid across the ties. Iron wheels wore the wood severely, however, and according to the railroad's historian, the company plated the stringers with strips of steel. According to the Slow-Train-through-Arkansas school of historians, the plating was "Mexican iron" — rawhide.[2] Cowhides were more plentiful than steel. Strips of them moistened, stretched, cleated down and dried resisted wheel-grinding. But they were not tough enough to resist an element that had not been taken into account. That winter the coyotes chewed them up. However extravagant the joke may be on the Walla Walla-Wallula railroad, its fidelity to coyote chewing is unimpeachable.

A coyote is apt to take any kind of joke literally. Back in the days of the Texas Republic, as salty old Noah Smithwick chronicles the incident,[3] two men named Dickerson and McGeary were crossing the wide coastal prairie on horseback. Dickerson had just arrived from the States; McGeary considered himself a seasoned frontiersman. While the two were making their pallets down one night, the Texan told his fellow traveler that coyotes were bad about carrying off shoes and hats and that he must secure these articles under his pillow. Dickerson followed directions and went to sleep. The waiting McGeary then got up, very cautiously removed the hat and shoes from under the sleeping man's pillow and put them in a bush a few steps away. In order that the joke might appear more practical in the morning, he put his own shoes and hat with them.

When Dickerson awoke at daylight and found his coverings gone, he was vocably disturbed. Riding barefooted and bareheaded under a hot sun is a serious matter for any person used to civilized trappings. McGeary pretended to be highly sympathetic. Ostentatiously, he looked under his pillow for his own hat and shoes and raised a howl at not finding them. After he had enough of the fun, he told his fellow traveler what he had done, and they stepped to the bush. Scattered about, fragments of the hats were visible. The shoes were not. Coyotes had carried them off for prolonged chewing. They were luckier than the Utah coyote that stole into a freighter camp and hung his head in a coffeepot he tried licking.

O. W. Williams relates that while he was surveying on the Staked Plains in 1886, his crew killed a yearling for meat one morning, dressed it, put the carcass in the wagon and then — without washing their hands — chained a line about fifteen miles before camping for the night. As usual, at the end of the day's surveying, the chainmen placed all the iron surveying pins in a pile. The pile was about thirty feet from the campfire. Each pin had a red flannel rag tied to a ring, so that the man following the one who had stuck a pin in the ground at the end of a length of chain could easily see it. When the chainmen started out to survey next morning they couldn't find their pins. There was much searching. Finally one was found about fifty yards away, then all but two were found, in various places where coyotes had dropped them. Not a red flannel rag was left on a single pin. Those rags had been handled by hands stained with the blood of the slaughtered yearling. In the opinion of Judge Williams, the coyotes had trailed the blood all the fifteen miles from where the yearling had been gutted.[4]

Not another American animal has had its food so extensively and thoroughly anatomized. The contents of tens of thousands of

coyote stomachs and droppings have been scientifically examined and catalogued.[5] Widely scattered observations of coyotes
eating many things have been published. Among the objects that
coyotes are known to have swallowed, either whole or in part,
are pieces of string, paper and cloth, rubber from an automobile
tire, harness buckles, snails, beetles, horned frogs, wildcat, house
cat, skunk, armadillo, peccary, grizzly bear carcass, eggs of birds,
turkeys, turtles, grasshoppers, crickets, any kind of mice, rats, all
other rodents, a great variety of wild berries, grapes, dates,
peaches, prunes, carrots, sweet peppers, tomatoes, watermelons,
plums, pumpkins, oranges, tangerines, bumblebees, flies, beaver,
crayfish, any kind of fish in reach, bull snakes, rattlesnakes, other
snakes, centipedes, apples, acorns, pears, figs, apricots, cherries,
cantaloupes, porcupines, ants, coyote meat and hair, all sorts of
water birds, all sorts of land birds, including the turkey vulture,
pine nuts, peanuts, grass, frogs, honey, green corn, bread, sugar
and spice and everything nice, new or old, hot or cold, cooked
or raw.

The coyote is, indeed, more nearly omnivorous than either
man or hog; but not everything found in a dead coyote's stomach
represents characteristic habits of diet. A coyote standing in a
steel trap, waiting sometimes days for death by starvation or
delayed man, chews on anything within reach and snaps up
flies attracted by his own wretched condition. In his freedom,
he is not a member of the flycatcher family, though at times he
is as sportive as the scissortail hunting the air on illumined wing.
I have a picture in my mind of a young coyote snapping up
butterflies alit in cow tracks on muddy ground. It is a sight, they
say, to watch coyotes after grasshoppers — at times an important
food to some of them — now slapping a paw down on one, now
leaping for another and catching it in the mouth.

Without the bear's power to rob beehives, the coyote has the
bear's sweet tooth. In his *Narrative*, written more than four hundred years ago, of wanderings along the Texas coast and then

across the continent, Cabeza de Vaca describes how in late summer coastal Indians would go to prickly pear flats and gormandize on the juice and flesh of the tunas. No Indian was ever fonder of cactus fruit than the coyote. Judging from droppings so plentifully evident in south Texas and Mexico in tuna season, many coyotes must at that time eat little else. Clusters of fuzzy thorns, easily detached when the tuna is ripe, grow out of the fruit, and Mexicans believe that the coyote switches the thorns off with his tail. This is sheer folklore. Any of the fine thorns that prick the mouth of the eater are soon dissolved by body juices. I know of a coyote that was shot while reared up on a prickly pear bush pulling off tunas with his mouth and swallowing them almost whole.* Sometimes, presumably when the thorns are unusually thick, coyotes roll them on the ground with their paws. Perhaps some coyotes with especially delicate mouths and manners — always roll the thorns off.

In Mexico, the coyote is a notorious thief of the *aguamiel* (honey-water) of the maguey plant, which is fermented into pulque and distilled into *mezcal* and brandy. When the astounding agave is about ten years old — not waiting to be a hundred, as the popular name *century plant* implies — it sends up from its hole a gigantic flower stalk. On maguey plantations, the base of this stalk, the heart of the plant, is cut out just as it is ready to spring up, the incision leaving a basin about two feet deep and a foot and a half in diameter. Sap, designed by nature to produce the mighty stem and ripen its candelabra-like panicle into fruit, seeps into this basin at such a rate that it fills two or three times a day for three months. *Tlachiqueros*, as the collectors of the honey-water are called, suck it into long gourds and pour it into containers. No coyote could alone get to the dagger-defended

* "I have seen grey fox in the tops of pears eating the apples, but the coyotes I have seen eating them stood on the ground beside the pears. In 1903 I saw three coyotes reared up on a Spanish dagger eating fruit from the stalk. This dagger stalk is far more formidably protected than pear apples." — Loyd Ligon, Fort Stockton, Texas.

heart of the maguey plant, but after man has hacked into it, the coyote's senses tell him of the *aguamiel*. The *tlachiquero* knows coyote appetite, and covers the basin with the maguey's own leaves or with a rock. Not infrequently a coyote manages to get his head through the covering and lap up the "*licor divino*." A servant on a hacienda in Zacatecas told me of snaring a coyote at the open bole of a maguey with a baling wire.

Mexicans say that the coyote robs bumblebee nests. One living in the Rio Grande Valley wrote me this description of the robbery: "The *jicotes* (bumblebees) build their *jicoteras* at the roots of tall grass. There are only a few of them in each nest, and they do not store a large amount of honey, but what they do store is very savory. When a coyote locates a *jicotera*, he sits down in front of it and begins swinging his tail around so as to make the *jicotes* come out. They fly at the tail and not at the coyote's face. As they get tangled in the hair, the coyote kills them with his paws. [Surely he must eat them also!] He keeps up this process until he is sure that all the *jicotes* have come out. Then he noses into the nest and eats the honey." *

Everybody who raises watermelons in coyote country knows how discerning the animal is of ripe ones. He may rush the season and break into melons before they are ripe, but he will pick the first red heart and thereafter nothing but red hearts will do. Often he leaves claw marks on an unripe melon. Perhaps he breaks the outer skin in order to smell better the fruit within. Whatever his method of testing, it is surer than thumping, peeling the rind with fingernail, examining the curl on the vine, or pressing down on the melon to listen for the crack. We used to put scarecrows in our melon patch; they did not scare

* A beekeeper at Marathon, Texas, asserts that the skunk goes to a beehive at night, strikes the hive with his tail until the agitated bees come out, and then eats them. — *San Antonio Express*, 16 March 1925.

"At times the skunk destroys great numbers of honey bees, scratching on the front of the hives and then stamping on the angry insects when they emerge. — Victor H. Cahalane, *Mammals of North America*, published by the Macmillan Company, New York, 1947, 214.

off the coyotes so effectively as suspicious-looking mounds of careless weeds piled over selected melons. Probably the smell of human hands on the melons or on the weeds was the main deterrent. A coyote disdains any soured melon. He is hard to deceive by a poisoned melon. After all, he is not an unmitigated pest around melon patches; he eats the rats that are voracious eaters of planted seed. What a joy to hear two or three of the raiders jubilating among the watermelons about an hour after dark — provided the hearer has only a platonic interest in melons.

Peanuts require sandy soil, where watermelons and sweet potatoes thrive. There coyotes dig out the planted nuts, soaked in the shell for quick sprouting. Later they truffle for the new crop. They feast after the underground nuts have been plowed to the surface for harvesting.

In one locality it is carrots that coyotes go for; in yet another, ripe tomatoes, and so on. To say, however, that *the* coyote always eats this or that, or does so and so, is as misleading as to say that *the* Indian, *the* Frenchman, *the* American will always think, feel, eat, act in a uniform way. Only the provincial-minded categorize all individuals of a given race or nationality. In *Wild Lone* B B says: "Just as children are more intelligent than we believe them to be, so, I think, it is with wild animals; they feel pain more acutely than we think, and, though within a beast's body, their grave eyes are aware of things we little guess or understand." And with sensitiveness and intelligence always goes variety — variety in food preferences as in other matters. About sixty years ago a man in Ohio named W. B. Hall tamed crows so that he might better study their feeding habits. "I had a male crow," he recorded, "that would eat the cabbage caterpillar (*Pieris rapae*) with evident relish, while his mate disdained such plebeian diet. They would both kill the sow bugs (*Oniscus*) and species of Myriapoda, but would not eat them." [6]

The more one learns about coyotes, the more pronounced appears their individualism in food habits. Of three coyote dens that J. W. Montgomery located in the same vicinity one spring, one was littered with little else but the remains of rabbits; the second showed that the pups were being fed solely on wood rats; at the third, feathers of blue (scaled) quail predominated over evidences of other food. Houston Lockhart, plow foreman on the King Ranch, was going along a pasture fence one winter morning in 1940 when he saw a coyote "come down to a point exactly like a bird dog." The coyote held the point for a minute or so, then broke and pounced into the center of a huddled covey of bobwhites, caught one, and made away with it into the brush. Coyotes have been observed lifting a foot in a pointing attitude while listening for an expected mouse, but a coyote that points quail and runs in among a covey in daylight and catches must be almost as singular as Hawthorne's Minister of the Black Veil. While riding one summer day over a ranch in the Brush Country on which coyotes appeared to be unusually numerous, I kept a rough count of the scaled quail I saw and estimated about eight hundred, besides several coveys of bobwhites — the most quail I have ever seen anywhere.*

The bird that coyotes pursue with expectation of catching, in treeless regions, is the roadrunner, on the border fittingly called paisano, which means "fellow countryman." A ground cuckoo, the paisano can fly, or volplane, only a short distance. In a tree, it is safe enough; but in a region where the trees are all bushes, coyotes can leap near enough to grab it or to make it fly again and, by repeated assaults, wear it down.

A particular coyote, it would seem, often becomes particularly skillful in capturing some form of meat for which it has developed a special liking. Certainly not all coyotes go for any snake they come across; some coyotes do eat bull snakes and some coy-

---

* "Stomach contents of coyotes killed in game refuges in California show that, although quail are particularly abundant (more than 300 were seen per day) in all parts of the area trapped, only two coyotes out of 563 trapped during the whole study had quail remains." — Grinnell, Dixon and Linsdale, *Fur-Bearing Mammals of California*, II, 493.

otes do eat rattlesnakes. About three o'clock in the afternoon of May 2, 1935, Jerry Johnson, of the Parker Creek Forest and Range Experiment Station in Arizona, heard, on a ridge he was mapping, the rustle of dead leaves. He looked. His own words best describe what he saw.[7]

"A coyote was standing on a dead sotol (*Dasylirion*) and sniffing at it. He jumped down and started to paw the leaves. Suddenly he jumped back and then cautiously approached at a different place. This time he began to tear apart the sotol with his teeth. He found a hole and stuck his head in as far as he could, then jumped back a couple of feet, looked around, and seeing nothing, began to paw the sotol again. For several minutes the coyote first pawed the sotol and then tore off leaves. Occasionally he jumped back and began at a different place.

"While the coyote was working at the sotol, I dodged along the opposite side of the ridge and came to a place, at a distance of about 200 feet, where I could see him more plainly. He then was dashing in and jumping back from a scrub live oak bush, coiled and wrapped around the branches of which was a bull snake trying to defend himself.

"The coyote dashed in, seized the snake by the tail and dragged it into the open. The snake, which was about four and one half feet long, prepared for battle by raising its head and part of its body a foot or so above the ground. When the coyote approached too closely, the snake struck at him. The coyote sprang out of the way and snapped the snake just back of the head, jumping away before the snake could retaliate. Every time the coyote came within range, the snake struck at him, and each time the coyote snapped the snake. The last time the coyote did this the snake collapsed. The coyote seized the snake and shook it until it stopped squirming. Being satisfied that the snake was dead, the coyote sat on his haunches and looked around, then started to eat the snake, beginning with the head.

"When the coyote had eaten about half of the snake I came

into the open and yelled at him. He dropped the snake, then grabbed it in his mouth, ran about 40 feet, stopped, turned around and looked at me for a minute, then went on eating. When he had finished, he trotted off through the brush."

Among coyotes trapped in Texas, a noticeable number have been bitten by rattlesnakes. The scars are unmistakable, mainly on shoulders and front legs, less often on hind legs, sometimes on the head. Hide and hair never grow back over the wound; it is covered, when healed, with a thin, bare, dark tissue. Joe Hill estimates that 20 per cent of the skins taken from coyotes on the southern plains of Texas show scars from snakebite. He has never seen a coyote kill a rattlesnake, but he has seen plain evidence on the ground of a coyote's scuffling with a rattlesnake, of which little remained but the rattles. Many coyotes, especially young ones, are no doubt bitten unawares — while investigating old rat dens, while passing a rattler waiting beside a trail for his prey to come by, and otherwise. "No," Luke Stillwell of the rattlesnake-infested Brush Country responded, "I never saw a coyote kill a rattlesnake. I have seen where a coyote ate a rattlesnake, and time and again I have seen where a coyote rolled on a rattlesnake carcass."

Many a rattlesnake killed and left on the ground in coyote country stays there until eaten by buzzards or ants or until it dries up. At the time, coyotes may be eating something else that is plentiful and more to their taste. On the other hand, a dead rattlesnake, buried under a bush or not buried at all, is a trapper's "Sunday bait." There can be little doubt that now and then a coyote becomes a special killer of rattlesnakes, just as an occasional dog or house cat becomes eager after them and expert in killing them. Charlie Stone, of Fort Stockton, Texas, used to have a hound that would turn aside from any trail to kill a rattlesnake. He was bitten numerous times and became immune to the venom. One day in the last century while, as boys, Houston Ellis and his brother were herding sheep in Frio County, Texas, they sicked their mongrel dog onto a big rusty diamondback they had stirred up. The rattlesnake bit the dog, but he got well. He became a rattlesnake-hater; he hunted rattlesnakes far and near. He learned to grab the snake at the right moment behind the head and, while biting down, to shake it violently. He was never seen eating one.

On a California desert one summer morning shortly after sunrise, Vance Hoyt saw a coyote intercept a sidewinder.[8] The rising thermometer had already registered more than 100 degrees. No rattlesnake can survive the direct rays of a sun like that. Whether the coyote knew this fact or not, he prevented the snake from going to shade by dodging about it and keeping it in a coiled position. The snake struck several times without hitting. In about fifteen minutes it "shuddered and lay quiet." Instantly the coyote severed the head * and trotted off carrying the snake's body. "I did not see the coyote eat it," says Dr. Hoyt. "I assume that he did eat it or else took it to his den for his young or his mate to eat. At my animal ranch, conducted for experimental purposes in wildlife behavior, I have placed rattlesnakes in the pens of coyotes. Their method of attack was always the same: to tease the snake at a safe distance until it became too exhausted to defend itself, and then leap in for the kill." Paul Fountain, an English naturalist of discrimination, says (in *The Eleven Eaglets of the West*, 1905): "On one occasion I saw a coyote seize a rattlesnake as it issued from a hole. It at once gnawed the reptile's head off . . . and then proceeded to feast on the writhing body."

Those coyotes that kill porcupines must be specialists. At least occasionally, an attacker whose daring is not matched by skill has its head so quilled that it cannot eat. The body of the "fretful porcupine" is armored with 20,000 or more detachable spines, or quills. With its tail it can drive the quills into the face and

* Perhaps all animals realize by instinct that rattlesnakes are poisonous and that the poison comes from the head. When an eagle with nestlings kills a rattlesnake, it eats the head, avoiding the fangs, before carrying the snake body to the nest. It will not carry a rattlesnake head.

other foreparts of all but the most expert attackers, among which the fisher of northern latitudes is notable. With one flashing pass the fisher turns the spined ball over and then as quickly rips open the defenseless under-belly. A coyote that has mastered the matador business with porcupines employs somewhat the same tactics. It will "fool around" a porcupine, tease it, sometimes allow it to start running for a tree, where it would be entirely safe, until there is an opening for lightning-like charge and deadly slash.[9]

The armadillo does not present a danger to any attacker, but its ability to keep inside its armor prevents just any coyote that comes along from readily feasting on its meat. However, there are undoubtedly specialized armadillo-eaters, just as there are specialized porcupine-eaters. One trapper goes so far as to ascribe the worn teeth of some of his catches to habitual biting on armadillo shells. In addition to playing with old deer horns, bleached bones, and dried shells of armadillo and tortoise, coyotes often gnaw on them. This may be to get calcium or some other element in bone that many animal systems crave. Range cattle chew bleached bones, one occasionally getting a bone lodged in its throat so that it cannot swallow and will starve unless man removes the impediment.

Whether it be a fact, as coast-dwellers aver, that coyotes on 120-miles-long Padre Island and elsewhere against the Gulf of Mexico fish for shrimp and crabs with their tails, I cannot say. Since time immemorial Mexicans have so believed. In South America, tradition ascribes tail-fishing to the jaguar. Mr. E. W. Gudger of the American Museum of Natural History would not be surprised to see someday a picture proving tradition to be fact.[10] "Anything but the impossible may be expected of a wild animal." It is certainly possible for a coyote to catch a crab on its tail.

Coyotes eat fish where fish are available, and coyotes are very numerous on Padre Island. A fisherman without guile who frequents this island assures me that coyotes have stolen redfish from him staked out in water two feet deep. One moonlight night he watched seven coyotes come close to his car on the beach. The next morning a rod and reel, with mullet-baited hook, was missing. A drag in the sand led to it three hundred yards away, where a coyote had released himself from the hook. Another man goes to Padre Island to fish for coyotes. He puts a mullet on his hook, leaves it in shallow water, at the edge of the sandy beach, retreats with rod into salt grass, lies down and waits until a coyote comes along and takes the bait; then he reels in the catch. There are all sorts of sportsmen. The sands of Padre Island are patterned with tracks of sand crabs. The coyotes dig down and get these "ghosts," especially in winter, when the crabs hibernate.

When the great sea turtles — spring by spring in decreasing numbers — come in from the deeps to lay their eggs in the sands along the unpeopled coast of Tamaulipas, Mexico, coyotes gather in great numbers to dig up and feast on the eggs. *Zopilotes*, those scavenger birds that used to take the place of sewer systems in Vera Cruz and other Mexican cities, follow them. In 1939, two Texas game wardens saw a coyote scooping large minnows out of shallows in the Canadian River. A forest ranger in the Yellowstone country found coyotes feeding on trout killed by the fall of ice into a pool.[11] On the Columbia River they have been seen slapping spawning salmon out of the water in the manner of bears.

Any view that anyone takes of the coyote leads ultimately to one basic fact: the animal takes advantage of whatever foods time and place make available. An unprotected carrot field in the "Winter Garden" district of southern Texas will draw coyotes out of the brush from far distances. Given a choice, they seem to prefer wild fruits to meat. Herbert Ward, game warden, has lived in the brush all his life and years ago became scientific in methods of observation. "Cut open everything killed to see what it eats" is his rule. "You may be killing your best friend." It is his observation that when, about the tenth of April, berries of the Texas lote (*Zizyphus obtusifolia*) begin to ripen, coyotes forsake rodents for this fruit. It is gone within forty days, and coyotes go back to rodents. Mesquite beans and tunas are ripening by June, while does are still dropping their fawns, and only if these fruits are lacking do coyotes to any appreciable extent prey on fawns at that season. If grass burs become too thick in one place, the coyotes move to another.

One day while I was waiting at the forks of a trail in northern Coahuila, I saw the head of an animal, down a slope several hundred yards away, moving high up in a bush. At first I thought it was a doe; then when the animal came down on all fours I saw it was a coyote. It was resting its paws upon branches of a brasil (*Condalia obovata*) bush and nibbling off the ripe berries as high as it could reach. After I walked down to the bush, I could not detect that the berries high up were of any better quality than those near the ground, which seemed more easily reached.

Vegetarians of Clemenceau's vigor and Sir Stafford Cripps's austerity would probably not agree, but most people regard a dog or wolf as sick when it eats grass. Scientific study of the food habits of coyotes led to the conclusion that "green grass forms a regular part of the diet, as beneficial, no doubt, as is lettuce or spinach to man." [12] Grass and hair are supposed to save coyotes from internal worms common to house-fed dogs. The meat diet of coyotes has undoubtedly been overemphasized. It was thought at one time that the animal was herbivorous only through necessity. Thus, Professor Richard Harlan in his *Fauna Americana* (Philadelphia, 1825) noted that it "is sometimes reduced by hunger to eat the wild plums and other fruits, to it almost indigestible." Sixty-five years later Professor St. George Mivart, in *Dogs, Jackals, Wolves and Foxes* (London, 1890), said that the coyote "will eat vegetable substances" only when it "cannot get animal food." The 1944 edition of the *Encyclopaedia*

Britannica virtually repeats the assertion. I have spoken sufficiently of the animal's avidity for prickly pear apples and other wild fruits of southern Texas. On the tablelands of Mexico coyotes subsist largely upon the wild dates in season. In the Montana country they begin eating serviceberries as soon as they ripen along in June, then switch to chokeberries and live for a while largely upon them.

But drama resides in the flesh. Coyotes are cannibalistic. There is no evidence that a pack will turn on some weak member, or that a male will kill pups as a tomcat kills kittens, or that, as one lay writer baldly says, "a coyote will eat her own young when they have died from other causes [than parental action]." [13] But, driven by hunger, coyotes coming upon one of their fellows in a trap — appetites probably whetted by the smell of his blood — sometimes kill and devour it. In December of 1917 or 1918, John F. Barnes went with Kalamity Bonner to hunt deer along the Rio Grande. A prolonged drouth had made the whole border country desolate. The prickly pear was withering; the rats, the rabbits and the quail had nearly all died; the deer were poor and dying; the starving coyotes were mangy. The hunters killed two bucks, far from fat, and put them inside their tent. The famished coyotes howled all about in the night, and some of the bolder ones pushed their heads under the canvas walls and tugged at the carcasses. Kalamity Bonner went outside, fixed a piece of liver on a tarpon hook he had along, and tied it to a mesquite limb. In no time he had hooked a coyote, which he killed and which other coyotes soon devoured. He hooked seven coyotes, and all were devoured. The next evening he set a baited steel trap about a hundred yards from camp. Not long after dark there was a great commotion about it; in the morning all that was left in the trap was a small piece of coyote leg. Five or six other coyotes caught in traps were disposed of in the same way. Coyotes like to eat the fat drippings from a coyote carcass hung on fence or tree and to sample the weather-cured meat.

The belief is widespread, in north Texas at least, that coyotes will not eat the carcass of a victim of anthrax. They are subject to anthrax. They are not subject to blackleg and sometimes eat animals that have died from that disease.

The one thing eatable that coyotes are traditionally supposed not to eat is a dead Mexican. Just as in other climes the flesh of sailors was once considered too salty for cannibals, the body of a Mexican was purported to be too impregnated with chile for any coyote to stomach. The idea seems to have developed after English-speakers began fighting Mexicans in Texas, about 1830; it held on long after border-fighting died down, and still survives. In the same period, both coyotes and gray wolves became notorious for clawing the dead of other nationalities out of frontier graves.

Noah Smithwick reached the San Jacinto battlefield, near Houston, in 1836, shortly after the Texans had defeated Santa Anna's Mexican army. "The dead Mexicans," he wrote, "lay in piles, the survivors not even asking permission to bury them. . . . The buzzards and coyotes were gathering to the feast, but it is a singular fact that they singled out the dead horses, refusing to touch the Mexicans. They lay there unmolested until they dried up." Later on, out in New Mexico, Smithwick came upon six hanging Apache bodies that had their toes "nibbled off" by coyotes but were "otherwise well preserved." [14] Veterans of the Mexican War used to tell that, after a battle, dead Americans would be found cleaned to the bone by coyotes, whereas the bodies of dead Mexicans on the same ground lay untouched.[15] When, in 1849, cholera swept San Antonio and the surrounding country, the dead had to be buried in makeshift haste. There were not enough gravediggers. In the cemetery at Castroville the coyotes feasted every night, according to the old-timers — but the bodies they held carnival over were of German-French Alsatians, not of Mexicans.[16]

In 1879, steel-eyed, steel-nerved, steel-true Jim Gillett of the

Texas Rangers crossed the Rio Grande in pursuit of Apaches and came to where they had ambushed and killed twenty-nine Mexicans. "All the bodies," Gillett later wrote in a graphic autobiography, "were in good preservation owing to the pure cold air of the mountains. It is a strange fact, but one without question, that no wild animal or bird of prey will touch the body of a Mexican. These corpses had lain on the ground nearly two weeks and were untouched. If they had been the bodies of Indians, Negroes or Americans, the coyotes, buzzards and crows would have attacked them the first day and night." [17]

Coyotes as carrion-eaters are no respecters of nationalities. On the immense Hacienda de la Babícora, owned by William Randolph Hearst, in western Chihuahua, I talked with an old vaquero named Antonio who had lived on the hacienda most of his life and had remained faithful to it through all the raids and revolutions. One year, he said, Pancho Villa's cavalry surprised a considerable detachment of General Carranza's infantry at Santa Ana, a subdivision of La Babícora. The Carranzistas scattered like quail before the hard-riding Villistas. They were shot down here and there over the big prairie, and those who surrendered were lined up against corral walls. All the Carranzistas ceased to exist, and Pancho Villa's men rode away, leaving their victims unburied.

It was several days before Antonio and a few other men got back from the mountains to which they had fled and undertook to dispose of the dead. Poor people had taken the clothes off the bodies, and almost every cadaver had been eaten on by coyotes. Antonio saw a coyote gnawing gristle from the bones of one naked corpse; he saw "twa corbies" making their "dinner sweet" on the face of another. Gus (Don Gustavo) McGuiness, manager of the Santa Ana, said that during these horrible times, a train on which he was a passenger had to stop near Guzmán while a railroad bridge burned by the Villistas was repaired. They had killed several Carranzistas in the little town. Wandering around,

Don Gustavo came upon a shallow grave in the sand whence three uncoffined bodies had been excavated by coyotes and torn to pieces.

It may be that coyotes will delay longer in eating a dead person than a wildcat will. Bill Gardner of Texas liked to whoop out the old backwoods boast: "The farther up the creek you go, the worse they get, and I come from the head of it." While he was living up in the Llano River breaks, he killed a Mexican. He was one of those frontier killers who "didn't count Mexicans," and he had several non-Mexicans to his credit. He attached so little importance to this particular killing that he left the Mexican's body lying where his bullet had dropped it. The next day, however, he got to considering the way times were changing. He took a spade and rode to the body. The head had been eaten on. It was wintertime; he was trapping a little anyway. He rode back for his traps. He set six or eight around the bait. The following morning he found five wildcats in them. He skinned these and, as he was doing so well, decided to leave the bait for another catch. During the next two nights, he caught six more bobcats. After that he dug a shallow hole and covered up what was left of the body. Wildcats are not very good excavators. It was the excavating of a grand jury that brought out these facts.

Along in the '70s, as A. Phimister Proctor, the sculptor, tells the story, a character in Colorado named Doc Buck rode up on an old Ute squaw who had been abandoned by her people and left with nothing but a dirty blanket. She was starving and sick besides. Doc Buck did a little practical practicing of medicine in addition to trapping and raising a few cattle on his squat. At this time he was on his way to Hot Sulphur Springs for supplies. With the poor old squaw in mind, he added some pills to his purchase of food and strychnine. When he got back to her two days later, he found her dead. Being a practical fur-taker as well as a practical practitioner, he put a little strychnine in the carcass. The thoughtfulness netted him several pelts from both coyotes and lobos.

Bert Sowell was a red-headed cowboy. In 1905 he was working for the Black Mountain Cattle Company in a "big country" north of Van Horn, Texas. He had a habit of sometimes leaving camp without explanation and not returning for a day or two — still without explanation. One night he failed to come in, and it was not until two mornings later that the boss said they had better try to trail him down. "Something might have happened." Riders scouted all day without seeing any sign. The next day one of them found red hairs on a greasewood bush, went on and found a defleshed leg, and then some other pieces of the man's body. Sign showed that Bert Sowell had ridden into a small pasture to put some cattle out and that in running them his horse had fallen, breaking the man's leg and probably injuring him otherwise. He had lain for a long time on the ground, kicking with his good leg until he made a kind of trench in the ground, very much as a cow brute down and unable to rise kicks out. Whether coyotes surrounded him before he died could not be determined.

"Why," asked an Apache of George Frederick Ruxton, "does the medicine wolf follow the buffalo and the deer? For blood." R. B. Townshend, an Englishman with a sense of the beautiful who wrote three civilized books around his ranching experiences in the West before barbed wire tamed it, had a chance to see the blood-followers at close range. One early morning he wounded an antelope, trailed it, killed it, and, in an attempt to make a half-broken mare drag it, received a kick that broke his leg and set some unhealed cuts to bleeding. He was about a mile from the ranch cabin; the other men were away hauling logs.

"I started to try to crawl towards the cabin and fainted," he tells. "How long I lay there I do not know, but when I recovered consciousness the sun was still high in the sky. I raised myself on my elbows and looked round. . . . The [prairie] wolves and the crows had arrived. Hop, hop, hop came a great black crow quite near me. Yellowish grey forms of a dozen coyotes sneaked round a little farther off. In a sudden fury I blazed away at them with four of the five shots in my pistol.

"At the shots the wolves ran off and the crows flapped heavily away. But as they saw I did not move, the wolves and crows soon came back again. . . . They smelt the blood on me. . . . They could wait. . . . Hour after hour I lay there and watched the sun sinking towards Pike's Peak, while the wolves lay down and yawned and licked their chops, and the crows croaked their impatience as they walked to and fro. Night would soon fall. Suddenly, when the sun was but a hand's breadth high over the Peak, I saw a black spot on the prairie two or three miles away. It was the wagon." [18] The narrator was so concerned with his own mutilated carcass that he forgot about the antelope's. The coyotes were probably interested in that only, and he was inconveniently near it.

I have never met a single account approaching authenticity of normal coyotes' attacking a live human being. Statements to the contrary by early Spanish writers on Mexico are echoes of absurdities still current in that country. At that, they contradict the coyote's nature not only historically but as expressed in legions of popular tales and traditions. Some people, of course, take farces literally. The editor of a New England hunting magazine once wrote me requesting an article on "The Perils of Coyote Hunting." Long ago it used to be told — as a lesson in orthodoxy — that a pack of wolves raiding a monastery tore to pieces every monk who had heretical opinions but piously avoided touching any orthodox monk. This tale is as well fortified by fact as — aside from cases of hydrophobia — any tale of coyote attack on human beings.

Here is the coyote at his deadliest as pictured by a blizzard-scorched Westerner to a tenderfoot Englishman. "One time," he told, "me and my pardner discovered a hot mineral spring that would cure anything. It was away back in the roughs. All any ailing person had to do was bathe regular in the water and bury himself regular in the mud. Even the Rocky Mountain bears knew about this here spring. There was one old grizzly all stove up with rheumatism that used to take the baths and mud-dyings regular before he denned up for the winter.

"Well, one time a rich New Yorker come out West looking for his health. His knees were so stiff he couldn't get on a horse from a log. The only way he could bend his elbow was to have a bottle in his hand. He had cricks in his neck and lumbago in the back and no telling what else. He got wind of our hot spring and offered to buy it at any price we'd set, provided it proved up on him.

"We agreed and rigged up an outfit to suit him. We put him on a stretcher between two gentle pack mules. Then we had ten other mules loaded with a fancy cook, canned oysters, French wine, Scotch whisky, Jamaica rum, Italian olive oil, Virginia ham, Boston baked beans, English plum pudding, and a lot of other such truck. It was slow going, but we got to the spring with the New Yorker still able to groan. We made camp under some cottonwood trees about a hundred yards from the main mud hole. He thought the mud was doing him more good than the water, and I guess it was. We'd bury him in it up to his chin every morning and dig him out and drench him off every evening. He improved like a starved mule turned loose in a corn field after the crop's gathered.

"In about a week he proposed one night that we celebrate his recovery with champagne. The cook opened a case. That was the first time my pardner or me either ever drunk any white mule like that. The next morning the New Yorker wasn't feeling so brisk. After we buried him in the mud, we felt mighty thirsty. Well, one bottle led to another, the cook joining in. By sundown we wasn't remembering anything. If the New Yorker yelled, we didn't hear him. When we come to next morning, we rushed down to dig him out. He wasn't visible. The coyotes had et his head off. I always will claim they're the derndest nuisance this country ever had. Naturally we didn't get our money for curing the New Yorker." [19]

*   *   *

The wild animals answer, consciously, no question about their conduct. But once in a while some human belonger to silences who has

a heart
That watches and receives

gets an answer. One such closes this chapter on the most adroit food-getter among American mammals. It is out of the semi-autobiographic novel, *Sundown*,[20] by John Joseph Mathews of the blackjacks and the prairie grasses.

"Chal backed up against a great postoak, and stood looking out over the emerald prairie. A coyote came trotting down the ravine that led through the blackjacks, stopping occasionally to test the air currents. 'I've got the wind,' Chal thought. . . .

"It was an old dog coyote and remnants of his last winter's coat hung ragged and matted from his neck. He stopped and nosed in the grass, then sniffed the ground like a setter. He started to trot off, then changed his mind and came back to a tuft of grass and re-examined it. This time a meadow lark flew up, then fell to the ground and made a queer little noise, and started flopping as though helpless. The old coyote stood with front legs apart and watched the bird, then nosed in the grass tuft, found the eggs, and was busy for minutes eating them; then he turned the nest over and examined it as if hoping to find more eggs. His pointed nose was yellow from his meal. He gave it two ineffective swipes with his tongue, then trotted toward the place where the mother bird had made her stage fall. She

[130]

flopped and made a sound like a young bird, but the coyote knew the trick, and she flew off on sound wing.

"The coyote half turned and looked intently across the prairie, then fell on his belly in the grass, and Chal could see only the tips of his ears, made translucent by the sun. Chal watched the horizon where the coyote was looking. He saw an object moving along the prairie — the crown of a Stetson hat. The rest of the hat appeared, then the head of the rider, and later a horse and rider came into full view. The horse was fox-trotting, and the cowboy sat with his hands on the horn. They passed within a few yards of the coyote and Chal, but the rider was looking straight ahead.

"When they had passed, but not quite out of sight, the coyote became nervous, got up and trotted down the ravine, looking back over his shoulder. Finally he stopped and looked back just as the horse and rider went out of sight over the next swell of the prairie. Chal stepped out from the tree and the coyote ran into the canyon, looking over his shoulder. Chal was suffused with happiness. He felt that he should like to make up a song about the coyote."

VI · SCENT AND CURIOSITY

IN SOME RESPECTS," Joe Hill said, "a man is a good deal like a coyote. Out here in the Pecos country, pasture gates are a long way apart. In the old days when a man drove his wagon up to a gate and got out to open it, he would very likely relieve his bladder on the gatepost. I got to noticing how coyotes were attracted to scent left in this way. One of them would scratch around and add a squirt of his own to the post. Gateposts in those days made good places for traps."

A Fish and Wildlife Serviceman had been setting traps in the trans-Pecos country with utmost care and not catching a coyote. Disgusted, he stopped on his way back to camp one late afternoon and roughly placed two traps in the ground, not far apart. He spat out a quid of tobacco on the earth covering one trap and urinated over the other. That night he caught a big dog-coyote in the second.

"Very well, then, I contradict myself." Ranch Mexicans claim that a coyote will not cross a circle scented with human urine. They, and also hunters not of the ranches, urinate all around a deer carcass to be left out on the ground overnight. The practice goes back to Indian times. A bandanna, a jacket, or any other human-tainted article tied on a buck's horn or leg is as effective as urine in halting coyotes. Some coyotes dodge away from any human scent they come upon; some do not. Trappers in the Rocky Mountains say that a coyote will jump a trail made by snowshoes, and then maybe follow beside it but not in it. On the other hand, I have seen coyote tracks in my own tracks only a short time after I had made them. One cold night in Arizona, while Louis C. Slothower, a mining man now of Colorado Springs, was stretched out fully dressed but blanketless on the ground beside a dying fire, he awoke to find two coyotes nibbling at his shoestrings and eight other coyotes sitting around in a semicircle. This was in October, 1910; not many coyotes would nowadays be so familiar. After losing a glove at two or three traps and catching coyotes in them just the same, John W. Crook quit wearing gloves for the purpose of keeping his odor away from sets. Nevertheless, nearly any trapper after an alert, cautious animal will wear clean gloves and take all other possible precautions against betraying with human odor the location of a trap.

All old-time trappers had their special scent-lures — secrets to be guarded as carefully as "an old Spanish waybill" to a lost mine. Modern trappers have them too. The common base for all is urine. The professional trapper ties a coyote up or confines it in a cage in order to obtain its urine. Now and then one keeps a coyote for years, giving it liberty to exercise and making a friend of it. Cooped up in the ordinary trapper cage, a coyote lives only a few months. This cage has a zinc floor, rimmed up all around, with a gap at one end to allow the urine to drain into a pan. Some trappers distrust the zinc, claiming that the smell of it gets into the urine and warns coyotes off. A distruster will tie a cord around the penis of a captive male coyote or sew up the vulva opening of a female, pour water down the mouth of the animal, wait two or three days, kill it and take the bladder. The cruelty of this method does not affect the users of it. However, a freshly trapped coyote kept chained sometimes does not urinate for a day or two and can be killed for its full bladder. The idea that urine will have a stronger drawing power if it is stale, dark and even bloodshot, is a part of trapper folklore. Fresh urine is, in fact, more effective.

One of the characters of New Mexico back in the early years of this century was George Jackson. His knowledge of the wolf world was, like Sam Weller's knowledge of London, "peculiar and extensive." His wife ran their ranch and he trapped. He claimed that the ranch and five hundred head of cattle on it had been paid for out of his bounty and fur earnings. Both his legs and two of his horse's legs had been broken by a fall at a prairie dog hole. He shot the horse, set his own fractures, and for ten days lay on the lone prairie before a searcher found him. After that he went in a wagon loaded with traps, grub, and all his personal belongings. To set a trap, he walked out on a strip of canvas twenty feet long, unrolling it in front of him, and then walked back on it. He wore cotton gloves to handle the steel traps. He selected every trap site with respect to the whole surrounding terrain. But what he mainly depended upon was the few drops of lure sprinkled at the trap site.

It was pure urine, undiluted and untinctured with anything else, taken from a bitch that had been shot dead instantly, before she was trapped, wounded, or even scared. He cut out her bladder while the body was still warm and poured the contents into a dark bottle. He claimed that if the bitch had been scared or injured before death, she injected a "sign," some sort of indication of her experience with man, into her urine and that this "sign" would be detected and understood by any coyote who came along and smelled even one drop of the urine. He said that again and again when he used urine from a female that had suffered or become frightened before she was killed, he watched a coyote go freely up to the lure, smell of it, instantly become cautious, and backtrack from the bush.

A trapper who imagines that he can "think like a coyote" wants urine only from an old dog (male). "You see, when a coyote smells this vinegar, for him it's just like seeing a picture of whoever done the sprinkling. You get the vinegar of some old, tooth-worn coyote and sprinkle a little of it on a bush. No matter what kind of coyote comes along, he says to himself, or she says to herself, 'Ha! Old Solomon's been here. He knows. No fear for us.' That's the way to fool them into a trap."

The more usual mixture with urine is the anal glands of either male or female coyote, some fish oil, and perhaps a few drops of glycerine to act as a preservative. It is the anal glands or the secretion in them that dogs smell on each other — not the anus. A tincture of the secretion probably adheres to many coyote droppings. Coyotes habitually take notice of each other's droppings; for that matter, so do range horses. All kinds of animal flesh are added to the urine base to make it more alluring, one trapper swearing by burro meat, another by wildcat meat. The rule is that it must be rotten. J. R. Alcorn of Nevada, scientific-minded fur trapper, concludes that some of the esoteric mixtures used by trappers repel instead of attract coyotes, and that an unexcelled assortment of lures is supplied by the animal itself. He recommends coyote brains, footpads (which emit scent), anus and bladder soaked in a jar of coyote urine. This mixture turns into a paste and is most effective, used as a smear, after it is a year old.[1]

In the absence of a coyote, a hound will do, especially on a range where dogs are not running. To quote Ross Santee, "An old trapper I once made camp with in Arizona had a hound named Brownie. The first night I was with him he tied Brownie in the tent. Early next morning he fixed a part of an inner tube over the dog's sheath, released him to kick the bushes, and then bottled the contents. One day he noticed both a cat and a dog

[135]

scratching and wallowing on a well-seasoned rattlesnake carcass. Whenever he killed a rattlesnake after that, he cut it into pieces, put the pieces in a bottle of the dog urine, and let the hot sun blend the mixture."

Joe Hill used to keep wildcats as well as coyotes caged for their urine and has, he says, "enticed lots of coyotes into traps with a mixture of the two kinds." Louis Martin, who has caught the last smart coyote out of many a sheep pasture in the Devil's River country of Texas, is especially fond of whiskey. Now and then he spares a sip to make the basic lure irresistible for some coyote that has refused to come to anything else.

To lure wolves in Louisiana, biologist Stanley P. Young took urine from a wolf trapped in Arkansas. Not all scientists agree on his theory. "Experiments with various scents used in wolf trapping," he explains, "have shown that urine taken from wolves far removed from the area in which trapping is to be carried on, when placed on scent posts along the runways, causes intense excitement, much sniffing, and tarrying around such spots. The antics of wild wolves when they sniff foreign wolf scent are similar to the commotion that results when the country dog visits the city dog. . . . As the wolf periodically passes over its runway, it instinctively stops at a scent post, either to sniff, void urine, or defecate." [2]

In the bizarre and extensive lore of trappers, female odors of the human species have a powerful effect upon wolf-kind. Nat Straw of New Mexico was about the last of the great grizzly hunters; he cooked for cow outfits, lived with Indians to discover the secret of the Lost Adams Diggings, trapped lobo wolves, and was one of the three or four most interesting outdoor men I have ever met. He said:

"My most remarkable observation on the power of scent over animals was made one winter while I was trapping for the V Cross T outfit. A man and his wife were living alone at one of the ranch outposts in a roomy cabin, and I made arrangements to stay with them. There were lots of lobos in the country; they were destroying a good many cattle, and there was a good bounty on them. I got to noticing that regularly every month lobos would come up around the cabin at night and for hours at a time keep up their deep howling.

"One morning before daylight while I was making coffee, the man came into the kitchen.

" 'Did you ever hear such howling as went on all last night?' he asked. 'Those lobos kept us awake most of the time.'

" 'Yes,' I said. 'Your wife is unwell, isn't she?'

" 'She is,' he replied in a startled way.

" 'That scent,' I told him frankly, 'is what draws the wolves about the cabin once every month. I will give you five dollars for a quart of her urine.'

"He got the urine. I began trapping with it. I caught thirty-two lobos that season. Later on, the daughter of a merchant at Pinos Altos [a village in the mountains] showed me some close-up pictures she had made of a big lobo. One day while she was out alone on the edge of the woods with her camera, she said, the lobo came up in a friendly manner. She was not afraid of animals. Though she did not realize the fact, I knew what had drawn the lobo to her and tamed him."

The male coyote is stronger on "passion scent" than the female, trappers say. Though they breed at only one season of the year, the male remains perennially interested in female smells. From puppyhood up, the male is less cautious and more inquisitive than the female. "I can make one of these fellows come hither every time," a trapper told me, "if I can get the urine of a bitch in heat, mix her anal glands and uterus with it, let the mass season in a bottle, and then sprinkle a little of it on a bush." Another trapper who had a tame male coyote used to bring trapped females in and keep them tied near him with the idea that he would bring them into heat — for him to "milk." Some trappers hold that ovaries preserved in alcohol have the same attraction as the urine of a female in heat. Ginseng and asafetida are common additions to the base.

In my mind's eye I can see now a certain ancient trapper of the Brush Country. No concoction that he mixed smell louder than he. He claimed that if he changed his smell, shy coyotes would take notice and leave. He would sit hunched up, silent, for hours. He walked and rode with a stoop from which his head protruded like that of an old terrapin. He ran his trap lines on a flop-lipped dun mare, and, according to him, she would locate by smell any coyote dragging a trap. He said she would take the trail, working her ears, until she came close to the coyote, then stop and point them. I never heard any other name for this trapper than Pegleg; how he lost a leg was not known by anybody in the country except himself. He told me that in trapping after one certain coyote he changed scent eight times before catching him. Tracks showed that when this coyote winded a scent — until the final one lured him — he would break and run as hard as if a bullet had knocked up dust under his nose. The really cunning coyote suspects man's deception in every smell in the air and proves his cunning by not letting curiosity overcome suspicion. His wariness tells him to avoid the curious and to deny his instinct for investigation.

One of the most able avoiders ranged over a big sheep country on the Pecos, going from pasture to pasture, but having no regular beat. He killed only to eat, and after he had made a kill he left the area. Five or six trappers tried successively to get him, each employing his own special scents and dodges. They all agreed that no lure whatsoever interested this coyote. They were unable to discover any scent post that he visited. He followed no trails or roads, and his passways from pasture to pasture were not discernible. After he became notorious, he was never heard by night or seen by day. He had been shot at once by a man on horseback. Tracks showed that he would shy at the imprint of a shod horse's foot but pay no attention to the tracks of a barefooted horse. Evidently, he associated horseshoes with man. The only possible way to trap him was with a blind — scentless — trap. The location of blind sets was a guess until Guy West saw where the coyote had jumped a fence twice at the same place. It appeared that he was springing to the top wire, between posts, balancing himself on it with all four feet, and then leaping. Guy West set his scentless traps in the dirt at the landing place — and caught. The section of wire he persisted in jumping seemed to differ in no way from other sections to the right and to the left of it. The Achilles heel of this arch-avoider of all scents lay in his instinct to follow his own tracks — in habit.

No scent, no method of applying it, works invariably. A lure that attracts one coyote repels another. If a coyote has discovered a trap in conjunction with a certain smell, perhaps been caught and got loose, he will, if he be intelligent, avoid that smell as poison. Another combination will have to be tried on him. A smart coyote that gets onto one trapper's methods and can detect his odors where the trapper does not think he has left any may be caught by another trapper who is less skillful but who has different methods and odors.

Many trappers dote on novelties to lure the animal. One in Montana is strong on rotten eggs mixed with fish oil and decomposed ground squirrel. One in Colorado always boils his traps in sage tea when he is trapping in a sage country, in piñon tea when trapping in piñon country, in pine tea when trapping in pines, and so on. "The iron smell makes them suspicious," he says. "Neutralize it with the vegetation that the coyotes in any particular locality are used to."

A good trapper, by his knowledge of coyote habits, readily locates scent posts — bushes, rocks, tree trunks, mounds of one kind or another — on any range. Nearly every coyote has a series of scent posts on his or her beat — maybe fifteen on a ten-mile round. A coyote that has left notice on a post will upon revisiting the vicinity, whether a day or a month later, investigate to see if some other coyote has passed. Any coyote coming to another's scent post leaves a notice, written in urinal ink or in dung, saying plainly, "I have been here." These notices are not necessarily love notes at all, but to coyotes they are as plain as the letters posted by Shakespeare's lovers on trees in the Forest of Arden. They are, in coyote land, the country newspaper chronicling the comings and goings of John Doe, Mrs. John Doe and other home-town inhabitants — and are on just about the same intellectual level.

Trappers often plant a scent post — a bush or a log — in an open glade or some other spot bare of extruding objects. On it they sprinkle a bit of the lure — not too much — and hide a trap in the ground where the investigator is likely to step. Most modern trapping is done with scent "bait," rather than with something to eat.

The coyote has three, perhaps four, hungers that respond to man-concocted lures: stomach hunger; sex hunger; a hunger for enjoying certain smells, usually expressed by wallowing in them; then, if it can be called a hunger, the investigative instinct. Scavenger that the coyote is, he is as fond of clean, fresh meat as anybody. This fact must not be forgotten. At the same time, to the wolf-dog kind any smell is as interesting as the most attractive-looking booby trap ever appeared to an acquisitive soldier. The scent may be familiar; it may be utterly foreign. Dried herring and seal oil, both undreamed of by inland coyotes, arouse lively interests in them.

Animal hungers overlap each other. Exactly what hunger inside a coyote responds to the loud-smelling stuff smeared as a lure on the bulb of a cyanide gun, or "coyote getter," * is much debated. Probably a combination of responses draws the coyote to it. The Fish and Wildlife Service prescribes for this lure a compound of rotten meat, especially horse, armadillo or prairie

* The instrument is described on page 48.

dog; rotten brains; a tincture of beaver castor; a little artificial musk. Siberian musk, which comes from between the toes of Siberian deer, is very desirable but is scarce and costly. One trapper adds a little skunk musk; another, a flavoring of port wine. A coyote freshly gorged will come to the reeking bulb — no bigger than the forefinger of an alderman and no more conspicuous than a lump of dirt — pull, and, instantly permeated with the charge of exploded cyanide, make his last kick. If a bucket of the stuff were put out, no coyote would eat it. One carrying a rabbit came by a cyanide gun, put it down and pulled the gun. Freedom from belly hunger seems to leave the animal freer to indulge other hungers.

Often a coyote wallows on the bulb before biting it, sometimes without biting at all. Perhaps the coyote wants to take the smelling object off and play with it; quite likely his desire to pick it up is identical with human instinct to handle any curious object. Perhaps in the way that human selfishness operates, the coyote wants to have the thing for himself and prevent any other coyote from having it.

A Nevada trapper noticed scratchings and pawings in a patch of ground perhaps twelve feet across. Investigation showed a scented powder puff in the center of the scratchings. He set a trap beside this lure and caught nine coyotes, one after the other.

Melman Standish, a trapper at Dillon, Montana, had a tamed male coyote about two-thirds grown loose in the yard when a woman came one day to call on Mrs. Standish. Usually very shy of strangers, the coyote was noticeably attracted to her. Her handbag was the object of his attention. She and the Standishes stood in the yard remarking on the coyote's behavior. "What do you have in your handbag?" Standish asked. "Why, nothing especially," the visitor answered. "Open it," Standish requested. The woman opened it and took out, first, a handkerchief. The coyote grabbed it, dropped it, and was about to urinate on it when Standish rescued it. "What kind of perfume is on the handkerchief?" he asked. "Just cheap ten-cent variety," she replied. He persisted and got the name of the brand and of the store where it could be bought. He bought some of it, sprinkled it on tufts of cotton, and used them, successfully, as lures. Half the trappers in south Texas add a bit of "Night-in-Hongkong" perfume, which is comparatively cheap, to the stinking mess smeared on cyanide guns.

Coyotes wallow on ground soaked with crude oil from a leaky pipeline — some say, but they are merely guessing, to get rid of fleas. A trapper in New Mexico noticed a coyote smelling investigatively along the high center of a country road impregnated with oil drippings from automobiles. Next, he noticed where a coyote had wallowed on such a place. He tried putting a few drops of oil on the earth over hidden traps and found that the lure worked.

Back in the ages while man was in the process of losing his tail, he probably had a much more active and keener sense of smell than he now has. He was not so introspective and intellectually curious, however; he left no description of how the sense of smell activated him or of how he responded to olfactory appeals. Modern man's comprehension of the sense of smell in the lives of keen-scented animals is analogous to a blind person's comprehension of colors. Modern man is not even aware of the part that smell plays in his own life. "Scent," said Emerson, "reveals what is concealed from the other senses." Some day I shall write an essay on Love at First Smell.

An English fox will kill a stinking stoat, not eat a drop of blood or a mite of flesh, but wallow on it, carry it somewhere and wallow on it again. Watch a clean dog wallowing in a putrid mess of offal and gloating with satisfaction. Members of the family Canidae are possessed by an appetite for identifying themselves with all sorts of smells offensive to most human beings. Long after it had passed from me, I came to recognize through memory a faint kinship within myself to this canine passion.

When I was about sixteen years old, my father bought around a thousand steer yearlings several days' drive away from our ranch. It was about the first of July when we received the yearlings and branded them, and that summer was one of the wettest south Texas has ever known. The creek flats grew up in tall bloodweeds; the grass was too sappy to give strength; the blowflies, which thrive in damp shade, and the screwworms hatched from their eggs were a plague. As the fresh brands peeled, the flies deposited their fast-hatching eggs on the raw places. Many yearlings had ticks, and when a tick dropped off, leaving a tiny raw place where it had sucked blood, screwworms worked in. Many animals had worms in their ears — a location that no animal can lick and self-cure. The yearlings had stampeded on the drive, and for weeks after they were turned loose in our pastures they would drift together in small bunches at night, run into barbed wire and cut gashes, which blowflies promptly found. Some got stomach worms and became too poor and weak to resist the slightest enemy.

We rode from daylight till dark every day doctoring the things, and often skinned dead ones by lantern light. I had a horse named Buck who could smell a wormy animal a hundred yards away in the tall weeds and brush, where sick and wounded cow brutes take refuge. When Buck smelled the animal — that is, the suppurating flesh of its wound — he would lift his head and, looking in that direction, work his ears slightly. He knew what we were hunting. He seemed to enjoy the smell. I came to the stage of rather enjoying it too. My hands were so impregnated with the odor of cresylic ointment, applied on the wounds to repel flies, and with the odor of rotten flesh that they could no more be washed clean of the stain than Lady Macbeth's hands. I not only grew used to the smells but came to take a kind of pleasure in them. True, I never got down and wallowed in a worm-writhing carcass, as I have many times luxuriated amid

[145]

fragrant bluebonnets, but the sensory condition I experienced enables me now somewhat to comprehend the response of dog or coyote to what man calls foulness. Only in kind, not in degree, does this response differ from the ecstatic sensations of

> Zephyr, with Aurora playing,
> As he met her once a-Maying,
> There on beds of violets blue
> And fresh-blown roses washed in dew.

The coyote has many rolling places — maybe where a cow has urinated, where a peccary has lain down and left the smell of its musk, where a possum has died. Often man cannot even faintly detect an attraction that shouts to the coyote nose. Occasionally a coyote with a passion for impregnating his hide with skunk musk becomes, it seems, an inveterate skunk-killer, sometimes eating the flesh as well as soaking up the odor, sometimes only wallowing in it. There is probably nothing to the popular idea that coyotes and foxes wallow in foreign-smelling substances in order to kill their own body scent and throw pursuers off the track. They are sybarites.

The keenness of an animal's sense of smell cannot be measured as intensity of sound is measured by a microphone. It does appear, however, that the coyote can wind as sensitively as the best hound or shepherd dog and trail as delicately. When a coyote pup wanders a short distance away from its den, it returns, without using its eyes at all, by backtracking with nose to ground. Tracks showed Fred Messer, near Sealy Lake, Montana, where a coyote had made a right-angle turn to go to a bait of meat covered by two feet of snow, fifty yards off. When the legendary hero of the Yosemite Indians sought to give his son all of nature's virtues, he wrapped him in the skin of a grizzly so that strength and fearlessness might pass into him, fed him fish and venison so that he might derive the power to swim expertly and the power to run tirelessly, and dressed him in a robe of coyote skins to make him keen-scented. Despite superstition concerning the transmission of virtues, the Indian's estimate of coyote superiority in the world of smell was scientific.

The coyote can see better than the greyhound; his sense of hearing is probably as sharp as that of the deer. It is no trouble to attract his attention. His senses are open to all sorts of invitations. In him, sensory appeals and the pull of curiosity must often overlap each other. A coyote with power to resist both makes trappers lie awake at night thinking up new dodges.

Curiosity, despite abuse of it, goes always with intelligence. Shyness and curiosity duel with each other in many animals, in deer and antelopes especially. Domestic goats, brazen and shameless, are unrestrained in exercising curiosity. Trust in man long ago made dogs take many things for granted. Coyotes are more curious than timber wolves; their unsleeping desire to investigate anything unusual often outpulls wolf caution. If a wolf suspects or detects a trap, he will avoid it; a coyote wants to examine it. The wolf is more direct. Upon sensing a quarter of horse that has been poisoned as bait, he will, if he is going to it at all, go directly. A coyote that locates it will go to a hill, if there is one at hand, stand on it and look, go to another lookout and look some more; then he will approach the quarter and examine it from all sides.

William James Burns told me of a sheep-killing coyote that carefully avoided every trick and lure until one day he wound up an ordinary alarm clock, put it in a tin can, and buried the can with a sprinkling of dirt over the lid along one of the ways the coyote was using. A trap was buried adjacent to the clock so that if the coyote investigated he would almost have to step into it. Hearing that ticking in the ground was too much for this coyote. Curiosity about something that was none of his business made him negligent of what had become the main business of his life aside from eating.

Another time Burns caught an unsophisticated coyote near a fence. After he killed it, he scraped dirt with his feet over a pool of clotted blood that had run out of the animal's nose and mouth. Back at the spot next day, he noticed that a coyote had dug up the clot, sniffed it and left it. He suspected a particularly crafty coyote that had been eluding him. He reburied the clotted blood and set a trap near it. The crafty one came again that night and followed his inclination, fatal this time, to satisfy the itch of curiosity.

One meddling Texas coyote caught himself in a trap that had been put aside against a tree and covered with a flat stone to prevent anything's stepping into it. A Montana coyote learned the trick of digging traps out and turning them over. Evidently he derived satisfaction from this procedure. Finally, a trapper buried a trap upside down. When the coyote tried to turn it over, he caught himself. He was smart enough to dig up traps but not smart enough to leave them alone.

A coyote that must know a bone-dry tortoise shell turned over on its back has no nourishment or other significance for him feels an impulse to sniff it, give it a turn with his paw. Making camp at a tank one day, Ray Brotherton noticed a big rattlesnake that a tanker had left hanging from the limb of a mesquite tree, tail down. Two mornings later he noticed that a coyote had pulled the snake down, torn it into four pieces and played with them without eating a mouthful. He set a trap in the midst of the pieces. The next night the coyote, probably on his way to water, came again to "monkey" with the pieces of rattlesnake, and got caught. Another time Brotherton set a trap at hazard beside the buzzard-picked skeleton of a bull snake and caught a coyote.

One of the dodges employed by lobo trappers was to bury a pair of deer ears, leaving the tips an inch or two above ground, near a trap. To attract coyotes, William James Burns sometimes buries the ears of a sheep or a jack rabbit in the same way. He has burned a beef bone and buried it. "Give the animal something new to investigate," he says. "Make him catch himself. In the end, curiosity will kill any cat."

One of the most difficult coyotes that William James Burns ever trapped after was a female sheep-killer. Her tracks became readily identifiable to him. She had no set range, but wandered from pasture to pasture, avoiding any area in which she discovered a trap. He had a dog that often called his attention to obscure details. One day while Burns was studying the coyote's tracks in a cattle bed ground against a fence, he noticed the dog smelling and resmelling a low bush rooted under the wires. He got down on his knees to see better. He picked eight or ten coarse javelina hairs and one soft coyote hair off the wires. They were slightly loose. The coyote was using a passageway made by javelinas. Burns set a trap at the bush. The coyote did not return that way, but did come back to the bed ground. Out in it, Burns set a blind trap where cattle would not step. The next day he saw that the coyote had come and walked around the trap.

He has not figured out yet why she did not, according to precedent, leave that part of the country. He set another blind trap out to one side of the first. She surprised him by coming back that night and walking around the second trap. It seemed as if she had taken a notion to play a game with this man of traps. He kept setting traps, all without scent, until he had a labyrinth of six. Then he killed a jack rabbit and buried it within the maze. In the night the coyote stepped within two inches of each of three traps, dug up the jack rabbit, and left it without having tasted it. Burns next buried a mixture of skunk, house cat and armadillo meat and set a seventh trap hard by. That night while the coyote was pawing into this lure, the trap caught her. She disgorged a full stomach of lamb before dragging the trap away.

"By indirections find directions out." A trapper in the hill country of Texas discovered that a stock-killer he had been unable to glimpse for months traveled a certain trail about every eight days. He killed a goat and hung it from a tripod of poles over the trail. The poles and the goat were as conspicuous as a roulette wheel would be on a church altar. Not far off was a knoll, up which a dim trail led. The trapper buried his traps on and around the top of the knoll. He figured that if he were the coyote, he would go up there, take a view of the country and reflect on the meaning of the goat gallows below. He figured correctly.

After studying the habits of a certain coyote that had out-coyoted several other trappers, W. S. Hall named him Frogger. Frogger would kill eight or ten sheep or goats and disappear. Often he merely drank the blood of his victims, not eating the flesh. After he had made a big kill, he would travel ten or fifteen miles before making another. Hall found that he was visiting tanks along his beats and amusing himself catching frogs; tracks in mud showed where he often leaped and slid. Sometimes he turned aside at a tank to go frogging soon after he had left a collection of uneaten sheep carcasses. Hall concentrated his traps at tanks, and at one of them finally caught Frogger.

Perhaps twenty coyotes are lured into traps through curiosity to one lured through hunger. While Ray Brotherton was being repeatedly foiled by a certain coyote preying on sheep, a drive over a bare, flat piece of ground that the coyote sometimes crossed gave him an idea. He happened to have a dried coyote's foot in his pickup. He tossed it out on the naked ground, then concealed two scentless traps, one on either side of it. If the coyote came along, he might feel an impulse to sniff that dried foot. That is what the coyote did three nights later. He was very suspicious of scents, but did not suspect a trap here. He had suspected, justifiably, and avoided successively a dried badger carcass, a mummified skunk, an armadillo shell.

Every coyote has his price — although it sometimes takes a trapper a long time to find out what it is. Alert senses as much as intelligence keep coyotes out of traps. The skillful eluders exercise a combination of the two, plus restraint against answering the never-ceasing calls of the senses and of curiosity.

VII · TRAPPER AND TRAPPED

IN THIS BOOK there are many citations to the printed works of travelers, hunters, naturalists, biologists and other observers of wild animals. There are more citations to the oral words of men who have never thought of writing but who have spent all their lives, mostly alone and silent, in the brush, amid mountains, on the prairies. If one who has lived thus be only fairly intelligent and alert, the mere law of chance enables him to see things in nature that no scholar who only makes excursions out from his study ever glimpses. On the other hand, there is no discounting the perspective, given by learning and thought, that relates particular instances of animal behavior to the whole pattern of life. The binoculared scientific searcher for truth, even though limited in field experiences, has some advantages over the out-of-doors liver, no matter how eagle-eyed, who always goes with a gun and the purpose of killing. But give me talk with a true *hombre de campo* who has spent forty years outside, and I will see things never reported by bookmakers.

It was about four o'clock on a warm Sunday afternoon at the end of November that I drove up to the house of Luke Stillwell on a sheep ranch bounded on one side by the Rio Grande and bisected by the Eagle Pass-Del Rio highway. This ranch of ten thousand acres, fenced with sheep-proof wire, is the spear-head of a vast sheep range jutting out into cattle range where coyotes breed free because they are not regarded as a menace to cattle. After it was stocked with sheep about thirteen years ago, a contest developed as to which should survive — sheep or coyotes. Though cleaned of coyotes time and again, the pastures are constantly infiltrated by predators, and warfare against the infiltrators remains constant. The warrior-in-chief here is Luke Stillwell, employed jointly by the United States Fish and Wild-life Service and the rancher whom he protects. He has been here going on five years. All his other years from childhood up were spent hunting, trapping and ranging.

As I drove up to his house, a dog barked, and Luke Stillwell darted out to meet me, as wiry as a ga'nted steer breaking from a thicket, bareheaded, thin-haired, maybe sixty years old, his deep-set eyes gleaming like two mesquite coals. "We've been expecting you," he said.

His brother Charlie had just come for a visit from his goat ranch up on the Divide. I liked Mrs. Stillwell at once. "We are about to have coffee," she said in a voice soothing to the nerves. We sat in the kitchen. There was apple pie to go with the coffee. We three men occupied most of the dining table; her coffee cup was beside the water bucket on a small side table. Water is brought into the kitchen from an outside hydrant, connected with a windmill that pumps for stock. The water is too mineral-ized for human beings to drink, and the Stillwells haul drinking water. Some day the ranch owner is going to pipe water into the house.

It has three rooms, one big room and a partitioned shed room. A daughter who had occupied the front room was gone. As we lingered over the coffee, Mrs. Stillwell told how her pet blue quail like to stand on top of the woodpile and how they eat with the chickens. She told about a pet spider in the front room and his leaps after flies. She showed pictures of two little javelinas.

One night soon after she got them, a snow fell and she awoke thinking they must be frozen in their pen outside. But when she rushed out, she found that they had dug two small parallel holes in the earth and buried themselves, their snow-covered backs barely showing. She told about the pet toads which all the past summer came into the kitchen through a hole in the floor, exterminated the cockroaches, and went out through a hole in the screen door that Luke made shooting at a hawk on a tree over the chicken house. The toads had hibernated not long before my arrival.

After a while Luke Stillwell said that he had to get some jack rabbits for their caged coyote, a dog and about twenty-five cats. He fiercely resented a suggestion that his cats killed quail. We got into his car and drove until he and Brother Charlie had shot three jack rabbits. One of them caught by the dog while only wounded made squeaking cries of distress that would have interested any coyote.

"The coyote will not eat while we are looking," Luke Stillwell said, as at dusk he put a big jack rabbit into a cage under some live oak trees, far enough removed from the house that its stench did not permeate the domestic air. "In the morning there won't be anything left of this rabbit. Coyotes have to have hair with their meat. One would starve on clean beefsteak." The tin-bottomed cage in which this coyote is kept drains the animal's urine into a pan on the ground. Luke Stillwell hates the cruelty of tying up a coyote in order to get scent bait from it.

Hot biscuits, venison, honey, gravy, lettuce and tomatoes (from irrigated fields not far away) for supper. Then another pie for dessert, but not for the crustiest and creamiest of all pies baked could I forsake honey of mesquite blossom, hot biscuits and fried venison — surely one of the perfect combinations of foods in the world. I had not intended to stay all night, but wanted to, and accepted the hearty invitation with the understanding that I would use my own bedroll. When the time came,

I brought it in and spread it on the floor in the front room across from the bed in which Charlie Stillwell slept.

After supper Luke brought out two books on wild animals that he had marked both approvingly and disapprovingly. He said that as a boy he read over and over Captain Drannan's *Thirty-One Years on the Plains and in the Mountains*, and that he wished he could get hold of it again. Some remark made me remember George Frederick Ruxton's account of the wolf that followed him for days, waiting each evening for his part of an antelope or deer, and often at night coming close to the campfire. Charlie Stillwell exclaimed that he wanted to buy Ruxton's book. "It has long been out of print," I explained, "but can be procured at not too high a price."

Very often in the country I meet natural men and women who are not regular buyers and readers of books but who have a deep hunger for good books, particularly on country life, that they don't know how to procure. The slick writing on slick pages and the imprint of pulpy brains on pulp pages piled up in the drugstores they go to and the canned insincerities and manufactured sensations that come to them over the radio never feed their undefined hunger for wholesomeness.

It was mighty pleasant and natural sitting there in the kitchen by kerosene light talking with the Stillwell brothers and Mrs. Stillwell. Luke was not bothered by my jotting down a note now and then. I asked him if coyotes eat dry land terrapins. He thought not. For one thing, a terrapin can lock himself up, head and feet, in his under-plated shell so that a tooth hold on any part of its body would be very difficult to get. "And the coyote can't make a fire," I said, "like the Indians and old-timey Mexicans to pitch the live terrapin into. I'd think the coyote would enjoy the meat as much as an Indian does, if he could get to it."

Luke Stillwell doesn't deal much in speculations. He went on to describe the hibernation habits of the dry land terrapin as he has watched them. One, he said, will find a softish place under a bush and begin excavating in his awkward way. He can't pull the dirt out into a mound in the manner of a badger. Most of the dirt he digs loose will fall back into the hole, but he slowly works himself down into the cavity and after three or four days is maybe a foot under ground level and is completely covered. He goes into hibernation in late October or November and comes out about March. I said I had never seen this, but once down towards the toe of Texas saw what I took to be a migration of terrapins. I was driving south, and I saw many terrapins crossing the road, going east. Charlie Stillwell said that one time while driving south in the Brush Country he saw hundreds of terrapins moving eastward, all going the same way. The road was studded with them, and many had been run over. Sometimes when I see one of these slow creatures trying to cross a highway, I stop and get out and lift him across so that the next car will not crush him.

We went back to the subject of lobos, which in his youth Luke Stillwell trapped. "In the tradition of American wildlife," I said, "the Custer Wolf and other cunning, man-eluding stock-killers loom big. Have there ever been any individual coyotes with so much character?"

He was silent for longer than a minute. He shifted in the raw-hide-bottomed chair. A wrinkle stood on his forehead.

"I called her Old Crip," he began. "I set my first trap on this ranch the twelfth day of September, 1943. There had been trappers ahead of me, and they had taught some coyotes a lot. I began right away catching crippled coyotes that had escaped from their traps. I caught fourteen crippled coyotes and then there were two left. They were really educated. Finally I caught one of them, and the trap held. It took me, in all, fifteen months and five days to get Old Crip.

"She had two toes off her left front foot. While I was still clearing the other sheep-killers out, she put her right front foot into one of my traps. She pulled, gnawed, twisted and broke

[156]

that foot off just above the steel jaws. What she left there was all I ever saw of her until the end. The average coyote when caught in a trap becomes frantic. It bites bushes, the trap cover, steel, sometimes its own tail. The part of its foot below the steel jaws becomes numb, and often the animal will chew that part, not with the purpose of cutting itself loose but in blind desperation. Another trapper told me about a coyote that chewed both front feet out of a trap and then just sat there without a struggle while he came up to kill her. I am absolutely sure that Old Crip knew what she was about when she set to work to free herself.

"Within thirty days the stub had healed and she was killing sheep again. She killed sixty lambs within a month's time. She went from one pasture to another and killed $3000 worth of sheep during the fifteen months and five days I kept after her. I didn't let up for a day. Her track was unmistakable and her habits were individual.

"She killed often for sport. Any killing leaves plain signs. But Old Crip never seemed boastful and reckless in her killing like some coyotes. One night four bold ones came into a clean pasture, killed sixteen lambs, gorged, went on, met a skunk, killed him, tore him up and rolled on him without taking a bite of his flesh, went on, met a big fat possum, killed him, and left him untouched beside the trail. These coyotes were out to shoot up the town. Old Crip would slaughter sheep right and left; then she was gone. When a coyote with any sense kills a sheep, he knows he is in danger. He eats in a hurry. He takes one gulp and then looks up. As soon as he is full, he makes tracks — no lying around the carcass for him. This was the way of Old Crip. She killed without reason at times, but always on the alert. After the killing was over, she seemed never to be playful or loggy. She stayed unceasingly careful.

"She never traveled stock trail or road. Coyotes that travel in that way — and it is natural for a coyote to trot down a road — are easily caught. All the time I was after Old Crip, fresh coyotes were coming into the ranch from the big cattle pastures joining us. They had regular entrances, and they regularly got into traps. A coyote seldom learns anything by seeing or smelling the carcasses of his mates. A dead coyote seems to mean nothing to a live one — excepting always the highly intelligent like Old Crip. During a period of five and a half years trapping on one big ranch before I came here, I caught 54 coyotes in a single trap at one location, just resetting it and hanging the carcasses of the victims, one after the other, near by. This was at a wire-netting fence corner. I had some other traps close by, and altogether caught between 110 and 115 coyotes at this location. The easiest kind of coyote to trap is a young male. The females even when young are more distrustful.

"Old Crip had already depredated on the ranch for several years when I took up her trail. She would never go under a fence unless another coyote preceded her, showing that the way was clear. She had probably been caught at a hole under a fence. She avoided all lures, scent or bait. I caught her that first time in a blind trap — just a naked trap hidden in the ground — placed where I thought she might go to water. That was on the night of October 31, 1943. She had miles of Los Moros Creek to water in and she was not fixed by habit to any one watering place. After she stepped down the bank to water and had drunk, she backed out, putting her feet in almost the exact tracks they had made coming in.

"In the spring I found her den with the pups in it. Her mate had no doubt been caught. I set a blind trap at the den. A sheep got into it and fell into the hole, rather large at the mouth. That night the mother coyote beat a trail around the sheep and the den. I took the sheep out the next morning. Old Crip never returned to her pups. The mother instinct in coyotes is strong; in Old Crip it was not blind. She plainly suspected — and she was right — that a hidden enemy would not let her pass if she stepped into her den to move her young ones. She left them to perish.

"In any coyote country you frequently see coyotes moving about by day, though it is their nature to be nocturnal. I never once saw Old Crip. It is my belief that she never roamed during daylight hours but kept herself absolutely hidden. So far as I know, she never howled. Except at mating time, she ranged alone. She killed alone. She went in the night and she went in silence.

"It is a habit with some coyotes, not all by any means, to gorge a bait of sheep meat, six pounds say, go off maybe forty or sixty yards, in open country farther, to where there is brush and shade, and there dig out a hole. Then the animal throws up the meat, still fresh and undigested, into the hole and covers it with earth, just as a dog buries a bone. The coyote that does this will almost invariably come back the next night, dig its meat out of earth that has kept it fresh, and eat. By that time flies and buzzards would have ruined the carcass, provided other coyotes had not made away with it. A coyote will rob another coyote's cache if he finds it. The caches make good trapping places; sometimes I bury a piece of meat or bone, mound up earth over it in a natural way, and set traps. After a coyote fills up on meat for the purpose of burying it and has buried it, he goes straight back to the carcass and eats again, either to digest the food or to carry it to the young.

"Now, if Old Crip ever buried a piece of meat, I did not know it. If she ever ate carrion, I did not know it. She had lost the scavenger habits of her species. She was always choosey about her meat. She liked it warm and fresh, and she was particular about the cuts.

"It was on the night of December 17, 1944, that I caught her the second time, in a blind trap, on a bluff overlooking water. She must have realized that she could not free herself this time. I found her drowned. She had dived off the bluff and gone under some wire netting in the water. The hook on the trap chain caught in this wire. She aimed to kill herself, so it seems to me.

She had just cut the throat of a choice lamb, had eaten, and was on her way to water. I examined her stomach. It contained five or six pounds of select meat — kidneys, small intestines, leaf fat, loin, and tenderer ribs. I never heard of a lobo smarter than Old Crip. I came to admire her while she was baffling me. She seemed to belong to the hills that I belong to. I think of her lots of times in the night. I'll never forget her."

*   *   *

The wariest coyotes are not always those that have learned by being caught and getting away. Many of the wariest avoid all traps until the final one. A dull coyote that gets out of one trap will step into another. J. W. Montgomery caught a coyote by two toes; it pulled loose. Soon thereafter he caught it by the other foot, which it gnawed off, getting away. It lived mostly in Mexico but crossed the Rio Grande at irregular intervals for mutton. Next, Montgomery caught it in two traps, side by side, the foot with the missing toes in one and the stub in the other. It lay down right there and gnawed both feet loose. Two years later a cowboy roped this coyote and ended its career. One Mexico coyote Montgomery caught on the Texas side had been completely scalped, probably by a Mexican shepherd to collect a bounty on the scalp. A gristle had healed over its head. A few coyotes after they are caught give up and die — *acalambrado*, as the vaqueros say of an outlaw steer that after running free in the brush for years, developing eagle alertness and Spartan resistance to thirst and hunger, is finally roped and tied and then just dies, paralyzed by emotion. It is liberty or death with this kind.

Frequently a trapped coyote begins barking as soon as it sees its man-enemy approaching. Now and then, as the man-enemy nears, one will lunge towards him, only to be held back by the fastened chain. Males show more fight than females. One time as Ray Brotherton came close to a large dog-coyote that had dragged its trap into some lechuguilla, the animal sprang at him fiercely. The trap chain was free. Brotherton clubbed the coyote down with the butt of his rifle. A few coyotes, only a small percentage of thousands trapped each year, turn aggressive at the last extremity and put up a fight that lasts as long as breath remains.

The immediate reactions of a coyote upon feeling itself trapped are thus described by Elliott S. Barker of New Mexico: "The big dog-coyote was jumping as high in the air as the trap chain would let him. He was beside himself with rage and fright. He barked once or twice as my car neared him, a rare action in my experience with trapped coyotes. He would run on the chain and be jerked into a somersault upon reaching the end of it. Then he would grab a bush just within reach and chew and shake it viciously, as if it were the cause of his misfortune. Then he would make two or three jumps high in the air. Another coyote that I saw step into one of my traps acted in the same way." [a]

VIII · BIOLOGICAL

THE WORD "DEN" carries with it a popular misconception. While severe weather in harsh climates may drive adult coyotes into shelters, and while, as has been said, they sometimes in summers go into the earth for shade and coolness, during most of the year they live out. The great majority seldom enter a den except to feed the young. In warm regions it is not uncommon for a female to litter under a bush, later carrying the pups to some convenient hole. The typical coyote den is a shelter for pups only, the mother withdrawing from them increasingly, except at feeding times, after they are a week or two old. In a country of ledges, boulders, canyons and caves, the den may be extensive and have more than one opening; on prairies and in the low-lying Brush Country, it is likely to be nothing more than an enlarged badger hole; in timber, it is occasionally a hollow log. One litter of pups was found in the skin-covered skeleton of a horse; another in cotton lint under a gin platform. Some coyote mothers are exceedingly stupid. A trapper in Colorado found a litter of pups in a pack rat nest of spines, two of them dead and the others thorn-punctured. Coyotes do not as a rule line their nests with grass and other soft stuff in the manner of rats and rabbits. However, A. B. Bynum says that he once found nine pups in a grass-lined oval scratched under a bush.

Den sites seem often to be selected for adjacent lookout places rather than for secrecy. In a rainy season coyotes are likely to den on higher ground than in a dry season. In a country where early spring rains are unusual they sometimes place their pups in gullies subject to flood waters, but I have never heard of a drowned pup. They like a location, on south or eastern slopes, that will enable the pups to come out into spring sunshine. Nearness to water seems to be favored at times, but many dens are far from water. No fixed rules for the location can be laid down. If left undisturbed, a pair of coyotes will use the same den year after year. On the drainage of the upper Rio Grande, in Colorado, a certain female's persistence in using the same den gave her the name of the Spring Creek Coyote. For seven or eight years she annually lost her young and her mate in the same vicinity, but was wily enough to escape herself. In the end she avoided all holes in the ground and kept her litter under a bush. She found a new mate each year.

Whether coyotes mate for life, as Ernest Thompson Seton asserts and as timber wolves, left alone to live out their lives, unquestionably mate, cannot be answered with a flat nay or yea. Nobody has ever studied them long enough in an undisturbed area to find out. In the rutting season, a female sometimes attracts several contending males — probably not all of them unattached. John W. Crook says that for half a day he has watched, through glasses, "a dozen" male coyotes after a single bitch; other trappers tell of seeing three or more males strung out after a female. On the other hand, R. E. Bateman of Billings, Montana, widely experienced and very precise in observation, says that he has never seen more than two coyotes — a pair — together in the mating season.

There is no reason to suppose that male eagerness is constantly restrained in coyotes. Hearing coyote yips one warm morning, John Joseph Mathews took his glasses and viewed this singular procession: A big blue wolfhound bitch belonging to a neighboring ranchman was stepping daintily across the prairie. Close behind her came Old Buck, a male wolfhound noted for his viciousness and credited with killing coyotes alone, apart from the pack. "Behind him were four male coyotes — one big one in the lead, singing his song of amorous confusion as he trotted, and behind him the smaller ones strung out, stopping occasionally to nose for possible messages, then resuming the eager trot. Old Buck would stop when the blue bitch in her apparent unconcern paused to nose among the grasses, and bare his fangs to the coyotes, who in turn snarled back. Several times before they trotted out of sight, Buck made a rush at the leading coyote, but the wolf eluded him easily and circled back when Buck turned to follow the blue bitch again."

Mr. Mathews, who chases coyotes with dogs, goes on: "I

have always known about the truce between male wolfhounds and female coyotes during the coyote's love moon. I have seen the best wolfhounds embarrass their masters by running up on the side of a female coyote during this season, then turn back without harming her, while she, realizing that hounds are males, made no effort to run fast but loped along, looking back over her shoulder like some coquette. The female coyote knows when there are female dogs in the pack, however, and at such times stretches out. This male understanding between Old Buck and those lovesick coyotes was something new." [1]

It is certain that male and female coyotes pair off to raise their family, and no doubt many pairs, if one or the other is not killed, remain constant year after year. Ross Graves observes that whereas an old male frequently lives in solitude, nearly any female deprived of a mate seeks a new one when she comes into heat. In mating, coyotes seem a good deal like human beings: some are strictly monogamous and some are unstrictly polygamous. Some mated males, like many professedly orthodox husbands, would apparently relish more variety and less responsibility. The brief season of sex activity among coyotes no doubt retards promiscuity.

A scientific study by the Biological Survey of more than 800 reproductive tracts taken from coyotes of both sexes, and of the records of approximately 3000 litters and pregnant females, from thirteen states, shows that the male is sterile during at least eight months of the year and the female during at least ten months. Positive sex activity of both males and females is confined to a few weeks. Not all adult females come into heat. The period of gestation is from 60 to 63 days. April and May are the main littering months, though in Montana and Wyoming a heavy proportion of females litter in June. [2] Variations in coyote behavior during the mating and parental seasons are probably as pronounced as variations in eating habits.

The affection and fidelity of mate for mate have often been

observed. "All night long," says Loyd Ligon, "I have heard the mate to a coyote caught in a trap barking near it — not howling, just barking." Occasionally a trapped coyote howls. Upon the approach of a person, the trapped one often calls for its mate. "The one called for will seldom appear while man is around," Joe Hill says, "but will come after he has left." Neither bark nor howl of an animal in agony has the sound of one that is free.[3]

Some males are much more solicitous for the welfare of their mates than others, and some are better providers for the young. Males have been known to bring food to pregnant mates.[4] Many females will not allow the male too near the den until the pups are weaned. Observers in California found males bringing food no nearer than a hundred yards to dens and meeting the females (to go hunting) about a hundred and fifty yards off.[5] On the other hand, trappers have many times found both male and female in a den. A long-time trapper, Arthur Meile of Valentine, Nebraska, writes in a letter that he has shot several male coyotes as they emerged from dens containing pups. Beyond controversy, the male does his share of guard duty over the den and is often more ready than the female to challenge an enemy and try to lead it away from the pups.

The "laying-up places" around a den shift with the wind. A coyote prefers to approach its den against the wind, and will generally circle it, raising the nose frequently to test the air, before entering. As the pups advance in age, the parents tend to take stands farther off.

If the female is killed before the sucklings are old enough to eat meat, the male can do nothing for them. Many times males have been observed bringing meat to pups that had lost their mother. Orphans old enough to scramble about may exist on grasshoppers and bugs. If they can get to water and catch millers, and if a wildcat, an eagle or some other enemy does not sight them, they stand a chance to survive.

It is at denning time that their worst enemy — the government trapper, who is not out for fur — is most active. Having located a litter of pups in the ground, he twists a "feeler," an easily carried length of stiff but flexible barbed wire, after them. The point of the twisting feeler will find any pup in any corner or crevice of the den and screw hide and hair into a hold that will not loosen as the wire is pulled out with the whimpering puppy.

When danger threatens, the male as well as the female moves the pups, carrying them one by one in the mouth to a new den, sometimes only a few hundred yards away, again for miles. A male coyote under the observation of J. W. Montgomery carried four pups, one by one, five miles in a single night — forty miles of travel. As an experiment, John Morris of the Brady Creek (Texas) country took six out of seven pups that he found in a den and put them in an open enclosure near by. Neither male nor female parent approached them. A few days later he located the female and the one pup left to her at a den seven miles from the original den. Parent coyotes, as if anticipating trouble, seem often to have alternative holes ready for occupancy. Now and then suspicious parents scatter their pups soon after birth. If hard-pressed, they sometimes scatter them for temporary hiding, reconcentrating them at the first opportunity. Some trappers claim that some experienced coyotes move their young every night. The moving is often for no other apparent reason than to get away from fleas.

Mates commonly start out together from near the den to hunt, the hour not being fixed but early night being the usual time. The male is likely to make a longer round than the female. One may specialize on sheep-killing, the other on rabbits. Some parents, acting apparently to prevent reprisal, are careful not to kill near the den. A pair that denned for season after season near a ranch house in Oklahoma ignored the chickens until August, by which time the whelps were rustling for themselves and had to be guarded against.[6]

Time and again coyotes have been known to pass by sheep

in the vicinity of their dens and to kill other sheep miles away. One pair carried parts of a carcass eight miles to their pups. A sheepherder in Montana stopped his wagon at a certain place and after bedding his flock there for several nights noticed, one evening, his sheep drawing back from a spot and making a circle around it, facing inward. He walked over to investigate and discovered a coyote den. He could hear the pups inside. He stopped up the hole with rocks and the next morning dug it out. He killed not only eleven pups but the mother coyote with them. She had, no doubt, been coming and going during all the nights that the flock was bedded about her den, but had carefully avoided molesting any of the animals at hand.

Back in the early days, Joe Hill says, coyotes, both male and female, would habitually bark at a man approaching their den. This was to draw attention to themselves and away from the young. Now, made cautious by continual trapping, poisoning and hounding, some coyotes will quietly slip away from their dens without trying to lure an intruding man after them. A few are so wary that if they suspect discovery of their den they leave the young to die. Joe Hill has trapped parent coyotes at a den after they had stayed away from it a month, finally returning to investigate — but "no two pairs of coyotes are alike in behavior." One female turned over two traps that John W. Crook had set at the mouth of her den, and moved seven pups, their eyes just opening, to a den half a mile away. Traps set at this den scared her off and she began returning to the original den, where she was eventually caught.

A female that Ray Brotherton trapped showed that she was suckling a big litter. He wanted the pups but did not know where to find them. He used the mother to direct him. He released her foreleg from the heavy No. 4 trap into which she had stepped and fixed a light No. 2 trap on a hind leg, tying the jaws together with wire so that they would not work loose. Then he put a sheep bell on her and let her go. This was in the evening.

The next morning he took his dog to the place where he had released her. After trailing about three quarters of a mile, dog and trapper came upon her in a clump of bushes on a hillside, shaking her bell and barking faintly. The poor thing could not run. She seemed to be doing the best she could to distract attention from the denned pups just on up the hill. Had she not been severely crippled in one foot and hampered by a trap on another, she would no doubt have moved her pups that night. There were ten of them. Another mother coyote on which the same ruse was tried refused to go towards her den at all. A female upon discovering an enemy near her den is said to look towards it instinctively, thus betraying its location to the knowing.

Astute females smell out and otherwise test the ground at the mouth of a den every time they return to it. If one finds the hole stopped up with rocks, she may or may not try to dig them out. She encourages the pups to try to dig free. If she discovers man tracks, instead of going into the den, she whines to her pups to come out, to be carried, or, if they are old enough, to be led away. If dogs at a den give chase to a female barking at them and then quit running to besiege the den again, she will follow them back and bark, bark. Paul Lambert once located a coyote den on an Alberta (Canada) prairie not far from a spruce tree and climbed the tree to observe. "After waiting a long time," he reported, "I saw the mother coyote following my tracks that led to her home. She did not go into the lair, but merely stopped at its entrance for a second. I heard her notifying her young ones not to come out. Then she began following my trail [by smell] toward the tree. Soon she got the air in the right direction and discovered me." [7] Lambert shot her, blocked up the entrance to the den, came back next day with a dead rabbit and camera, opened the mouth of the den, placed the rabbit at it, withdrew, and snapped a picture of the famished pups as they came out to eat. Where was the male? Very likely somebody had killed him.

As in other species, the maternal instinct among coyotes some-times leads to extreme conduct. In late April of 1935, Guy Givens, a trapper in Idaho, found a den of nine coyote pups, their eyes still closed, and killed them. He shot at the mother, who bore peculiar markings, but missed her. A few days later he saw this individual emerge from another den, investigated it, and found two collie pups. The desolate mother coyote had stolen them from a dog at a sheep camp. Joe Hill, who used to keep several coyotes at a time in roomy pens, once had a female so foolish over an adopted dog-pup that she would vomit up everything in her stomach every time it whined. This, of course, was her way of offering it food.

It is generally taken for granted that a family group among coyotes and other wolves consists only of parents and pups. In *Wolves of Mount McKinley*, which contains more intimate information on the daily life of timber wolves than any other work ever published, Adolph Murie sketches the personalities of two unmated males and one unmated female that for months lived in comradeship with a pair of wolves around their den of six pups, hunting with them, keeping watch, bringing in food, and then, as the pups grew up, remaining with the group. Like-wise, odd coyotes, especially unmated yearlings,[8] often live with a pair of parent coyotes during the denning season. Also, not infrequently, two litters of pups are found together. At a den where he found two litters of distinctly different ages, A. B. Bynum took two female adults and one male.* W. S. Hall found two litters, fourteen pups in all, that had been brought by their parents from two "brush nests" about two hundred yards apart to a common den three quarters of a mile away. Tracks in soft

* "At a den where two litters are found there is usually only one male, which would suggest polygamy." — Stanley Paul Young, *Sketches of American Wildlife*, Baltimore, 1946, 10. Evidence on coyote harems seems to me too haphazard and casual to warrant assertion of their existence. If they do exist, they are rare.

ground following a rain told the whole story. C. R. Landon found in one den three pups four or five weeks old and two pups with eyes still closed, all five being, apparently, suckled by one female. It appeared that the mother of one set had been killed and that the mother of the other set had adopted the orphans.

Females do not as a rule breed until they are two years old, and many seem to be either barren or only sporadic bearers. The average litter is from five to seven pups, nineteen being the highest number on record, in Utah. The eyes of the pups open in from nine to fourteen days. They suckle from three to eight weeks; they usually begin eating predigested food before they are weaned. The mother sometimes chews meat into bits for the little ones.

Many a trapper has located a den by watching crows and buzzards attracted by meat the parent coyotes disgorge near the entrance. Often there is such a surplus of disgorged meat that it decays and smells far off. Only to very young pups do parents bring meat in predigested form. After the pups are well weaned, they want the meat strong with hair and hide on it. Joe Hill is sure that coyotes sometimes bring water in their stomachs and regurgitate it to the pups, just as they do meat. They seem generally to bring in food for pups before they themselves eat. However, some coyotes that kill early in the night apparently eat first. Distances to be traveled and the amount of meat at their disposal determine conduct.

When puppies make their first sorties out of the den, they play and exercise only around the entrance, ready to scramble back at the slightest warning. Day by day they explore farther and farther out. The parents give them first lessons in catching such small game as mice, rats, rabbits. After they are able to travel alone, they do not as a rule all stay together, but go off by twos and threes. Later they become part-time solitaires, but even then often reunite for concerts and fellowship. The fraternal spirit is strong in them. A half-grown coyote alone on his own resources is at the most helpless age. Luke Stillwell says that a mother coyote sometimes scatters her pups before she quits feeding them, making the round of food-providing visits periodically until they are able to rustle for themselves. Some families stay together longer than others. One day Joe Hill saw a family of fourteen moving across the prairie, the mother coyote in the lead, "encouraging the half-grown pups along by occasional curious calls, the male parent keeping guard at the rear. No doubt this big family had just been disturbed."

After the denning season is over, adult coyotes probably hunt over a more extended territory than while anchored by the young. The hunting ranges of individuals certainly overlap. An extra supply of food, like a dead cow, will bring numerous coyotes together. A dearth of food in one area will force coyotes to seek elsewhere. In 1932 the Biological Survey ear-tagged twenty-four coyotes on a Western range and released them. Within fourteen days one had traveled 125 miles, crossing four mountain ranges; thirteen months after the tagging, one was caught 100 miles away. A number of the tagged animals were retaken in the vicinity of their original capture.[9] J. W. Montgomery noticed watermelon seeds in coyote droppings twenty miles from any watermelon.

Under normal conditions, the average coyote ranges habitually within certain boundaries. This is his *querencia* — his haunt. He knows all the wrinkles and cracks upon its surface. If he is disturbed while making an excursion away from it, he heads back to it. Estimates of the extent of territory covered by coyotes vary widely. Much depends upon the character of the land. Coyotes themselves vary widely in roving habits. In plains or semi-plains country well stocked with food, a coyote's beat may not be ten miles across; in rough, arid country in which game is scarce, the beat may be twenty-five miles across. It will not average half the extent of a lobo's beat. A suspicious lobo will get up and leave a country; a wily coyote who realizes that he is being waylaid will shift around and shift far but will seldom "clear out" in lobo manner. The coyote is not so regular in making a beat across his range as the lobo. He is more casual, less punctual, in making the rounds of his scent posts.

"The devil is wise because he is so old," the Mexicans say. That is not the reason for coyote wisdom. The average age of the animal seems to be from ten to fifteen years — the same as that of the gray wolf. Most of the figures on longevity are derived from observing captives. A country man will solemnly assert that he has never found a coyote on the range dead from natural causes — as if coyotes, like the white mules of folklore, never die. "They live to be so old that they finally turn into Mexicans," a border saying goes. "Nobody ever saw a coyote starved to death and nobody ever saw a fat coyote," is a range saying. It expresses the ignorance often attending familiarity. Many coyotes are fat, and during hard seasons some starve.

A coyote staked out under an intense summer sun will not die so quickly as a rattlesnake thus exposed, but he will die before the sun goes down. Coyotes must have water.

Coyote readiness in voiding the stomach is equaled by readiness in voiding the intestines when frightened — a distinct advantage in fleeing for life. In a book meaty with trapper lore, *When the Dogs Barked "Treed,"* [10] Elliott S. Barker relates an illustrative experience. One winter, accompanied by two dogs, he found where two coyotes had run a deer off a mountain. He followed the trail through four inches of fresh snow that recorded plainly what had happened. The deer was a two-year-old doe, in good condition. The coyotes had chased her to a creek and then worried her up and down it a good while before killing her at the edge of the water, where she made her final stand. They were still at the carcass when Elliott Barker came up but had eaten an enormous amount of meat from the hams as well as inside fat.

"Gorged as they were, they would not be able to get away

from the dogs, I thought. I urged Pup and Puse after them. The coyotes separated, both dogs taking after one. They pressed him hard for a while up a rough, rocky hillside. He doubled back, crossed his own track several times, and dodged around rocks and thickets; finally the dogs became confused on his criss-crossed trail and paused. Taking advantage of the respite, Don Coyote stopped to disgorge his meal. I estimated the mess to weigh ten pounds — enough meat in the animal's stomach to equal a third of its own weight. Relieved of the handicap, the coyote now easily outdistanced the dogs and they soon gave up the chase."

Some coyotes, like some men, deer and certain other animals, evince astounding vitality. The only morbid coyote-hater I ever heard of was a sheepman up the Frio River in Texas. He hated coyotes with the frenzy that raged increasingly in Jeff Turner towards all Indians and in Bear Moore towards all grizzlies. He would saw off the lower jaw of a coyote caught in a steel trap and turn the mutilated animal loose for his dogs to tear to pieces. One winter day he skinned several coyotes that he had brought in from traps and then threw the carcasses into his wagon to be hauled away. As he was driving off, he heard a slight noise behind him, turned, and saw one of the hideless creatures leap out. The dogs caught it as it ran off. It was, the coyote-hater said, "a fearful looking thing." [11]

Pasteur's name is probably more familiar to country people in western America than that of any other great Frenchman, including Napoleon's — not through pasteurized milk but through the Pasteur treatment of rabies. The "hydrophobia skunk" is more feared than rattlesnakes; probably more people have been bitten by skunks than by coyotes, but coyotes have been more active in communicating the disease, during epidemics, through dogs. These epidemics seem not to occur now with such intensity and frequency as in past decades. In the grisly lore of the range country, descriptions of death from hydrophobia, especially of the victim's madness at sight of water, have first place. An epidemic of rabies among coyotes that began in central California in 1909 had by 1915 extended into Oregon, Washington, Idaho and Nevada, and it soon passed into Utah. According to government figures, by the end of 1923 over 2000 people of these states had been bitten by rabid coyotes and dogs, 56 of them dying. The infection seems to have been more severe in Nevada, where in two years it resulted in livestock losses totaling half a million dollars. Mad coyotes entered the yards of dwellings and stock pens, attacking cats, dogs, hogs, cattle, sheep and human beings. A single coyote bit twenty-seven steers in one pen.[12] In my boyhood a cousin and I walking along a wagon road were followed for a mile by a coyote that took refuge, at the end of our walk, in a cow shed, where a man shot it before dogs attacked. It manifestly had hydrophobia, and like many mad coyotes it was mangy, but it did not act in a vicious manner. Matt Martin of the Brush Country recollects an example of the vicious:

"This was many years ago. The death of a boy from being dragged by a horse had drawn a number of men to the Fitzpatrick Ranch in McMullen County. The house was built on a slope and the rear of it was several feet above the ground. The sleeping place for the ranch dogs — and there were always plenty of dogs — was under the floor. After dark, bedlam broke out among them. We soon discovered that a mad coyote was attacking them. They would stay under the floor and not push the fight when the coyote retreated, but when it came back to attack, they fought furiously. The only gun on the ranch was in a servant house several hundred yards away. Nobody wanted to get out in the dark to bring it, but finally Jay Martin and I made the run. Then, while he held a lighted lantern over my head, I picked out the coyote under the house and shot it. Before daylight, bedlam broke out again. This time it was the mother of a litter of pups that was mad, and we had to shoot her. After a mixup of this kind the only thing to do with dogs was to kill all that might have been bitten or keep them tied up for watching. During the epidemics we lost many cattle bitten by mad coyotes. When a cow brute went mad, it would make the most mournful and distressing kind of bawling imaginable. It would turn vicious and charge a man on horseback with its horns. I saw a ranch Mexican who had been bitten by a mad coyote die screaming in that same horrifying way that mad cattle scream. This was before there were any Pasteur institutes." [13]

Sometimes people who had been bitten would ride hundreds of miles to get to a mad stone — taken from the stomach of a deer. Its efficaciousness was purely imaginary, but even doctors thought that it worked. In those times ranch mothers in the hot country never had mad dogs and mad coyotes out of their consciousness. Before wire screens came in, some ranch people nailed wire netting over the lower half of the windows to keep mad coyotes from entering.

Biologists have classified coyotes into eighteen subspecies; some of the distinctions are too fine for any but dental and cranial experts to detect, and certainly not all coyotes observe them at mating time. Climate and other physical factors make for variations in color, but it is characteristically grayish or tawny, often yellowish, graduating into white under neck and belly, the legs trimmed with black. In habits, general appearance, voice and psychology, all coyotes are *Canis latrans*. The mountain coyote is the largest, an exceptional weight of 68 pounds being recorded for California. A coyote caught in Wyoming is said to have weighed 71 pounds. The smallest of the subspecies is the desert variety (Mearns's coyote), which often weighs not more than 20 pounds. The average weight of the Texas varieties is between 25 and 26 pounds. During a good season, coyotes on the plains probably average 30 pounds. Males average somewhat above females in weight.

*   *   *

Multi-tomed Riva Palacio says, without adducing evidence, that domestic dogs introduced by the Spaniards into Mexico soon crossed with the coyotes and formed "a new species easily distinguishable" from either native or Spanish dogs.[14] This brings up a subject on which science has spoken but has experimented very little.

Indians of the Plains and the Rockies did not hunt with dogs, to any extent at least. Dogs would have interfered with the mass slaughter of buffaloes, source of both food and shelter. The Indians kept, nevertheless, hordes of dogs. Until they acquired horses, the dog was their only beast of burden as well as their only domesticated animal; pups were the caviar of their most important feasts. All early observers were struck with the character of the dogs of the Western Indians. Frontiersmen called them "coyote dogs."[15] The first biologist to observe the coyote, Thomas Say, in 1819, regarded the animal as "probably the original of the domestic dog so common in the villages of the Indians, some varieties of which still retain much of the habit and manners of the species."[16]

Paul Wilhelm, Duke of Württemberg, unflagging searcher for facts, after living among the Plains Indians during the years 1822–1823, wrote: "Their dogs have pointed ears and a drooping tail. They constitute a species as unique as the dingo. They seem to have been bred up originally from the coyote. They howl, but do not bark; they growl and bristle up their hair; they approach one quietly and bite without warning. They dislike Europeans especially. The [prairie] wolves will follow bitches in heat and breed bastard dogs, as I myself had occasion to observe."[17]

In the Dakota territory in 1843, Audubon found Indian dogs virtually indistinguishable from wolves. "I was assured," he wrote, "that there is much cross-breeding between these Dogs and Wolves, and that all the varieties actually came from the same root."[18] The naturalist J. K. Lord characterized the dog of the Spokan Indians as "beyond all question nothing more than a tamed Coyote." [19] Sir John Richardson saw in the Hare (Tahl-tan) Indian dog of British Columbia — famous because so little is known of it — nothing more than a prairie wolf, bearing "the same relation" to it as "the Esquimaux dog bears to the great grey wolf." [20] Following Audubon by thirty years, learned Elliott Coues marked the resemblance between Indian dogs of the Plains and coyotes as extending from skulls to "the remarkable mode of outcry. . . . Indians picket out their female dogs over night to procure a cross, with constant success [as the Gauls, according to Pliny, tied their female dogs in the woods to cross with wolves]. In every Indian community there are mongrel dogs shadowing into coyotes in every degree." [21]

Research has added much to the world's store of knowledge since the time of Darwin, but the world has not added such another mind for bringing the stores of knowledge together and arriving at deductions. Darwin proved that fertile crossing of various kinds of dogs with wolves was common in many lands over centuries of time.[22] The hordes of dogs that once followed their nomadic owners over the plains of North America had dwindled to a fraction of their original number, and what remained had been mongrelized beyond value as historical evidence when, in 1920, Glover M. Allen attacked the subject of their origin.[23] He based his conclusions mainly on examinations of dog teeth recovered from ancient refuse heaps. "The teeth of American aboriginal dogs," he asserted, "are those of true dogs rather than of coyotes or wolves. The domestic dogs of both Old and New Worlds are closely related and of common ancestry." Instead of domesticating coyotes, the progenitors of the Plains Indians "must have brought their dogs with them to America, presumably from Asia."

This conclusion does not alter the evidence on the coyote qualities of Indian dogs. Scientists agree that the ancestors of all breeds of dogs were wolves, just as certainly as all the widely variegated races of pigeons go back to the wild rock pigeon.

Whether the remote ancestors of the dogs of the Plains Indians came from the Old World or not, the breed must have been thoroughly coyote-ized through centuries of infiltration of coyote blood. Hybrids still occur, though they seem not to be uniformly fertile.[24]

The frequent association of dogs with coyotes and larger wolves is more natural than their aversion to wolves. The aversion was acquired through the dog's lackeyism to man. Jack London's *The Call of the Wild* is the universal call to freedom. How a collie answered the call by taking up with coyotes is related by Enos A. Mills in *Waiting in the Wilderness*. When a civilized man forsakes civilization, to take "some savage woman" and rear his "dusky race," he may not be noble; he is countering human evolution; but he is acting more naturally than a domestic dog that turns against his free brothers. Perhaps the dog turns against the wolf merely because the wolf is foreign, without respect to freedom. In that case he is on as high a plane as any nationalistic or race-prejudiced man.

IX · IN FIELDS OF PSYCHOLOGY AND SPORT

DERISION IS NOT necessarily witty, but dullards do not excel in it. Coyotes do. C. B. Ruggles, who has trapped from Alaska into the Sierra Madre of western Mexico, told me that he once rode up on two coyotes baying a wildcat on top of a stump. He said they were prancing around the stump and evidently enjoying themselves while the wildcat snarled and spit frenziedly. Coyotes have been taken with little wildcats in their stomachs and also with the flesh of adult wildcat, but the merry fellows that Ruggles saw apparently had something else than meat in their consciousnesses.

They were teasing the bobcat in the same spirit that an agile pair described by George Bird Grinnell [1] deviled a big gray wolf on slippery ice. "They could turn much more quickly on the slick ice than their larger cousin. One of them would dance in front of him and annoy him, while the other ran by from behind and nipped him as it went past. Then the big wolf would try to turn and chase the little one, but would slip and get another nip from the second coyote. Thus they worried him until the observer tired of watching the performance and rode away."

In *The Land of Shorter Shadows* (William Morrow & Company, New York), Erle Stanley Gardner tells how a very captivating pet coyote named Bravo would sneak into a room where a dog, big enough to devour him almost, was sleeping on a quilt in front of a warm fireplace, "brace himself for a good hold, grab with his jaws, jerk the bed out from under the dog and go scampering away, dragging the bed with him." Just before the highly irritated dog could catch him, Bravo would drop the quilt and run under a couch too low to permit the dog's following.

Vance Hoyt avers that when he was a boy in Oklahoma he saw a coyote sledding along ahold of a steer's tail. "Now and then the steer would stop, but before he could kick, or whirl or charge, his tormentor would let go and bound a short distance away and there sit, lolling and grinning." [2] This sounds a little extravagant, but it is in character.

A pet coyote on a Montana ranch was a playmate to greyhound pups and very friendly with the grown hounds. It would wander far out alone, and was not infrequently sighted at a distance by the hounds while they were hunting. They would take after it as just another coyote, and it would run until it tired or was overtaken, when it would roll over on its back with paws in the air and there wait innocently and confidently until the hounds came up and recognized their friend, whereupon it would jump around in a joyful manner. [3] Coyotes that night after night willfully provoke ranch dogs into futile sorties justify Mary Austin's epithet, "the Charlie Chaplin of the plains." Trappers regard the "card" that a coyote frequently leaves atop a trap he has avoided, sometimes even sprung, as an expression of conscious derision.

How much of the dog's readiness in aptitude is owing to long and intimate association with man cannot be determined. Certainly a high percentage of it is. Back of the beautiful and intelligent skill of shepherd dogs lie centuries of training and selective breeding. Native potentiality is one thing; cultivated application is another. In his book on *The Minds and Manners of Wild Animals*, William T. Hornaday rates twenty selected animals of the world for intelligence, basing his averages on ten qualities: hereditary knowledge, perceptive faculties, original thought, memory, reason, receptivity in training, efficiency in execution (of whatever the animal is trained to do), nervous energy, keenness of senses, use of voice. Out of a possible 1000 points he gives the chimpanzee 925, the highest average, and 850 points each to the orangutan, Indian elephant, domestic horse and domestic dog. He rates the gray wolf 625 and the coyote 500, placing lower only the giraffe and the rhinoceros. Explaining that he will not explain,* he gives the dog 100 points on voice, and the coyote only 25; the coyote 50 on reason, and the dog 75; the coyote 75 on perceptive faculties, and the dog 100. The coyote and the gray wolf both get zero on receptivity in training and efficiency in execution. In *Camp Fires on Desert and Lava*, Hornaday makes it clear that he regards the coyote primarily as a camp pest.

The men I know who have had most experience in the field mark coyotes up as high in native intelligence as they mark their own dogs. Coyotes have never made the sagalike stories that some man-eluding gray wolves have made; they are too slight to be heroic killers. But most men of experience with the two kinds of wolves would agree with George Bird Grinnell that "the coyote is a much more interesting animal than the gray wolf" and has "far greater intelligence." The fact that coyotes and gray wolves will not accept captivity and do tricks for their captors lowers their intelligence quotient in Hornaday's estimation; in

* "Explanations are tedious." — Matthew Arnold.

[182]

mine, it makes them far more admirable than imitative monkeys and fawning spaniels.

They cannot forget freedom, and they will not lick the feeding hand that bars them in. Their self-reliance and the free exercise of their intelligence belong only to conditions of freedom. Their spirits wither with the clank of chains. The hanging nest, from four to six feet long, woven by giant cacique birds in the delta of the Orinoco is one of the most intricately and skillfully wrought nests in the whole world. As further protection, apparently, against the depredations of prehensile-tailed monkeys, a dozen or so giant caciques build their nests in close proximity to that of a wasp resentful of monkey intrusion. This is certainly intelligent behavior. No giant cacique has ever woven a nest in captivity. Irrational though it may be, the coyote's never dulled yearning to be free indexes intelligence as justly as servile tractability indexes it in certain other animals.

In the spring of 1878, sportsmen of Virginia City, Nevada, procured a coyote, fed him well at Rock's Livery Stable for several days, then put him in a box, loaded the box on a wagon and, accompanied by numerous hounds, rode out into a big alkali flat to have their sport.[4] The wagon was driven by a livery stable attendant called Little Martin who had a sympathy for the coyote. It was agreed that the hunters would hold their hounds in leash until the released coyote got across the alkali flat to the edge of sagebrush, about three miles away. The hounds had been bawling at the coyote all morning, and when Little Martin opened the door to the box, he lost no time getting away. In about fifteen minutes he reached the edge of the sagebrush; the hounds were slipped, the riders spurred and the chase was on.

Not more than twenty minutes after the dogs got into the sagebrush and boulders, rising dust showed Little Martin that the coyote had circled. In a little while it shot back from cover into the open flat, bee-lining for the wagon. Before long, hounds and horsemen cleared also, and now the whole chase was in sight.

The hounds were rapidly gaining when the coyote spurted into his box and Little Martin closed the door. After the hounds had yelped until they were tired and the coyote had presumably rested, the hunters decided to have a second run. The coyote reached the sagebrush in less time than he took on the first run, and as he disappeared, the field opened up on the trail. Dust rising out of the sage showed that the coyote was doubling more frequently than on the first run. Again he shot back into the flat. Little Martin decided to drive the wagon to meet him, but he left the box behind. About fifty yards from the wagon, hounds overtook the coyote. The leader bit into his shoulder; he took a part of the leader's ear and gained cover under the front axle of the wagon, which Little Martin now turned back for the box. Surrounding the wagon, the hounds would now and then dash in for an attack, but the coyote managed to send every assaulter back. He held his position "like a coach dog." When near the box, the hounds seemed to anticipate the next move, but the hunted animal made a dash, cut his way through them, got into his fort, and was secured by Little Martin. The hunters agreed that the coyote deserved a place in Rock's Livery Stable, and there, under Little Martin's protection, he led a lively life to the end of the story.

George Bird Grinnell relates a similar demonstration of coyote behavior at a ranch on Dismal River in northern Nebraska. The adobe walls of the ranch house were about two feet thick, and the window sashes were set flush with the interior walls, leaving deep embrasures outside; the sashes were swung from hinges within and, when raised, could be hooked to the ceiling. The ranch dog was a bull terrier that the cowboys regarded as a prodigy in fighting. One snowy winter night a cowboy happening to look through the south window saw a coyote curled up asleep on the sill, his side against the glass, well sheltered from the wind. It would be no fun to shoot it. The thing to do was to get the bull terrier, stealthily raise the window, pitch the bull terrier onto the coyote, and then run outside and see the fight.

The coyote did not know when the window was opened. The instant the bull terrier was pitched upon him, he disappeared — and the window closed. Everybody rushed outside, only to find the dog running around and around the house, all the time barking furiously. This form of fun soon got old and the cowboys came back inside. Presently one of them went to the window to see that it was securely fastened down. There the coyote was, lying cozily against the glass as he had been when discovered. He had evidently made one run around the house and leaped back upon the sill. The bull terrier was brought in again, the window was swiftly opened and once more the chase was on. Again the coyote returned to his refuge. The cowboys decided that he had won a right to it. He had measured the dog's intelligence.[5]

If the coyote can't rationalize, he can make a deduction. Ed Bateman, who runs coyotes with greyhounds on his ranch in northwest Texas, says that no coyote will use a pasture until he has located all the gates, both wire and wooden. This would be hard to prove, but Ed Bateman has found that when a coyote is headed towards a fence, riders cannot veer him to a gate. He seems to know that the proper place for him to go under is where men on horses will be halted — not at a gate. He aims to leave them behind, and his aim is not blind. Again, a coyote hardpressed by hounds will twist through a bunch of cattle or other livestock, seemingly to kill his scent or to confuse the vision of greyhounds.*

* "A forward rider saw a weary fox dragging himself over a grass-field spring up on a manure heap and roll himself in it. The rider judged that the fox was trying to obliterate his own by a stronger scent. It is well known to huntsmen that manures and fertilizers are bad for scent. Is it not possible that this is known to the fox also?" — Thomas F. Dale, *The Fox*, London, 1906, 118.

"Probably on good scenting days, foxes lie under ground, or in places not disturbed by hounds; for as they live by the use of their noses, they cannot but know their danger of being hunted on such days." — Thomas Smith, Esq., *The Life of a Fox*, London, 1843, 131.

Charles W. Brown, a rancher in the Sand Hills of western Nebraska, tells of riding after one coyote that upon reaching a fence took down it, instead of crossing. A hound is shorter-haired, has a thinner skin, and is taller than a coyote. After Mr. Brown's lead dog had shot under the fence six or eight times behind the dodging coyote, his back was shredded by the barbs on the bottom wire. I have heard of one coyote pursued by hounds that was running along a railroad track when a freight train overtook him; he leaped upon a flatcar and, while taking a rest, left his enemies behind.

As among foxes, it is the especially astute and experienced that accomplish such dodges. American hunters who have chased both animals say that the coyote can outfox the fox. Probably it would be more accurate to say that some coyotes outfox some foxes. Both animals are constant in variations. The fox has the advantage of the coyote in being the subject of a cumulative body of literature that arouses admiration for his intelligence and sympathy for his existence.

William T. Hornaday, whose spiritual understanding of nature was not commensurate with his services to physical conservation, said: "The coyote carries his tail low — humbly — as befits a cowardly animal." Mark Twain in a caricature more verbose than witty called him "spiritless and cowardly." A news dispatch from Connersville, Indiana, a few years ago read: "Coyotes are cowardly animals, but housewives are perturbed over one of the species eating out of town garbage cans." No discernment whatsoever is required for epithet-throwing. Everybody calls the coyote "cowardly." The epithet has been bestowed upon the coyote more frequently than upon any other American animal. He is neither brave nor cowardly, any more than a plant is brave or cowardly. What passes for bravery among men is often only obtuseness, anyway, or fear of public opinion. Why is it cowardly for an animal weighing hardly thirty pounds to keep out of reach of a panther that can kill a grown horse or to avoid a man with a gun that throws a bullet a mile? When this creature goes to attacking bulls instead of rabbits, he is mad. He may win against one dog; he cannot possibly win against a whole pack. He is not a tiger; he knows his own limitations; he must use his wits or perish. The only way he can survive his big enemies is to slip around them. In his tactics he is no more cowardly than a soldier taking advantage of a foxhole. To brand him as cowardly is to show a sentimental ignorance of life.

The rank and file of coyotes seem to learn little from the experience of others — the tragedy of the human race. Judge O. W. Williams tells of poisoning a dead horse one evening and the next morning counting fourteen dead coyotes in sight of it, beside an irrigation ditch, five the second morning, and then more coyotes until the carrion was all gone. Certainly some of the victims must, before eating, have seen preceding fatalities among their kind. An experiment in poisoning watermelons convinced Judge Williams that crows are more apt in learning from their fellows than coyotes are.[6] "The crows," he relates, "would light upon the top of a melon just beginning to ripen and peck a hole down to the heart. I had a large crop, and had they continued to feed upon the melons thus opened, I would have cared little. But a melon once opened in this way would sour within a few hours under the hot sun, and the crows were too epicurean to return to it when there were fresh melons everywhere. So the loss became considerable, and I made an effort to stop it. I scared off some crows that were just beginning to open some melons and placed strychnine down in the holes, then concealed myself to watch results.

"The crows returned and while some proceeded to open up new melons, a few returned to the melons with holes already pecked in them. In a few moments some of the latter rose into the air, fluttering, whirling in short circles, and uttering cries of distress. The entire flock then rose and, circling around and over the poisoned ones, kept up a Babel of noise. Some of the sound ones would fly down to and hover over the poisoned ones, keeping up an incessant cawing, which was apparently answered by those poisoned. I was never able to poison any more crows. While they did not entirely cease raiding on my watermelons, they had learned not to return to a melon in which they had even so much as barely commenced a hole. Their wisdom exceeded that of the coyote.

"This animal was as fond of my cantaloupes as of watermelons. It did not destroy unripe melons, for it infallibly picked ripe ones, but damaged the vines greatly by trampling and rolling melons over them. Every night apparently the number of raiders increased and the damage became greater. Tracks showed that they were coming over my garden fence at the same place. I picked the smallest cantaloupes I could find, small enough to be almost bolted whole, poisoned them, and placed them just outside the garden by the coming-over place in the fence. Night after night the coyotes ate the poisoned cantaloupes and died until the last one acquainted with my preserves turned up its toes."

Country people of Mexico who will with one breath say, "Next to God the coyote is the smartest person on earth," will with the next breath begin a fable that substantiates Judge O. W. Williams's deduction. One time in Sinaloa I came upon a boy with a sling guarding a small field of ripening corn against crows. He proved to me that he was a good sling shot, but he seldom got within slinging distance of the crows, he said. The boy's father came to the field while I was still there, and after we had talked a minute or two about the depredations of animals he told me this story.

One time a crow in a tree and a coyote on the ground under him were having a conversation, full of wisdom. This did not keep the crow from looking around.

Presently he said, "Right now we shall have to stop our talk."

"Why?" the coyote asked.

"Because yonder comes a man."

"I see him," said the coyote, "but he has no gun."

"That's true."

"He has no stick."

"That's true also."

"He has no rock."

"Not in sight."

"Then," went on the coyote, "why should we leave yet? I am afraid of an armed man, but I am not afraid of an unarmed man."

"Well, I am," the crow said. "I have a disconfidence in all men around corn fields. That man we see might have a rock hidden in his pocket. Adios."

And the crow flew over the river — without "a raw lump of liver in his mouth."

*   *   *

Hunters are naturally more sympathetic towards coyote cunning than are owners of chickens and sheep upon which some coyote is preying. The hunter point of view is expressed by John Joseph Mathews — who raises chickens. "I like," he says, "the story of the British hunting lady who was asked her opinion of a certain diplomatist. She replied, 'I don't really know, but I rather suspect he'd shoot a fox.' That's the way we feel in my country [the Osage country of Oklahoma]. We shoot coyotes only if they are actually killing our flocks or if they become calf-killers. Even then we prefer to hunt such bandits with hounds. Of course, this prejudice against cold murder is not so deep as it is in England in regard to the fox, but it is growing."

It is probably growing more among horseback hunters than among the other kind. There are two ways of hunting coyotes with dogs. One is to take dogs in a trailer, drive until a coyote is sighted and approached, and then release them for the chase. That is the machine way. The other is the way of spirit-releasing freedom — on horse. The coyote drives, or surrounds, sometimes accompanied by airplanes, in Nebraska and adjacent states, in which hundreds of armed people encompass a whole township of land and kill not only all the coyotes but pheasants, rabbits and every other wild thing that the human wall closes in on cannot be classed as exercise in sportsmanship.

Head-lighting coyotes is hardly in the calendar of sports either. All head-lighting — "fire-hunting," as it was once called — is outlawed in most states. Deer keep both eyes open and gaze into the light, unable to see the head-lighter, who carries an electric or carbide lamp on top of his head so that its rays will light the sights of his gun as well as the eyes of the quarry. The eyes bracket the target, the center of the head. Colts, mules, cattle respond in the same way as deer and are shot by mistake by illegal night-hunters. A coyote, all the eye-shiners say, will seldom "give you both his eyes at the same time." Often he will move around the head-lighter to get the wind on him and find out the source of the light. Mexicans apply to human beings a saying based on this behavior: "With one eye he sees the person and with the other he sees where he is going." A coon, it is claimed, will put a hand over first one eye and then the other to prevent being entirely blinded by a light.

I shall say nothing of the mechanical methods of those animal murderers who keep airplanes fueled and shotguns loaded for any coyote or eagle reported by sheep ranchers within their zones. For them the wild scream of the eagle in sunlight and the free howl of the coyote in starlight mean less than the price of some snotty-nosed old ewe's offspring.

Charles M. Russell painted with realism the joyful cowboy sport of coyote-roping. Not every expert at twining a calf can pull the loop up on a little dodging prairie wolf. The roper must cast his loop a second or two before he would be ready to throw it at a calf. If he waits to gain a few feet, the coyote dodges back and, except for experts at casting the loop backwards, is out of rope reach before the best cutting horse can wheel. The sport can be practiced only in fairly open country. Exercise of it by American cowboys has been casual and occasional in contrast to the arranged roping fiestas in Mexico of bygone days. A traveler in the state of Zacatecas in 1826 wrote: "When a chase is meditated for some holiday, an old horse is killed on the plains. A herd of coyotes soon flock to feast upon him. They are watched attentively, and when any leave the carcass, which is only when they are replete, the active horsemen are rarely baffled by the wily turnings of their victims."[8] H. G. Ward, another traveler over the Mexican mesas of the same date, saw thirteen coyotes roped beside a road in Durango. More than one snapped the tightening reata in two and got away.[9]

The most highly organized form of coyote hunting in America is by the South Texas Wolf Hunters Association. Its members seem to feel that by calling themselves Wolf Hunters instead of Coyote Hunters they add at least one cubit to their own stature. Once a year, gathering from Alabama, Washington and other states, including Texas, they camp somewhere in the Brush Country and for three days and nights drink coffee, talk, listen to hound music, car-hunt and trade dogs. The dogs include pot-lickers, Walkers, Julys, Triggs, Sugarloafs and other strains. Some hunters keep a nucleus of dogs in the brush the year round. Adaptability to thorns, which comes only from experience, is here a greater advantage to a hound than a pedigree is. The two most important dogs in a pack are the top trailer and the killer. Multiplicity, rather than coldness, of trails baffles many of the dogs. When a coyote is bayed, sometimes after a run lasting up to six hours, he is played out. The dogs are played out also. A tenderfoot among them that ventures too near before the killer comes up is apt to pay with his life. The victim dies game.

Nearly every town in the Brush Country has a few coyote hunters who follow their hounds in automobiles every month in the year. Most of them have chased some coyote that can't be bayed. Almost any night, for instance, "the Schoolhouse Coyote" can be jumped in the vicinity of a certain one-room schoolhouse out in the brush. During the school term he visits the place regularly for scraps of lunch left by the children. He will not leave the country. Perhaps he enjoys the chase as much as the baying hounds and the listening men. One morning he circled around after a very hot chase and ran under a cotton gin about a mile from the schoolhouse. The hunters rushed up while the dogs were scratching to get through the little hole the coyote had threaded. Everybody was sure that Old Schoolhouse had been run down at last. While the dogs were frantically working on one side of the gin, he got out on the other side. They were too hot to resume the chase.

X · THE COYOTE COMES TO MAN

THE CALL OF WOLF-WILDNESS to run utterly free from all human tameness has been answered by many dogs; it must stir in all noble dogs. Correspondingly, the wild canines possess intimations of whatever it is inside domestic dogs that, apart from hunger for food and shelter, draws them to man. "I feel within me two spirits struggling." Of primordial simplicity, indeed, the individual who is torn within by only one pair of dualities. For this man-creature, "begot in a pair of minutes," compasses within himself everything from a worm squirming in corruption to the Pole Star fixed in eternal chasteness. With Empedocles, the lowliest may say, "I have been both a bird and a stone and a fish in the glittering sea." The most foreign thing to man should be denial to other mammals of some share, however dim, of those elemental kinships, potentialities, sympathies, those vague, complex, contradictory stirrings brought from afar that make the paragon of animals a composite of all terrestrial life.

Curiosity, and nothing else apparently, pulls many a coyote into following a human being on horseback, afoot, even in a car. The coyote that stole a side of bacon from under a saddle on which a sleeping circuit-rider pillowed his head [1] was manifestly motivated by hunger. But now and then an urge entirely apart from hunger or curiosity seems to draw the animal to man. One night on a roundup, Sloan Simpson, Theodore Roosevelt's hunting companion, awoke at the touch of something on the tarpaulin against his feet. When he roused, the thing ran off and he saw in the moonlight that it was a coyote. It came back and a cowboy shot it. [2] It was not mad; it was not cold; there was no food at the pallet for it to come to. It seemed to be responding to a yearning for companionship — a yearning that to some ears often sounds in coyote voices around the haunts of man. A Scot rancher in northern Mexico told me of seeing a wounded coyote come to his house and crawl under it; it was one, he said, that had been shot several miles away two days before. He knew of other coyotes in distress coming to ranch dwellings.

The process of domesticating all animals is, however, tied up with feeding them. The accounts of pet lizards, pet coons, pet birds, pet rats and such all begin with food. In Yellowstone National Park, where all wild things are protected, coyotes are beginning to come to people for food as bears come.

Many years ago a character known generally as Old Man Carpenter, but called Carp by a few intimates, lived alone in a dirt-floored, thick-walled, verandaed, adobe house amid the spruces and pines of the Sandia Mountains of New Mexico. J. J. Phelan used to drive out from Albuquerque, twenty-five or thirty miles away, with his wife and daughter Edith to visit him. In the evening Carp liked to sit and tell of freighting days over the Santa Fe Trail, but often there on the veranda he and these friends joined the silence of the trees and darkness. All this I know from Mrs. Edith Phelan Lane of El Paso.

One twilight while they were sitting silent, a dark, doglike form came down the mountain road in front of the veranda, stopped without sound and then made towards the kitchen entrance. Carp rose, speaking some Spanish words softly, and went to the kitchen. When he came back, he said, "Poor thing, she doesn't dare show her head till night. I keep some meat and tortillas out for her."

Mr. Phelan said, "Feed a coyote and it'll kill all your chickens."

"Well, I've been feeding this one for over a year," Carp answered, "and she hasn't bothered a chicken yet. Maybe you've killed a chicken when you were hungry. When no one's here but me, she'll stay close by for hours sometimes. Coyotes make good friends. They don't lie, and they mind their own business."

Early one morning the following spring, on another visit to Carp, Edith Phelan heard "a queer, plaintive low cry" outside the house. She ran and found Carp taking up a diminutive pup that the mother coyote had laid at his feet. By her actions — actions that many people have understood in dogs — the coyote indicated that she wanted Carp to follow her. He put the pup in a box and he and Edith followed. The coyote led them to a shallow den, where she nosed another living pup apart from two dead ones. Carp wrapped it in his coat and gave it to the little girl to carry, the mother coyote coming back with them. Carp said that a bear had killed the pups and that it must have been frightened away suddenly or it would have eaten all four.

And now I come to the most remarkable account of coyote behavior ever published. A copy of the original manuscript was sent to Dr. Joseph Grinnell of the University of California and used by him and his associates in their excellent *Fur-Bearing Mammals of California* (1937). The author, Mrs. Lila Lofberg, with the help of David Malcolmson, rewrote the account for the *Saturday Evening Post*, in which it was published December 9, 1939. In 1941 it appeared as part of *Sierra Outpost*, a book by the same authors.[3]

The Lofbergs lived at Florence Lake in the sierras of California, tending a power dam, more than 7000 feet above sea level. For eight months of the year their home was snowbound. They always fed nutcrackers, chickadees, other birds and Douglas squirrels through the winter. One spring a coyote stole four chickens and paid the penalty imposed by a rifle; examination showed that she was a female nursing pups. For six years no other coyote came near the house. Sometimes the Lofbergs saw one in the mountains. "A coyote would pass through a flock of ground-feeding birds; the birds scarcely moved from his path and he, in turn, ignored plump quail within a foot of his nose." At night they heard the song of the coyote, which came to be for them "the saddest, the most beautiful and the most triumphant music in Nature." Each winter they wondered what the coyotes lived on. From droppings it appeared they were eating little else than juniper berries. The winter of 1931–1932 was unusually severe, snow following snow. The deer had been gone to lower country for weeks before coyote tracks began appearing near the house. The Lofbergs threw out scraps of food — what could be spared from the supply for chickens, birds and squirrels — over the fence outside the kitchen door. Tracks showed that coyotes found the food.

On January 20 a blizzard raged all day. About four o'clock, while the lone couple were eating supper, Ted Lofberg suddenly jumped up from his chair, put his face to the glass of the south window and peered out over the snow level with the sill.

"Look!" he cried. "That poor starving animal!"

What follows is, in condensed form,

LILA LOFBERG'S STORY OF THE COYOTES

About thirty feet away stood the poorest coyote we had ever seen. We guessed it was a female, and the guess later proved to be correct. The snow-whirling wind flattened the fur against her famished body as she stood, head down, tail between her legs. She made a step towards the house. The soft snow yielded under her padded paws. She could move only flounderingly. She came on slowly, her belly dragging the snow.

Ted pressed bread and cold meat into wads that he could throw and that would not sink too deep into the snow. When he opened the back door, the coyote held her ground, without cringing. She stood facing him while he raised his arm. The food went down in powdery snow. She had come no nearer to it when darkness blotted out the view.

During the night the snow stopped. Ted went the morning rounds by starlight. At dawn I looked out the window and the coyote was not visible. I shoveled snow from the doorway, and then as I was carrying out the regular two trays of food for birds and squirrels, I saw the coyote sitting on her haunches some distance away. She looked like a patient shepherd dog that had been abandoned without knowing why.

Nutcrackers swooped down in the half-light and crowded the trays even before I placed them on the snow. Then juncos and chickadees joined the greedy big birds. In addition to crumbled bread and chopped suet for the birds, there were shelled peanuts and walnut kernels for the squirrels. Instead of rushing in their accustomed gay way for the trays, the squirrels clung to the tree trunks, switched their tails and chattered furiously at their visible enemy. The enemy did not move. One daring squirrel leaped, disappeared in the snow, flashed up, and in three more cometic jumps was at the tray, where, with a shake and a curse, he snatched the nearest kernel. Other squirrels, noting that the coyote remained motionless, followed. They did not, however, sit as usual in the middle of the trays until gorged, surrounded by amiable, fluttering birds. Without stopping their shrill denunciation of the silent gray watcher, they grabbed nuts, raced through the soft snow in six-foot jumps, and climbed to tree-top safety to eat, then repeated the whole performance.

The coyote watched me, making no move toward trays or fresh squirrel meat. What did the food-providers have in mind for her? she seemed to be asking. I met her straw-yellow eyes and she held the gaze. Without saying a word, I tried to tell her not to worry. I was worried. There simply would not be enough food for us and for the wild guests we had already welcomed unless the road this year were to open earlier than usual, in July. The prospect was for late snow-melting.

Inside the house, Ted was telephoning his morning report. "Clear. Minimum temperature four below," he finished.

Turning to me and rubbing his cold hands, he asked excitedly, "Have you got her food ready? Don't be stingy. Give her some meat. She needs it more than we do."

I fished out a chunk of kidney from the can of suet. Ted took it outside in plain view of the coyote. His idea, and mine, was to establish a feeding ground to the south, visible through our windows. The feeding ground for birds and squirrels was on the north side of the house. The chickens were located on the west side. The lake, now frozen over, was to the east.

"Come on, Jerry. Come on, Jerry," Ted called.

The coyote's manner of sitting and watching the house had reminded him of a German police dog by that name.

"Come on, Jerry." Ted retreated as he called, trying to lure the animal forward. Within five minutes she had circled the house. When she appeared south of the window, in almost the exact spot at which we had seen her the preceding evening, Ted called again and tossed the food towards her. He came inside, and together at the window we watched.

Jerry began a floundering series of approaches and retreats,

each advance bringing her a little closer to the splash in the snow. She sniffed and backtracked half a dozen times. Finally, she reached down for the suet, carried it back a few feet, crouched, and began to nibble. A kitchen window enabled me to watch while preparing breakfast. Now we sat down to food.

We talked about the supplies. As he arose, Ted said, "Give her some of that meat with her pancake."

Stepping out, he called in his most endearing way, "Come on, Jerry. Come on, Jerry. Come on, Jerry."

He threw the morsel and came inside to watch. Again Jerry approached cautiously, testing the ground forward, then back-tracking. Before tasting the mouthful, she took it to the spot where she had eaten the suet. She did not bolt the pancake and meat in dog fashion. She ate with leisurely elegance.

Ted went out again, this time with a doughnut. After he tossed it into the snow, Jerry came directly to it, carried it to her place and put it on the snow. But she did not eat. She stood watching the house expectantly. We could not resist. Another doughnut went her way. She laid it beside the first one. Not until minutes passed without another handout did she crouch on her belly and daintily begin her meal.

All through the light hours of the next few days, she was con-stantly within sight of the house, usually lying in the one spot amid the limitless snow that she had taken as her station. She ate there. The absence of tracks in the snow indicated that she did not roam off during the night. Within three days Jerry came to trust us; when either of us snowshoed past her to the intake house, she stood up but did not make off. When called, she came forward and all but caught the falling food before it dropped into the snow. She got no food without first hearing her name called. She carried whatever was given her to her station and stood beside it watching us until we made it clear that nothing further would be coming. Then she ate as becomes the well-bred. Her mealtimes were at daybreak and an hour before dusk.

Between times she would curl up in the snow, head and feet tucked into her belly, in the position of an unborn embryo. Her bushy tail came around to cover her feet and face and on over the back of her neck. New snow blanketed her, making her form a white mound. At mealtime she would get up, shake off the snow, and after a while recurl to sleep in the gathering blanket. She put herself into the condition of a hibernating animal. She lay in the same position as that in which we found a cold, apparently lifeless, hibernating chipmunk wound in the rubbish of the water-pipe boxing. No doubt she could have lived thus for days without food. The difference between a balled-up coyote lying voluntarily in a semi-coma in the snow and a hibernating chipmunk that in the autumn blindly follows its inherited urge to lapse into winter-long sleep is a difference in degree only.*

On the fourth morning after Jerry's arrival, her mate sat beside her — waiting for breakfast. Had she gone somewhere and led him to food? Where had he been during those three days of separation? During nighttime there had been no howling back and forth between the two.

Jerry was slightly larger than her mate. A year later, we were to observe the same superiority in size of the female over her mate in another pair of coyotes, but this disparity is not typical.

* Every animal, including man, seems to have the potentialities, however latent and feeble, of every other animal. "I do not believe that the hibernating instinct is dead in those animals which appear to have lost it," writes Thomas Firbank in *I Bought a Mountain* (London, 1940). A great snow in Wales late in the spring of 1937 caught Firbank's sheep out, covering them under banks of snow; more snows kept making the drifts deeper. The rescuers used poles to prod through the banks along stone walls against which the sheep had sought shelter. They found many sheep smothered and others with their wool chewed off. The natives said that a buried sheep does not live after nine days. On the eighteenth day Firbank found eleven buried sheep in one place — six dead and five alive, one so vigorous that "when daylight was opened over her head she took a standing jump out of her tomb and ran off." (I saw a Welsh "mountain sheep" jump flatfooted, from a standstill, to the top of a rock fence about eight feet high.) On the twenty-first day a lone ewe was rescued. She had chewed the wool off her own sides. After swallowing some gruel, she tottered away. "A fortnight later she bore a lamb and subsequently raised it."

Jerry was grayer than the male, and the black band of her white-tipped tail was wider than his. He was more reddish about the face, and the edging of the long fur over his shoulders was lighter in color than hers. Except for size, he was handsomer.

Jerry's mate could deserve no other name than Tom. When an animal understands that he is set apart and is being called by a particular name, he is as flattered as any human being is at being individualized. Every bird, skunk and squirrel that set himself or herself apart as an individual during our years of associating with hundreds of them received a name and quickly, with pride, responded to it.

Tom's was a new personality. From the beginning he gave us his trust. He must have been famished, but his buoyant manner seemed to say, "I'm fine!" He did not beg hungrily with his eyes as Jerry had manifestly begged with hers before her first few feedings. He seemed to expect hospitality as something due his presence beside Jerry.

As Ted and I, both elated, looked at the pair, force of habit prompted me to say, "But what will we do for food?"

"Food," Ted exploded. "Look at all the food in the attic and in the storeroom."

"I have looked," I said. The day after Jerry's arrival I made an inventory. The insulated storeroom had shelves of canned goods and bins of apples, oranges and root vegetables. In the attic were a hundred and fifty pounds of corn meal, oatmeal, flour, rice, and assorted prepared cereals. The screened meat house held less than half a beef, half a lamb, a quarter of pork, slabs of bacon and two hams. Twenty-gallon garbage cans in the woodshed contained eight hundred pounds of stale bread and smaller quantities of dried fruit and peanuts for the wild guests and four hundred pounds of grain for the chickens. From the roof hung twenty sacks of suet. According to my chart, based on the experience of years, the storage was less by far than it should be at the middle of January. The birds and squirrels were feeding in unusual numbers. Jerry had come and now Tom was at the table. I could afford dieting. Ted was underweight.

But no one can tell Ted Lofberg to go easy on groceries when a friend is at the door. He heaped meat trimmings, suet, pancakes on a tin plate and went out the door. At his emergence, the coyotes rose from their haunches. The newcomer showed no sign of alarm.

"Come on, Jerry," Ted called.

Jerry ran forward. Tom remained standing. Jerry carried the morsel back to her station, dropped it, and stood attentive. The bit of food was hardly more than two feet from Tom's nose. He made no motion towards it.

"Come on, Tom," Ted called.

This was the first time he had heard his name. Whatever the processes of his brain may have been, he came forward without any of the caution and hesitation that Jerry had demonstrated before she took her first bits of man-provided food. He wagged his body and tail like a happy pup. Without apparent sniffing, he took the piece of food and carried it to his place beside Jerry, dropped it on the snow and, like his mate, stood waiting.

"Come on, Jerry."

Turn by turn, each coyote came for four portions. Only after Ted entered the house did they begin to eat, Tom in the same mannerly way of his mate.

With pencil and paper I computed that by careful rationing all around, each of the two coyotes could have six square inches of cake a day. This cake I made of cereal, meat scraps, suet and canned milk. We had more of apples than of any other food item. Ted tried out one on Tom. Tom picked it up and carried it to his station and then took small bites through the rosy skin. In a day or two both he and Jerry were racing forward at the call of their names and leaping up to catch the apples in the air.

When on the seventh morning after Jerry's arrival we looked

out at the pair of coyotes, we saw beyond them, and off to the right, a pair of sharp ears and two eyes poked up over a snow-bank.

I told Ted that if we were going to make supplies hold out for Tom and Jerry and all our other guests through the winter, he would have to shoot this newcomer.

"If we shoot one," Ted replied, "we lose all three."

"Well," I said, to put off the decision, "feed Tom and Jerry and maybe this stranger will go away."

Ted took out the food.

"Come on, Tom," he called.

Tom came and got what had been pitched for him. The intruder stood behind the snowbank, watching. Only his head showed. He was ready to run, and two days of sunshine and the hard freezes of nighttime had formed a crust over the snow that made traveling easy.

"Come on, Jerry."

Jerry came to where the cake lay on the snow crust. She sniffed it but did not open her jaws. She turned and trotted to the coyote unwanted by man-people. We could not see all the action. Presently Jerry returned to her cake, looking back over her shoulder every few steps. The new coyote stepped into full view, watching her. He was a fine specimen. These mountain coyotes are larger than the desert, or plains, specimens; the cold gives them richer coats.

But the newcomer would not follow Jerry. She went back to him a second time. Again she walked slowly towards the cake, but he made not one step forward. Now Jerry put her muzzle down on the food, without biting it. The stranger took two steps forward, stopped dead still. Jerry trotted back to him and put her nose against his. The smell on her snout of that fatty cake must have spoken loud.

Meantime, Tom said nothing, did nothing but stand beside his own uneaten cake. He showed no concern for his mate's nose-to-nose solicitude for another male coyote. We could at first tell the sex of these animals only by their behavior, but in weeks that followed this evidence was unmistakable.

Now Jerry started back to the cake again, and this time the stranger followed her. Very likely he was not a stranger, but a friend to Tom and Jerry. When the new coyote was within reach of the cake but before he had taken it, Jerry went to Tom's side and stood.

Left to himself, the newcomer behaved very much as Jerry had behaved the first day. He could see us watching through the window. Nearing the cake, he ran back and forth lightly; he stopped and considered. He approached the cake from all sides, drawing nearer and nearer. His nose, no doubt, told him that here was something good. His ears gave him no warning. His eyes told him that the man-enemy was at hand. Finally he made a rush, grabbed the cake, and hurried with it to the distant snowbank. But, as nothing happened, he did not hide behind the bank. He put the cake down and, standing nervously alert, seemed ready to break away.

Ted now went outside with another plate of food. The stranger did not run. "Come on, Jerry," Ted called. Jerry came, took the mouthful to her station, and dropped it. "Come on, Tom." Tom took his second portion.

Since Jerry was eager to share and Tom evidently had no objections, Ted and I were now ready to share also. We'd make out somehow. Hastily, Ted and I decided to name the new coyote Dick.

"Come on, Dick."

Whether he understood the summons or not, Dick seemed to know that he had been accepted and that it was his turn. He wanted another cake, though he had not yet taken a nibble of the first. He came by himself and took the cake to the snowbank and put it down beside the other. Jerry made no demonstration of pride in the aptness of her pupil. At the window inside the house we watched Dick eat as deliberately as the other coyotes ate.

It took Dick only two days to lose all fear of us. On the fourth morning when Ted appeared with the food plate, Dick brazenly rushed up without waiting to be called. Ted called Tom, and when Tom started to come for the cake, Dick chased him back to his place, nipping at his heels. Ted called Jerry, and when Jerry responded, Dick made for her. Dick got both cakes. Ted returned to the kitchen, refilled the plate, and this time tried to throw the cakes to Tom and Jerry directly. Dick got to them first.

"Shoot him," I cried.

"Wait till I get him alone," Ted said.

He was tolerantly amused. I might have been less vindictive had I not known that now, on the crusted snow, the coyotes were hunting both by day and by night. On Lower Jackass Flat I studied their droppings, and saw that while they were living mainly on juniper berries, they were also catching a few mice and rats. For a week Dick bullied the feed grounds. Then Ted had to leave on the February steam-gauging trip.

On the first morning that I was left alone, after placing the food trays for squirrels and birds and scattering grain in the chicken house, I took out the plate of coyote cakes.

"Come on, Tom," I called.

Tom got up and started for the cake. Dick was beating him to it.

"Stop it, Dick!" I screamed in a murderous voice. Tones speak a universal language.

Dick stopped short. "Come on, Tom," I called in the gentlest tone I could shift to. While Tom came, got his cake and took it to his station, Dick remained absolutely still. All he needed was firmness. I called Jerry, and she got her portion.

"Come on, Dick." Instead of running up on all fours as the other coyotes ran and as Dick himself had run up to this time,

Dick now stood on his hind legs, holding forepaws loosely before his chest, and began dancing towards the food in two-footed hops. The light tan of his belly was beautiful in the light. He minced forward like a ballet dancer until he reached the cake. Then he lowered forepaws to the ground, took the food and carried it — not to the snowbank, but to the spot where he had stopped when I screamed at him. Thereafter, that was his sleeping and feeding station. For the remainder of the winter and through the following winter, Dick danced up on hind legs to his food when his name was called. No other coyote tried to imitate him. All coyotes are individuals, just as all people are individuals. Dick was especially individualistic. After the one calling down, he did not try bullying the other coyotes.

Occasionally the three romped, Tom and Jerry beginning the play. Tom would stretch out on his back and start to roll over. Jerry, who had been curled in a lifeless position at his side, would instantly be on her feet over him, while he slapped at her face and she nosed him. Then Dick would trot over and for fifteen or twenty minutes the three would roll, tussle, chase each other, all without making any noise or showing anything but good humor. Then back to the curled-up positions in the snow they would go, Tom and Jerry side by side, and Dick at his station.

One morning I saw five, instead of three, coyotes tussling. I stepped outside and in a determined voice, at the same time waving my apron, told the two strangers to scat. They scatted. The other three waited to be called to breakfast.

On February 18, Jerry's nervousness was observable. During the next few days her "jitters" became more pronounced and Tom became more interested. On February 28, the two mated; on March 1, a second time. Jerry's behavior was abnormal for thirteen days; she was in heat, apparently, for six days. Dick kept entirely apart from the pair, so far as paying rival attention to Jerry was concerned. He had his own Missy, as I discovered, but she never accompanied him, in daylight at least, to the house.

Thursday was my free day from employment by the power company. One Thursday in May, at which time the coyotes had ceased to require regular meals, I was lying on my back in a flat trying to identify a warbling vireo in a pine tree. Suddenly I heard a "woof, woof" right at me. Ted had taught the three coyotes to say "woof," always rewarding them with apples and other treats. Tom and Dick, but rarely Jerry, got so that they would occasionally come near the house and woof between meals.

Now on the flat I looked and there was Dick. "Yes," I said to him, "there's a doughnut in my pack." I broke it into quarters, and threw one of them out about halfway to the beggar. "Come on, Dick," I said. He began dancing up on his hind legs. Just as he reached the piece of doughnut, what sounded like war cries from half a dozen coyotes broke out behind me. A combination of police siren, fire engine screeching and hounds closing in for the kill could not have made a more terrifying sound. I whirled to look. At the same time Dick was trotting back in the direction whence the cries came. Then I made out, under the trees, a single coyote racing back and forth in great agitation. She had been making all the noise. She calmed down at Dick's approach. I called him again, and when he started his two-legged dance, she broke out again. It took several tries before Dick succeeded in assuring her that neither he nor she was in danger. Probably the den of pups was very near. Finally Dick gathered all the doughnut bits at the place where he had first woofed. He ate them deliberately without regard for his nervous mate. Lingering on my way home, I watched him kill five or six Belding ground squirrels. He followed me home and had a lone supper, Tom and Jerry not having made their appearance at the house for several days. Two weeks later I saw Dick and Missy again in the locality where I had learned his secret. This time he was not interested in getting food from me.

By the end of May, Jerry was staying away all the time except when called. Tom frequently showed up before meals without his mate, and then he and Dick would have to wait a quarter of an hour after the call for Jerry went out across the hills. On June the fifth Jerry did not come at all. We supposed that she was keeping close guard over her pups, now reaching the exploring age. For eight days she did not come.

On the morning of June 13 I stepped into the winter shed to get some grain. On top of a packing box Jerry was stretched out on her belly, head down on her feet. She looked at me without moving. Then I saw that the paw had been severed from her right foot. An inch of splintered bone stuck out from the blood-clotted hair of her ankle.

"Oh, Jerry, did you find one of his traps?"

Her straw-yellow eyes never flickered. During the past two years I had found fifteen traps, eleven of them unsprung, left by a coarse-grained trapper too shiftless to gather them up at the end of the trapping season.

For three weeks Jerry lay on the box, eating the food we took to her. Every day I swept her platform clean. Instinct told her that her wound needed rest. Eight old hens frequented the shed for shade and scratched in the straw. The coyotes that came to us were given to understand that they must leave the chickens alone. They paid no more attention to them than the ordinary house dog pays.

In July the road opened. All at once campfires of vacationists flickered in the night around us. Jerry left us in the night. We never saw her again. Beyond all doubt she was killed. For two more winters Tom came, alone.

On October 15, 1932, the last deer hunter broke camp at Florence Lake. The road was still open, but few people used it so late in the season — the most beautiful time of year. On the morning of October 16 Tom and Dick were at their accustomed stations, waiting for breakfast. Dick's Missy was not with him;

perhaps she had ceased to exist. A week later a young female appeared, Dick's own daughter, we judged. We named her Nelly. She was the most playful of the three. Her station was halfway between the stations of her elders. She soon learned to woof for an extra bit, and became Ted's favorite. Tom was mine.

On November 4 Skäta arrived. She had been with us the preceding winter. She was a black-billed magpie, a spectacular bird of the jay-crow family, with long black-and-white tail, long green-black body, and wings marked white and black. Black-billed magpies are numerous on the eastern slopes of the Sierra, and yellow-billed magpies range the San Joaquin country to the west of Florence Lake, but no other magpie of any kind came to us. Instead of eating with other birds from the trays, Skäta picked up meager scraps by the back fence and salvaged crumbs dropped by the coyotes. She came to food very irregularly. She refused to respond to her name. If she grew impatient for a coyote to finish and came too near, he was likely to slap at her.

This second winter, eating alone at the place he used to share with Jerry, Tom became more than tolerant of the big bird. He allowed her to take bits of his unfinished corn meal cake. She became as punctual as he was at feeding time, invariably perching on a pine branch above him. She would remain there until Tom, obeying the accustomed calls, had carried all his portions to the station before beginning to eat. The coyotes got an apple every evening now for dessert. The minute Tom crouched to eat the collected food, Skäta sailed down to his side. While he nibbled on a cake held between his paws, she pecked at it. She took her part of the apple. She ranged with him; she slept in the tree over his station. The two became inseparable.

When Ted left each month on his ten-day steam-gauging trip, I had to make the company readings, traversing a big triangle on snowshoes. Tom had taken to accompanying me. Now we were three companions, Tom running light circles around me, Skäta sailing through the air to wait on tree, boulder or snow for the earth-bound slowpokes. She was not my friend, however — only Tom's. When we came to a steep place and Tom went ahead to await my ascent, I would upon coming up see Skäta beside him, a splotch of black at his tawny hip against the background of snow. She spent the summers elsewhere.

Early in the afternoon of November 8 of our third coyote winter, I heard coyote yipping and went outside.

"Tom," I cried. "It's you."

He leaped down from a boulder just outside the fence and ran up as close to me as the fence would permit. He kept running back and forth and leaping up, yipping wildly. While he was still cavorting and my heart was singing, I saw a shadow skim the ground. I looked up and there was Skäta in a branch above her coyote friend. She had evidently found him out on the range. Together they had come to the house of their Lofberg friends.

Dick did not come. Under a deserted cabin in his range I found a coyote carcass that Ted identified as his. Some deer hunter had probably wounded him and he had crawled under the cabin for shelter. Of all the coyotes that came to us, Dick came the nearest to being bad. Completely selfish, he was nevertheless the most engaging of them all.

Nelly was back that third winter, and with her was a wolf that according to circumstantial evidence, appearance and behavior was a cross between timber wolf and mountain coyote. We named him Lobo. Nelly was as endearing as ever, but Lobo never trusted Ted or me; he lacked charm altogether; we could not share Nelly's fondness for him.

I have spoken of Ted's monthly stream-gauging trips that left me alone. Even during the first coyote winter, while Jerry was Tom's constant companion, he became my guardian in Ted's absence. Dogs often assume special guardianship under special circumstances. Why should not a friendly coyote, as intelligent as any dog? As time went on, Tom became so watchful that while I was alone he did not leave the house by day at all, probably not by night. I could see him after dark, sitting not far off, looking in through the window. One night I pressed my face against the glass and saw him faintly lighted, a dark pyramid against the snow.

"Hello, Tom."

"Woof," came his answer.

"Go on and hunt," I told him. "For six winters before you came . . ."

"Woof, woof, woof."

On my shorter rounds during the mornings, Tom could watch me from his station. When I made the circuit, to the dam a mile away, Tom accompanied me. In summer on his range, my "Come on, Tom" brought him wagging to me time and again. He was wise in ways of keeping out of sight of strangers.

Our third winter with the coyotes was our last on the mountaintop at Florence Lake. On the evening before we were to leave, Ted and I went outside, as we had gone many a time, to listen to the circle of singing coyotes and to see the full moon come up over the ridge. One singer in the darkness was nearer to us than any of the others. As the moon came up, we took a step to the right, and there silhouetted against it, sitting on his boulder, his mouth pointed straight up, Tom wailed us — unawares — his farewell. No words can convey what he and the other friends of his kind had meant, and, in memory, still mean to us.

XI · ROMA, CARLOS AND OTHER CAPTIVES

PEOPLE WHO HAVE RAISED COYOTES as pets all say that they are shy of strangers, and that they never yield themselves to a master like a companionable dog.[1] They refuse to be touched while eating; some out-of-doors dogs are this way also. "They always do things from the back side," Ross Graves said. "After one has run from a stranger, he will slip around and watch him from a hidden position." There is a saying that it takes five generations to produce a tame coyote, but I have never heard of anyone's trying to breed coyotes under normal domestic conditions through five generations. A cage does not fulfill the requirements of normal domestic conditions. Despite any gentleness in any coyote's behavior, all coyotes are wolves by nature. The Russians, the people in world tradition most associated with wolves, have a proverb: "You may feed the wolf as much as you like, he will always glance towards the forest."

Out of nearly any litter of coyote pups, one will incline to be more domesticable than the others. George Springer of Minneapolis discovered in a coyote acquired when it was only ten days old a constant craving for companionship.[2] It would play with its owner even in sight of a waiting steak. A Mexican on a hacienda in Zacatecas told me about a coyote — on the other side of the mountains — that had been captured as a pup, castrated, and put to suckle a nanny goat, in the manner of dog pups brought up for shepherd purposes. It grew, he said, to be an excellent *pastor* (shepherd), keeping a flock of goats together and guarding them against other coyotes.* A coyote that was christened Dingo and was raised by a collie bitch with California sheep became rather proficient in helping her shepherd the flock. Then, the very night after ending a twenty-mile drive, Dingo explored away from his charges and at a neighboring ranch liquidated sixteen turkeys; the next night he increased his score, was discovered, and thus brought to a close his shepherding career.[3]

The following narrative, presented to me by Miss Davis Monts, now of Washington, D. C., expresses more of coyote nature as seen in a pet than many pages of exposition might achieve.

"We lived about fifteen miles out from Plainview, Texas, on a half section of land. The usual windmill pumped water into a dirt tank full of frogs in the summer and, during freezes in the winter, covered with ice thick enough to slide and sit on. A pair of coyotes took to coming to the tank for water. If a gun was on the place, they didn't appear in daylight. If it wasn't, they would drink while we children sat on the kitchen steps a few feet away. As spring advanced, they showed such a fondness for our chickens that Dad set out one day with a gun to find the den. He found it and shot one of the parents, which got back into the hole. After he came to the house for a spade, he

* An American in Mexico told me that a pet *jabalí* (peccary) guarding a small flock of goats once assailed him when he rode near and made him retreat. Javelinas are easily domesticated but generally show emphatic hostility to any stranger.

had to let my younger sister, a neighbor's little girl and me go back with him.

"When Dad dug into the hole, he found the mother coyote dead and four pups, one of them dead also. Our little neighbor took one of the live ones, which soon died. My sister and I took the other two. They were probably not more than forty-eight hours old; their eyes were still closed. We named them Romulus and Remus and, until we could get a nipple to fit on a bottle, fed them warm milk on a clean rag. Their sharp little teeth cut it to shreds. They thrived beautifully, and while they were still too small to eat meat we acquired some baby chickens. We imagined that if the coyotes were brought up with chickens they would regard them the way dogs and cats do.

"The first time we introduced the little coyotes to the chickens, they seemed puzzled. Then Remus reached over and gingerly lifted a chick by the down on its back and started off. We rescued it, and then the pups went wild. We had to keep them tied up in daytime. Soon we acquired a collie pup. The three would play together. The collie, which was slightly larger, would bowl them over; then they would scramble up and chase her.

"At night, the coyotes, still very small, about cat size, would roam out until about eleven o'clock. We left a screen door partly open so that they could come in. They would come to the bed in which my sister and I slept, jump on a chair beside it, then to the cover, and dig at it as fast as their feet could go until we awoke and lifted it. Then they would crawl to their nesting place, turn around a time or two, sigh, and go to sleep. One day while Remus was tied, he got his soft leather collar twisted and almost choked himself to death. He died two days later. Romulus, shortened to Roma, continued to thrive. When a musical instrument was played or someone sang, she sat down, lifted her nose, and howled.

"We moved to a place that had sheep, and had to keep her tied constantly for about two weeks, bringing her inside at night. The sheep were shipped to market, and again she was free to roam at night. She came in, after her excursions, through an open window from which the screen was removed. No other entrance suited her. The only place that suited her to sleep was an old quilt on the floor of a closet in my parents' bedroom. Sometimes she stayed out all night, appearing for breakfast.

"One day we killed a big bull snake and dragged it to where Roma was sleeping, chained to a tree. She was stretched out like a lazy dog. I pitched the snake across her middle. She raised her head lazily, sniffed once, and jumped straight up in the air at least two feet. Then she jumped down upon the bull snake, grabbed it in her teeth, shook it, threw it down, repeated this act three or four times — and ate it.

"When she was loose, she liked to slip up behind us and nip our ankles, not biting in, but only enough to feel. Then she would sidle off grinning. There was no mistake about the grin. There were four big mules on the place, and I saw Roma nip them in the same way. They always kicked at her. She liked to walk along the rail at the top of a picket fence, like a cat. She always tried to run from strangers, but with people she knew she was gentle and at ease. Until she was half-grown she crawled into my lap to sleep, but she was too nervous to have been safe with very small children.

"One morning we found her limp and still warm. Our opinion was that she had not sidled quickly enough out of the way of a mule's hind ankle that she had nipped. She was full grown when she died. The whole family felt sad, and I wept very bitterly. We gave her a decent burial. Roma gave me an enduring sympathy for coyotes."

Several years ago while Miss Nina Sue Taylor, now of Fort Worth, was attending the University of Texas she wrote for my course in Life and Literature of the Southwest an account of a domesticated coyote that through her graciousness I now quote. The setting is her girlhood home on a stock farm in western Texas.

"Early one summer we took to noticing a pair of coyotes passing about a quarter of a mile from our house every morning. The larger of the two was the most beautiful of its kind I have ever seen. From his size and dark color we judged that he had been crossed with a fine dog. If left alone, the pair always went in the same direction, but if chased by our big shepherd, named Shep, or surprised by a volley from my brother's gun, they always turned back in the direction from which they had come. Knowing the habits of these creatures in protecting their young, we decided to search for their den.

"One morning after watching the pair go by in their usual manner, my brother Bob and I, accompanied by Dad, set out to follow them. They were soon out of sight, but Shep kept their trail. We had gone about a mile when she let out a yelp that would have waked the dead. She had seen the master of the pair mount a little hill to our right. He loped away, Shep yelping after him, but, being slow and awkward, she soon gave up the chase and returned. We judged that the big coyote was trying to lead us away from the den, and we went on searching.

"Carrying her tail hoisted in the air like a flag on a battleship, Shep led us into a shallow ravine. We had not been in this place more than twenty minutes before she gave us a signal and disappeared behind a chaparral bush growing against the ravine wall. She did not stay hidden long before she backed out, barking and growling with all her might. We rushed to her, and there, behind the chaparral, was the small opening to a little cave, and standing in it, the mother coyote was showing her teeth and growling as if she owned the world behind her and dared another being to set foot on it. Since Shep had puppies at home, we did not want her to be injured in a fight and so did not sick her on. I could see that Dad hated to take advantage of this poor coyote, trapped as she was, trying to protect her young, but he killed her. Then hurriedly we dragged her out of the opening, anxious to see the *coyotitos*.

"There were six of the little round woolly fellows, just about the size of Shep's babies at home. It is said that few trail dogs will kill a pup coyote, though greyhounds will. Terriers are trained to go into dens and bring the pups out, but generally they bring them out alive. The sight of the coyote pups had a peculiar effect on Shep. She nosed them around a few times, whined, and looked up at us with that expression of abject apology visible on a sheep-killing dog. Her behavior vindicated the cowboy who, after listening to a hunter's bragging on his wolfhounds, said, 'On my way in this morning I seen them hounds eating up one end of a dead cow and two coyotes chawing on the other.'

"Still, the pups had to be destroyed. The burden was heavier than that felt towards unwanted kittens. On first seeing the puppies, I had immediately picked up one of the largest. Now, I begged so to keep it that Dad gave in. The others were killed and scalped and we started home, I with my precious little bundle of fur and my brother with the scalps, which brought a bounty at that time.

"On putting my baby coyote, which I named Carlos, with Shep's family of three, I could see very little difference in their size or color. At first, Carlos appeared timid, but, with considerable whining, he explored his way among the other pups. When dinnertime came, Shep was still rather wary of her new baby, but after much sniffing and low-toned whining, she lay down so that her family could eat. She was not alone in the sniffing and uttering of sounds, but little Carlos, after a few tries and tastes, set into his meal in earnest. After this first experience, he lost no time when Shep announced that 'soup was on.'

"Carlos grew and developed rapidly, but not so fast as the dog puppies. However, he was larger and looked much heavier and sleeker than the usual coyote pup. The table scraps and raw meat added to the diet of milk made him develop rapidly. He had all he could consume. Bob liked nothing better than watching these puppies devour the rabbits he frequently killed.

"Carlos, like the dog puppies, had a passion for shoes, hats, bridles, and everything else he could chew on and tear up. One evening Bob left his pretty cowboy boots on the porch. The next morning he remembered his negligence. Experience had taught him where to look for missing articles. Giving the porch only a hopeless glance, he went out behind the chicken house to the favorite treasure mound of the dogs. There, among other puppy relics, he found the boots. One was still wearable, but the other had lost not only its glamour but a part of the toe. Bob's rage was terrible, but since he did not know which pup was guilty, none was executed.

"When the pups were about four months old, they began chasing chickens, especially small ones. It was quite noticeable that Carlos was not playing, but had an earnest purpose. Naturally this was not play to my mother. She declared that the orphan must be killed. Bob and I pleaded in a way that would have drawn 'iron tears down Pluto's cheek,' and finally succeeded in getting Carlos a stay, on condition that we break him of his chicken-killing habit. All of us were convinced that the coyote could never be broken of a deep instinct, but Mother let us try.

"For a few days we took turn about watching Carlos, and when we saw him start for a chicken went after him with a stick. Usually he escaped under the barn or some other place to which we could not get, but he plainly learned that it was not to his advantage to be detected chasing chickens.

"Months passed, and although we missed chickens and found chicken remains here and there, we had no proof that Carlos was guilty. A friend several miles away took two of the pups. Although Carlos had been gentle during his puphood, he now began to be less friendly. I think the punishment inflicted on him for catching chickens was largely responsible. As he grew older, he was encouraged in rabbit hunting. He was more successful in catching them than Butch, the other pup. They hunted well together and were good friends, but the time came when Butch refused to accompany Carlos on nightly excursions. His absences grew longer and his presence at the ranch house less frequent. Finally, he ceased to return at all, and we knew that he had claimed his birthright.

"About a year after Carlos's last appearance at our house, we began to hear stories from different ranchers about a huge coyote leading a band of chicken thieves. On one raid the band, so it was said, killed every fowl in a barnyard, eating and carrying away some of the chickens but leaving more lying about.

"One summer morning just before daybreak the squawking of chickens awakened our household. Dad grabbed the shotgun and rushed for the hen house, the door to which, because of the heat, he had left open. Before Bob and I could reach Dad's side he had already fired both barrels, but we were in time to see an astonishing sight. About ten coyotes were fleeing towards the pasture, the surrounding air was full of feathers, and, lying on the ground, not twenty paces away, was our old friend Carlos — dead. Also scattered about were eight of Mother's prize fat hens as lifeless as Carlos. Dad was somewhat disgusted because Shep and Butch had not given warning, but said he supposed they had been cajoled by Carlos. All that the dogs were doing now was to sniff at the dead form of Carlos instead of chasing the other thieves.

"Bob and I carried the body of our former pet to the shade cast by the tallest tree growing beside the tank and gave it the nicest funeral we could devise. We had no preacher and no songs, but there was at least one mourner. Now and then I go back to my childhood range, and always when I see a coyote or hear his cries in the night I have a sensation of sympathetic pleasure — and remember Carlos."

* * *

While my wife and I were walking along a street in Taxco, Mexico, we noticed the office sign of the Department of Forestry, Hunting and Fishing of the state of Guerrero. We stepped inside, and there for two hours an intelligent official by the name of Enrique Varela Antillón communicated knowledge. Near his home in the state of Zacatecas, he said, a family had a pet coyote that had been taken before its eyes were opened. At first they fed it only goat milk, and then no other meat than cooked. They never allowed it to eat raw meat. It grew up without any apparent desire to kill pigs, chickens and goats around the ranch.

When grown, it used to wander out, always coming back at night to eat — cooked meat. But in time this family began to miss pigs and chickens. They watched the pet coyote suspiciously; they offered him raw meat of several varieties, but he refused to eat any flesh not cooked. This does not sound improbable to me. There are people who eat lettuce only in fried form and who put sugar on fresh tomatoes. I could adduce authentic records of a mule and two horses that came to prefer roasted meat to any other food.

Anyhow, this ranch family were missing so many barnyard animals that they set a regular watch. They had several mongrel dogs, but the dogs had not once given warning of the marauders. A night or two after the watch was set, a watcher saw the pet coyote guide in three other coyotes, seemingly introduce them to the dogs, and then, as they started to raid, go to his accustomed bedding place. *Sí, señor, el coyote es muy astuto.*

In his unusual book *Animal Outlaws*, privately issued and now out of print, generous Gid Graham of Oklahoma tells this story of another captive: [4]

"He was a half-starved pup when we got him and named him for a dark spot about the size of a half-dollar at the root of his tail. Spotted Tail grew into a beautiful coyote, as gentle as a collie and as companionable — but when he saw a chicken his lip worried him and he could hardly withstand the temptation to rush. He rebelled against being taken into the house or into a car, but, once in the house, he investigated everything he could reach. He studied the doors intently, gave a ticking clock his closest attention, and became excited at looking into a mirror. We had to remove the skins of gray wolves used as rugs to prevent his chewing them to pieces.

"I often took Spotted Tail on long country walks, leading him past houses at which there were chickens and then turning him loose. He hunted rats and rabbits with great energy, but to my knowledge caught only one rabbit, which he got at a woven wire through which it was trying to pass. He was so proud and jealous of it that he growled loud when I tried to take it from him. He would tauten and cock his ears listening for a rat in grass or brush and make spy hops trying to locate it. At home I kept him on a thirty-foot chain and he became adept at ambushing rats that lived under the garage, in which he had his bed. He would lie very still, and then if a rat came within reach would streak for him and usually nab him. When bad weather portended, he would howl dismally during the night before it broke upon us.

"It was my habit to walk to the post office, a mile away, every morning before daylight, and going with me on these trips was Spotted Tail's delight. He was suspicious of everything he did not understand. He distrusted walls, telephone poles and electric lights. He rushed every cat he saw, and all the dogs were afraid of him.

"To the south of town was a field of kaffir corn between two forested streams. Several wild coyotes lived in the area, and one day while Spotted Tail and I were walking to the field I saw Jim Porter herding his cows on the kaffir corn and about the same time saw his dog racing towards him, yipping loudly. I knew that one of the wild coyotes was boosting him. The dog was so excited that he did not stop with his master but kept on towards home. About this time I looked for Spotted Tail, who was off the leash. I saw him standing, head lowered, tail straight out, in the path of the oncoming dog. He did not see Spotted Tail until he was right at him. Then he wheeled and ran back for his master, my coyote hot behind him. In about two hundred yards, Spotted Tail overhauled him, caught him by the hind leg, and turned him a flip-flop.

"During another walk, we entered a pasture in which a large Guernsey bull and some cows were grazing. When we were within about seventy-five yards of them, the bull charged. At first I was not sure of his intentions and stood still, watching him. Then I realized my danger and started for the fence. By the time I was halfway to it, the bull had caught up. Without any weapon of any kind, I pulled off my hat and hit him in the face. He stopped to butt and paw the hat, and I made some more distance before he caught up again. And now Spotted Tail was biting his heels and doing everything else he could do to distract him. Some passing motorists made a demonstration with their car that added somewhat to the distraction. As I made a flying dive under the wire, the bull struck the fence. For several minutes he walked up and down it, pawing the ground and bellowing; Spotted Tail did not cease for a second to nip his heels and harry him. Finally he lit out for a barn in the pasture, about four hundred yards away. Spotted Tail did not let up on him until he reached the barn. If it had not been for Spotted Tail, I doubt that I should be here to tell about him.

"How he resented the leash! It was a small rope about fifteen feet long, with a snap on one end for attaching it to his collar. I kept it hanging over his bed in the garage. One day I left the snap hanging within the coyote's reach. He cut it off and buried it. Later, after a rain, we found the tip of the snap sticking out of the ground. A few days later the rope fell from its hanging place. Spotted Tail cut it into four pieces and carried them as far away as his chain would permit him to travel.

"Having to be absent from home a great deal and not liking

to leave Spotted Tail alone to be fed by others, I placed him in the Mohawk Park zoo in Tulsa. He was given a mate and with her raised a family. Whenever I went to visit him, he would recognize me among many visitors and exhibit his pleasure by whining low and leaping about. Coming nearer to the cage, I would put my ear against the bars and he would lick it. This cage was floored with concrete, utterly unfit for any animal but especially for one that belonged to freedom like Spotted Tail. He died after about two years of confinement."

XII · PLAYING DEAD

IN PLAYING DEAD, as in other acts, animate life shows varying degrees of intelligence. The leaf-folding of a sensitive plant at human touch is purely reflex. If poked, the tumblebug, which has as little intelligence perhaps as any other species of the beetle family, curls up into a lifeless lump. The spreading adder, or hog-nose snake (of the genus *Heterodon*), higher in the life scale but unable to protect itself with venom or prairie-racer speed, reacts when threatened by first widening its head into a hideous form and then turning over on its back in apparent death convulsions. To say whether the opossum in "playing possum" exercises some small degree of volition or experiences only involuntary paralysis requires more than a flat *yes* or *no*. In the opinion of Dr. Carl G. Hartman, who has made a lifetime study of the opossum, the reaction is "neurochemical, has survival value, and is, of course, hereditary." The limpness of limbs, shut eyes, lolling tongue and reduced heartbeat that any cornered opossum demonstrates appear to come from sheer shock. W. H. Hudson was sure that during similar death-feigning by the common fox of South America, "the animal does not altogether lose consciousness," though it is so benumbed by terror that it is insensible to physical punishment.

The coyote sometimes goes into a death-simulating swoon as convincing as that of fox, opossum, jackal, or Australian dingo. One of Fido's best tricks is playing dead. As intelligent as any Fido, does the coyote also sometimes plan his act?

The coyote frequently gets credit for trickery when its revival from coma is as involuntary as the horrifying resurrection in Poe's story *The Fall of the House of Usher*. Henry Mayfield owned a big gentle horse called Old Roan that was never known to pitch but once. That was after Henry Mayfield got converted at the Bloys Camp Meeting in the Davis Mountains of western Texas, where all the ranch people are church people. The pitching episode caused Henry Mayfield to use language that he felt duty-bound to confess at the "prayer tree."

"Boys," he said, "you know that lone China tree down on the flat. Well, one day says I, that China tree is the scent post fer the coyote pestering my sheep. So I saddled up Ole Roan and took a couple of traps and set them at the China tree. Next morning, says I, I'll git on Ole Roan and see what I got. Riding up to the tree, I seen I had the coyote fast by one front foot. But, fool like, I'd gone off without my gun. But I knowed where I could pick up a club, and I got it. I tied Ole Roan and eased up to jest the right smacking distance and laid that coyote out cold, right between the ears. Says I, he's deader'n a doornail; I'll jest tie him behind the saddle and take him to the ranch fer skinning. After I got him tied, I climbed up and headed back fer the ranch. Then, sudden as hell, that coyote come to life and grabbed Ole Roan in the flank, and I was left setting out there in the flat. Ole Roan didn't stop till he got inside the corral, and I didn't stop cussing till I walked up to him. Boys, I hev made my confession."[1]

"A coyote must be killed till he kicks," a saying of frontier days goes. The wounded coyote that only blinks or closes its eyes is likely to make a more desperate move if pulled by the tail; it is dying when it wrings its tail and its eyes turn green. If hit, not necessarily hard, over the nose, a coyote is temporarily paralyzed in the same way that a mustang is when "creased" — shot through the nerve along the top of its neck. Like the stunned mustang, the stunned coyote recovers quickly and runs. One trapper used to tap caught coyotes over the nose with his trap spoon and then, putting one foot on the animal's neck to hold it down, stamp into its heart. If a coyote knows what it is doing when it plays dead, it generally keeps the secret. Some boys experimented on a female trapped in Wyoming that was plainly suckling young. The boys pulled her teats and she did not flinch. She lay with eyes open and expressionless. The boys made passes at them, and she did not blink. They tapped her teeth, and her mouth did not quiver. She flinched only at a deathblow on the head.

Immobility, aided by coloration that blends with ground and vegetation, is nature's camouflage. In country hunted over by airplanes, coyotes often freeze, stretched out on the ground against any coverage within reach. This behavior seems intentional as well as instinctive. The animal that deceives its prey by jumping around and otherwise acting conspicuously might, it would seem, be cunning enough to act inconspicuously. A correspondent in Montana relates the following incident. A farmer had a pet coyote that he kept chained to prevent its catching his chickens. The chickens had learned just how far the chain permitted their enemy to range. One day after the farmer had fed the coyote, he watched it take a portion of the food to a place within tempting view of the chickens and then retire to nap — apparently. No dog ever lay in profounder slumber than this coyote appeared to lie in. The chickens showed a distinct interest in the bit of food but manifestly doubted the wisdom of picking it up. Finally, the farmer said, they seemed to decide that a sleeping coyote could not see them. Two or three of them went to gobbling up the food. Like a released spring, the coyote leaped and caught one. The same trick has been credited to a captive fox in England.

A parallel story came to me from a priest in the state of Chihuahua. One day, he said, he saw a coyote that was trotting down a draw suddenly stop, fall to the earth and stretch out like a dead animal. He supposed the animal had been poisoned, as people in the vicinity were known to be putting out strychnine. The priest was in a comfortable shade, and he watched. Presently he noticed a buzzard wheeling earthward over the coyote. Before long it lighted on the ground near the motionless body and hopped near it. Just as it was within reach, the coyote sprang up, seized the buzzard by the neck, killed it and then ate. The fact that a story is traditional is not proof of its falsity. A writer in *Forest and Stream* reports watching a gray wolf play dead and catch an investigative raven.[2] Hundreds of years ago Reynard the Fox was credited with the identical ruse. *Quién sabe?*

The basic differences within the hordes comprising the human race lie not in color, creed, cranial conformation, linguistics, or belief in the folklore of this or that nationalism. They lie in the realm divided between literalists and people with imagination. I am not a literalist. I do not write to satisfy literalists. Not all of the *historias* of the coyote's playing dead are meant to be taken literally. This is a *quién sabe* chapter, anyhow.

One time there was a coon who lived up in a hollow tree overlooking a kind of open-air distillery where *mezcal* was made. This coon was curious and often sat back in the hollow of his tree and watched without being seen. He watched men bring in goatskins of honey-water from the maguey plant. Then, after it was distilled, he watched them pour it into bottles. Often when he was sleeping down in the hollow tree he would hear sounds of laughter and gaiety. If he came up and looked out, he would see the laughers drinking out of bottles, some acting like lunatics. He wondered about the stuff in the bottles.

One day all the people left the distillery to go to a fiesta. Then the coon came down to investigate. He was a solemn kind of person, but in his heart he loved laughter and wished he could laugh too. He took up a bottle of *mezcal*, stood on his hind legs just as he had seen men stand, and pulled out the stopper with his teeth. Then he took a drink. *Hombre!* Fire blazed through his insides! Zig-zags went up and down his backbone! He coughed, water flooded his eyes, and then he felt better. He felt springy.

He took another swig, not quite so much, and let it trickle down. Then he laughed, his spirits seemed so light. He took one more drink and shouted with glee. He wanted to find somebody to share his joy with, and so, carrying the bottle, he went walking down the road. Once in a while he would sip, just sip, the *mezcal* and laugh. His shoulders were thrown back, and he was looking at rainbows.

Now it happened that a hungry coyote passing across the country heard Señor Coon laughing. He stopped behind a prickly pear bush and looked. What fine eating the fat fellow would make, he thought; but he knew from experience that if he started after him, he would run up a tree out of reach. After he watched the coon dawdle along a little while, he said to himself, "This fellow is drunk. He won't ever get up another tree."

The coyote struck a long trot, keeping down low, and made a circle so as to come into the road ahead of the coon, but out of his sight. There he lay down on his side, kicked the dust as animals do when they are helpless, made other signs, and then became as lifeless as a chunk of mud. His face was turned in the coon's direction.

Coming up, the coon saw the dead-looking coyote. Before he got too close, he stopped, laughed out loud and said, even louder, "H'm, I've always heard that the way to see if a person is really dead and is not just acting, is to kick him in the stomach. Then, if he is dead, dead, dead, he will open his mouth and stick out his tongue."

Señor Coon took three steps forward, put down his bottle, reached into his pocket, pulled out his specs, put them on and leaned away over. "Absolutely dead," he said to himself out loud, "but it will be wise to make the test." Then, very cautiously, he approached nearer, but not too near, and poked a paw into the coyote's belly. When he did, the coyote opened his mouth and stuck out his tongue.

At that the coon ran up a tree and there he laughed more than he had laughed in all the rest of his life put together. And the Señor Actor passed out of sight without saying one word.

One time Coyote went out to hunt buffaloes. For five days he hunted without seeing one. He was getting hungry. Then he met Wolf.

"Where are you going?" Wolf asked.

"Oh, just traveling," Coyote replied. That's what he always said when anybody asked him where he was going.

Wolf went on and Coyote kept traveling. Before long he heard the rumble of a wagon. He circled around to get behind it and saw that it was loaded with meat. His nose told him that it was buffalo meat, but the wagon bed was too high up for him to grab a piece. Then he made another circle that brought him to the road, just over a hill in front of the wagon. There he lay down and stretched out in lifeless form.

The driver of the wagon saw him, stopped, got out, and felt his fur. "I'll skin him when I get home," he said to himself, and threw him in the wagon on top of the buffalo meat. Then he drove on without looking back.

Coyote lost no time. The meat had been cut up and he did not have to tear into hide and bones. He ate very quietly until he was stuffed. Then he jumped out of the wagon and traveled back the way it had come.

Before long he met Wolf, following the smell of the meat.

"Look here," Wolf said, "you're not the same fellow I met

this morning, are you? You look like him, but he was skin and bones, and you are as full as a pup."

"Yes, I'm the same fellow," Coyote said. "I've had all the meat any coyote could ask for, and the choice of the land at that!"

Coyote told him about the wagon and about the trick he'd played on the driver. "Your fur is finer than mine," he said to Wolf. "You gallop around and get beside the road ahead of the wagon and just play dead. The driver is sure to pick you up for your hide."

"Thank you," said the Wolf as he started off to follow directions. The driver saw him lying there beside the road, stopped his horses, got out and felt his fur. "Prime fur," he said to himself, "but nobody's going to play dead on me this time." He hit Wolf over the head two times with the handle of his big whip, but he did not quite finish him, and just as he was about to pitch him in the wagon, Wolf ran off.

He was furious at Coyote for playing such a trick and trailed him down. "I'm going to kill you right now," he said to Coyote. What Coyote said and how Coyote got out of this trouble do not belong to the story of playing dead.[3] Centuries before Columbus sailed, this identical story was related of Reynard the Fox over the Old World. Some tales seem to belong to all races — like ideas of decency to one's fellows. No matter what their origin, if they have vitality, they take the first ship out and travel across oceans and fasten themselves to fresh hosts.

At Christmas time in 1932, Dr. F. R. Seyffert, then employed by the Cusihuiriachic Mining Company of Chihuahua, told me this story. A ranchero named Rodríguez living at Saucillo had back of his house a corral of high and thick adobe walls. It was drained by a very narrow rock-lined ditch running under the wall. Through this ditch Señor Rodríguez's chickens entered the pen every evening and went out every morning. One night a coyote squeezed through and caught a chicken. Then the master ordered a servant boy to stop the ditch up with a rock at dark every evening.

One summer morning the master went out early to enjoy the sight of his fighting cocks in the corral. All he could see was scattered feathers, heads without chickens and chickens without heads. And over in a corner lay the gorged marauder. With maledictions, the ranchero kicked it. It showed no sign of life. He thought that perhaps it had died of colic from so much fresh meat. Perhaps it had filled itself so full that it could not squeeze out through the narrow ditch it had entered. In a harsh voice he called the servant boy to come now and take away the stinking carcass of the destroyer of his finest gamecock.

After the boy had dragged the carcass through thorns and sharp rocks about a hundred yards, he gave it a kick and was turning to come back when the master yelled for him to take it yet farther away, out of stinking range. The boy obeyed and dashed the carcass against a boulder. As he started back to the house this time, Señor Rodríguez, who was still watching and expressing himself, beheld the coyote leap to its feet and run away.

Not long after hearing this story, some version of which may be heard in almost any locality in Mexico, I went with a friend on a hunt for wild turkeys in Durango. Our guide was the *caporal* (boss) of the Hacienda de los Coyotes. "One time," he told, "a man had a bakery. A thief kept getting into it at night and stealing bread. Nobody could track him, for the bakery was at a very rocky place. The baker decided to poison some of his loaves and watch. He placed the little loaves in a conspicuous place for the thief, went outside, and hid. After a while he saw a coyote come up to the bakery and enter through a little hole he had not thought about. He stopped up the hole so that the thief could not get out. He was certain that the coyote would eat the prepared loaves and in the morning be 'well herbed' [strychnined].

"In the light of day he looked within, and there, amid pieces of bread, the coyote was all stretched out and swollen up like a bladder of warmed air. He flung the carcass into the street and began to sweep out his shop. Then he noticed that not one poisoned loaf had been touched, only the pure fresh loaves. He rushed outside to take another look at the coyote. It was running down into the arroyo."

XIII · FOLKLORE ODDITIES

IN THE TIMBERED SIERRA MADRE of northern Mexico I heard how the gunless Pima Indians catch wild turkeys. A roost having been located, a number of Pimas go to it after dark with a supply of pitch pine and gourd rattles. One Indian lights a torch and, holding it up in one hand and waving it, while rattling a gourd containing rocks in the other hand, circles around under the turkeys, all the while yelling and chanting. The turkeys begin to *put, put, put*, looking down this way and looking down that way, too distraught by what is under them to fly away, growing more and more uneasy. Before the pine torch is burned out, a second Indian relays the first, running, jumping, waving his light, rattling his gourd, splitting the air with his yells. Maybe two or three Indians run at the same time. They keep up their business until some of the turkeys lose their balance and fall out of the tree, *como borrachos* — like drunken ones.

I am not giving this method as historical fact. I am merely telling what I have heard. Old-timers north of the Rio Grande tell of similar methods used by northern Indians to bring down turkeys. I was discussing the matter with a kind and honest old Mexican in a village of Sonora.

"You need not doubt the facts," said he. "Coyotes catch turkeys in the same way. They run around under a turkey roost at night, barking and shooting fire out of their eyes up towards the watching birds. After a while the turkeys get dizzy — sick, and just fall out."

Many times, I have heard from Mexicans how coyotes draw chickens out of trees. The means employed by Don Coyote vary according to the tellers. The most remarkable account I ever heard came from Don Marcelo, gardener for the San Luis Mining Company's grounds at Tayoltita, in the state of Durango. Wonderfully pleasant grounds they were. Attending to Don Marcelo's words, I would forget their meaning while I became lost in the sounds of his soft voice and the vividness of his gestures. What an actor he would have made! Munden's "bundle of faces" could not have been more various than Don Marcelo's. Not content with acting out all his own characters, if I tried to tell something about a horse or a burro, he would throw his fiery sympathy into mimicry of every sound and motion made by the animal. He would crane his neck like a turkey. He would put up two fingers alongside his head to represent the sharp ears of the armadillo and then rustle a hand through leaves on the ground to imitate the armadillo's motion. He would contort his face into the jaguar's snarl before leaping on a dog.

We came to talking about the way the coyote catches chickens. Don Marcelo had seen this with his own eyes. Every morning at a certain place where he stayed, a chicken was missed from the tree roosts. There were dogs at this house, but the dogs never said anything against any thief of the darkness. Then one night Don Marcelo and another man sat up to keep watch. The moon was shining. They could plainly see the chickens in the leafy trees.

Perhaps an hour before midnight, they heard the chickens make soft noises. Neither of the watchers had seen the coyote come, but there he was. He had just appeared out of nowhere. He knew how to awaken the chickens without making any noise himself. There he was under them, looking up, and there they were, all awake, looking down. Then came an extraordinary exhibition.

The coyote caught his own tail in his mouth and began a mad whirl around and around under the chickens. They became so intent on watching him, trying to keep up with his dashing circles, that within a short time one of them lost its perch and fell to the ground. Some of the other chickens began squawking and cackling, but the coyote was already trotting out of sight with his chicken. As intent on the spectacle as the chickens were, the watching men had not tried to interfere with the performance.

I used to consider all such tales as pure folklore. Now I neither believe nor disbelieve. Mrs. W. A. Roberts, of Frio Town, Texas, is the daughter of W. J. Slaughter, one of the strong characters in southwest Texas during Reconstruction Days. He ranched on the Frio River. He was renowned for his honesty. A long time ago he used to tell his children of the following experience.

He was spending a night at some ranch down the Frio River. The moon was full. Out in the yard a number of chickens roosted in a mesquite tree. Slaughter's bed was a pallet on the floor of the unscreened porch looking out on the mesquite. He was a light sleeper, and had not been asleep long until he was awakened by uneasy sounds coming from the chickens. Looking, he saw three coyotes under the mesquite tree. They were not making any noise but were running around. Every so often a coyote would rear up on his hind legs and spring towards the roost. Slaughter was too much interested in the procedure to draw the six-shooter from under his pillow and shoot. He was seeing something that he had often heard his vaqueros tell about and had set down in his own mind as just another piece of childish fancy. Before long he saw a chicken flop downward. One of the coyotes caught it before it struck the ground and made off; the other two went with him. They got out of sight and no doubt divided the chicken. In about three shakes of a dead sheep's tail, here they were back again under the mesquite. By now, however, the owner of the chickens was up, and a shot from his gun put a stop not only to the coyote magic but to any further natural history observations on the part of Mr. Slaughter.

A trapper of the North Platte River country told B. F. Sylvester, Omaha newspaperman, of a method of catching coyotes that fits here. A dead chicken — though it would seem that a live one might do better — is tied to the top of a small tree ten or twelve feet above ground. A trap is set at the base of the tree. A wandering coyote detects the chicken and, regarding it, begins walking around and around, his circle becoming smaller and smaller until he is against the tree bole. Then, still looking up, he steps into the trap.

Coyotes, of course, do not confine chicken-getting to night. At any time of day almost, one will approach a farm or ranch house from the leeward side, keeping hidden until it sees an opportunity, then dash, seize a chicken before it can squawk, and be gone. The popular idea that the coyote always catches a chicken by the neck and thus prevents it from making a noise — from talking back in the way that fowls talk back to Reynard the Fox — is not borne out by facts. Often, but not always, the coyote does grab by the neck. Sometimes before fowls are stirring he secretes himself in a covert and remains there until a chicken approaches. Many Mexicans claim that a coyote lying in grass or weeds waves his tail to draw curious chickens, pullets being the most curious. *Quién sabe?* Again it is said that if a chicken flies from a coyote in broad daylight and alights in a tree, the coyote can make it fly to the ground by moving around under it.

A. L. Johnson, of Lakeside, Arizona, had a chance to learn something on the subject, but his sympathy was stronger than his intellectual curiosity. In July 1937, he was watching three wild turkey hens with eighteen poults when a coyote rushed them. The young turkeys flew into trees while the hens fluttered off as though crippled, disappearing into the woods. The coyote paid little attention to them but nosed around in the grass under the trees and then walked about, apparently not noticing the young turkeys over him. In about thirty minutes the hens began calling, and the young ones became very uneasy. They were craning their necks, evidently trying to decide on what ground to land. Considering that a flight was what the coyote was waiting for, Mr. Johnson revealed himself and ran the coyote off.[1]

One summer I passed some time on the Hacienda de los Cedros in the state of Zacatecas in Mexico. What are now empty mule stalls there used to be the *portales* of a convent. The owner who took over the convent built a bath fit for Roman emperors and a wine cellar ample enough for the most worldly monastery of the Middle Ages. During the Madero Revolution, which began in 1910, the wine drew bands of patriots as molasses draws flies, and to protect themselves from molestation the owners extirpated every grapevine in the orchard. In an immense rock corral enclosing the conventual mule stalls is a trough hewn out of a pine log thirty feet long and three feet through. The log was dragged by oxen from a mountain fifty miles away. In the old days when the million and a half acres of Cedros lands were stocked with goats, the trough was often filled with melted tallow.

It was by this relic of vanished times that Juan and I talked. No movement or sound around the hacienda's deep portals, the decayed bath, the sleeping church, the empty wine cellar, the scattered peon houses, and a pool where burros drank and women filled their earthen jars, seemed other than a part of the skimming of swallows over the water and the shadows of great cottonwood trees shortening and lengthening beside it. Juan and I had plenty of time. With him it had always been afternoon. He was not reticent. He told me many things that had happened to him during his fifty-six years on the Hacienda de los Cedros. He told how he had seen a panther wave its tail in grass and entice a filly within leaping distance. He agreed with the old woman cook who set down her jar of water to rest with us, that the coyote draws chickens from a tree by means of *"electricidad salienda de sus ojos"* — electricity coming out of its eyes. Yet he himself had never seen a coyote magnetize a turkey or a chicken.

One thing very *curioso* he had, however, seen one coyote do. On the great Mesa Central of Mexico a species of yucca called *palma real* bears wild dates — *datiles*. People eat the dates with gusto. Of course, coyotes eat them too, but it would be impossible for any coyote to climb the branchless trunk of a massive royal palm and pull off a bunch of dates. Ravens and coons knock some of them down when they are ripe, and some fall when they are overripe.

"But, Don Panchito," Juan went on, "you must never forget that the coyote is most astute, most sagacious. Listen! One time I was lying in the shade of a great royal palm just resting. It was one in a forest of palms. They were all loaded with the divinely delicious dates, and it was the time of ripeness. There in the shade I was thinking how good God is, and I was silent, making no noise, no motion. I was hardly alert, all the world was so peaceful with me.

"And then I saw a coyote come and set himself down under a *palma* loaded with especially ripe dates. There they hung ten feet, maybe twelve feet, maybe fifteen feet, above the coyote. He did not see me. Like me, he seemed very peaceful with himself and *el Dios*. He looked steadily at the dates, but he did not seem to have envy. I well knew how every coyote delights in

[242]

dates. 'Now I will see,' I thought, 'if it is true that this animal can draw dates down to his jaws.'

"Well, there the coyote was, first sitting on his haunches and then lying on his stomach and looking at one big cluster of the ripe dates. He began to wave his tail back and forth, back and forth, from left to right and from right to left. He was waving that tail toward the fruit as a serpent runs its red tongue out and dazzles the eyes of a bird. Slow the tail waved. At the same time the coyote pointed his ears towards the dates and looked at them intently.

"There may be people who doubt this, but I tell what I saw with my own eyes. I saw a heap, a whole bunch, of the *datiles* turn themselves loose from the stem on which they grew and fall right at the coyote's mouth. He ate them until he was full, and then, very contented, he went his way. You ask me how long it took this wise coyote to draw the fruit out of the palm. Perhaps a half hour, perhaps an hour, perhaps longer. Who can say? I was not thinking of time."

The Spaniards introduced sheep and goats into the coyote's country. Whether they, the Indians, or the coyotes introduced the fantastic theory enunciated by Clavijero in the eighteenth century, I do not know. "When a coyote invades a sheepfold and cannot find a lamb to carry off," Clavijero wrote, "it seizes a sheep by the neck with its teeth and, dragging it and beating on its rump with its tail, conducts it where it pleases." [2] The switching of a coyote's bushy tail on a sheep's woolly pelt would not be excruciatingly painful. The wisdom of a coyote's removing a victim from a flock guarded by man and dogs, before devouring it, is apparent.

My old friend Don Alberto Guajardo, as historian less skeptical concerning coyotes than concerning priests, assured me that long before he read Clavijero he "several times witnessed" a coyote dragging a sheep out while "lashing" it with his tail. Through him I met an old *pastor* (sheepherder) who gave me this particular account: "I had two dogs. One evening about dusk as I was penning my flock, two coyotes appeared. The dogs took after them. One coyote led them on while the other circled back to the sheep. When I saw him he already had a fat ewe by the neck-skin. His body was parallel with hers as if the two were necked together, and he was switching her gently with his tail as he led her forth." With more fanciful detail, H. L. Davis describes the procedure in his novel *Honey in the Horn*. A Mexican goat herder on the Rio Grande told me he had seen the Virgin of Miracles gently lift a drowning baby from the river and hand it to a man standing helpless on the bank. As all administrants, pious and impious, of opiates to the popular mind know, it is no trouble to produce witnesses for any wonder.

All factual men of experience whom I have questioned concerning this coyote-sheep business regard the idea as absurd. They say that coyotes habitually flush sheep before killing, whereas a wildcat leaps upon a sheep as it stands. A coyote chooses the most advantageous position from which to attack. He may try to drag a carcass to what he considers a preferable eating place. If he eats it where he has downed it, he will when full go back the way he came unless he is cut off from that direction. He generally cuts the jugular vein, seldom chewing on the sheep's rump in the manner of some sheep-killing dogs.

From time immemorial wolves have taken advantage of scattered sheep. Unless shepherds and dogs act decisively, a flock of sheep assaulted by coyotes is likely to scatter. This has led to the tradition that coyotes sometimes cut off a small bunch and drive them into a blind canyon or some other corner to slaughter them. Frightened domestic sheep run downhill, which is to any coyote's advantage and which is exactly opposite to the direction taken by fleeing mountain sheep. In a hilly country wise shepherds camp below their flocks.[3]

Extraordinary folklore develops around only extraordinary characters, though not all extraordinary characters inspire it:

Woodrow Wilson and William James, for example. At its best it is spontaneous, coming of its own will, as about Abraham Lincoln and Mark Twain. While such folklore is often false as to fact, it is oftener true to character, illuminating instead of betraying truth. Propaganda assimilated by a folk until it is a part of their lore — Japanese belief in the divinity of their emperor, for example — never seems natural and never has charm. White-faced Hereford cattle have been of large economic importance to the western half of the United States; the Hereford is an extraordinary bovine; but there is no folklore of consequence about the animal. The coyote is extraordinary in another way. He is extraordinary as a character, quite aside from economic, political and like importances. He has something in common with Abraham Lincoln, Robin Hood, Joan of Arc, Br'er Rabbit and other personalities — something that sets popular imagination to creating.

I have no philosophy to explain the belief, common among ignorant Mexicans, in the magical power of the coyote's eyes. The people who hold the belief live in fear of the "evil eye." In April 1933, I was at a village hotel in the state of Oaxaca owned by a communicative man who related the following experience. While he was a lieutenant in the Mexican army during the Escobar revolution of 1929, he went out hunting, taking a soldier for his *mozo*. Seeing a coyote followed by two little ones, he raised his rifle to shoot.

"No, *jefe!* Don't shoot," the *mozo* cried, greatly excited.

"Why not?" the lieutenant asked, pausing.

"Because the coyote has such a fierce and burning gaze that it will break the gun if you point it towards the animal's eyes."

The lieutenant leveled his rifle and was on the point of pulling the trigger when the excited *mozo* pushed the barrel up, thus diverting the aim.

About a year after I heard this instance of a common belief I was driving on the Texas border and picked up a Mexican. Before long we saw a dead coyote beside the road. The Mexican, eager to show his appreciation of the ride, warned me that if I ever came unexpectedly upon a coyote and tried to shout I should find myself able to do no more than bleat weakly. I said that I had never tried to shout at a coyote near me. He said that he had, and he demonstrated the feeble effort to cry out made by a person having a nightmare. Furthermore, he told me that if a vaquero running after a coyote to rope it allows his horse to run exactly in the coyote's tracks, the horse will stumble. "*El coyote es un mágico.*"

Upon separating in the morning, deer hunters in some parts of Mexico say to each other, "*Cuidado del coyote!*" (Look out for the coyote!) If a coyote runs across his path, a jinx is upon the hunter and he had as well turn back. Some hunters say that the spell may be broken by killing the animal, though if a man fires and misses, there is simply no use of his going on. What the hunter wants to see as he sets out for a buck is the luck-bringing paisano (roadrunner).

As I have said elsewhere in this book, Mexican belief in the diabolical power of the coyote runs back to unknown times. "When the animal wishes to kill," Sahagún wrote, "it breathes on its victim first. The breath suffices to infect and terrorize. Whenever any person deprives the coyote of its prey, the animal awaits a favorable opportunity and then takes revenge on that person by killing his poultry or other domestic animals. If the offender happens not to possess such, the coyote waits until he undertakes a journey, then places himself in his way, and barks at him as though he would devour him, thus inspiring terror. Sometimes the coyote calls several other coyotes to his assistance so as to terrorize the man more effectually. It does this by day as well as by night. On the other hand, the animal has excellent qualities and a grateful disposition." [4]

Some Mexican folk regard possession of some part of a coyote, such as a claw or a tuft of hair, as a warranty against harm from witchcraft. They believe that a coyote carcass roasted and fed to chickens will make them more alert against predatory coyotes. I have seen the skulls of coyotes hung around the necks of goats to make them wary of coyotes — or perhaps to make the coyotes wary of the skulled goats.

Skulls are probably no more effective than bells. The tradition of a belled wolf is as old as the tradition of a belled buzzard.* The theory was that a belled wolf would frighten other wolves out of the country and make too much noise to allow him to slip up on prey. An Englishman who tried belling coyotes in south-west Texas declared that every one with a bell on collected other coyotes, as a remuda mare collects horses. Shepherds in Manitoba who tried belling sheep found that the coyotes were repulsed temporarily but were soon depredating again, avoiding only the few sheep wearing bells. Next, the coyotes took to listening at night for the bells so that they could come directly to supper without the bother of trailing a flock down.[5]

One of the Old World traditions is that the fox rids itself of fleas by taking a chip in its mouth and backing slowly into water, the fleas coming up for air and crowding forward until they have only the nose of the fox and the chip in its mouth to stand upon, whereupon the cunning one releases the chip and ducks its nose. Some person with a Baconian passion for experimentation should get himself full of fleas and back into water and ascertain whether fleas can be got rid of in this manner. The Spaniards brought the belief to the Americas; in the Argentine it is applied to foxes and in Mexico to coyotes.

The old belief that male wolves deliberately emasculate each other has been extended, though not widely, to coyotes. Judge O. W. Williams[6] relates that a rancher coming in from a hunt one day with tired hounds noticed a coyote following the hind-

* Friedrich Gerstäcker, who wove much of reality into his tales of the South-west, set the action of "Bell-the-Wolf" (in *Tales of the Desert and the Bush*, Edinburgh, 1854) in Missouri.

most dog, and then upon reaching home found the dog bleeding from emasculation. The fact is that coyotes frequently gash each other on the rear parts, but it is not likely that they have any knowledge of the biological function of testicles. Joe E. Hill says that during fifty years of trapping, during which time he has examined thousands of coyotes, he has found — aside from those marked and castrated as pups by cowboys — only two males without testicles, and not one lobo.

I have a letter from an old cowboy of open range days on the Staked Plains offering ten dollars for a teat from either coyote or lobo that a pup has ever suckled. One of the absurdities of folk belief, prevalent throughout the West and in Mexico, is that coyote mothers do not suckle their young but feed them altogether by regurgitation. Anybody who believes this would believe that opossums are born through the nose.

The coyote in a *corrido* of the border country is more realistic. My troubadour friend Brownie McNeil, of San Antonio, heard a ranch Mexican of the chaparral sing it in 1942; in 1948 he took

CORRIDO DEL COYOTE

An - da pa' la no - pa - le - ra, Y pa - sa pa - ra el mo - go - te;

An - da y di - le a tu ma - dre Qu'en - con - tras - tes al co - yo - te.

the singer's trail to get all the *versos* for me, and found him in a *cantina* of Piedras Negras, on the Mexican side of the Rio Grande. "Zenon Martínez was wearing boot-style shoes," Brownie McNeil says. "He shook his iron-gray head and swore he knew no ballads, no songs, no tales, nothing. The Monterrey beer made him remember."

Pass through the prickly pear
And walk through the thicket;
Go and tell to your mother
That you met the coyote —

The male coyote on the little hill,
His mate being down in the valley.
Dawn songs have no ending,
Nor do these verses.

Sonora for the careless weed,
Chihuahua for the roasting ear;
For wisdom it's the burro,
And for jokes the coyote.

Passing by the prickly pears,
I was told by the coyote
That the wildcat howls
Because he wants his pug-nose.

The mountain road leads
To the village of San Juan.
— "Little Brother Scorpion,
They say that gold does not frighten." *

Fly away, fly away, little dove,†
Light on yonder fig tree.
— "What news, Companion Rooster?
I'll meet you in the henhouse."

Coyote was walking on a hill,
And look what happened!
There underneath a rock
He chanced upon the rattlesnake.

* The coyote here chooses, through a popular saying, to represent his color
as golden. He is expressing respect for the black and venomous scorpion of
western Mexico.
† The "fly away, little dove" line is a conventional refrain, attachable to any
verse in any ballad.

— "Good morning, Don Chillado;
I'm going to give you whatever you wish;
If you wish a picture, I'll paint it for you,
But I prefer to paint the violin." *

Fly away, fly away, little dove,
Light on yonder pear tree.
— "Señor Horse, loyal friend,
What do you carry in your nosebag?" †

The coyote said to us,
Passing over to the State of Texas,
— "Here I knocked over the honey jar,
There I leave you with the bees."

Fly away, fly away, little dove,
Light on yonder mulberry tree.
Here terminate these verses
About a valiant animal.

* To "paint the violin" is to "light a shuck," make tracks fast.
† The proper content of a nosebag is shelled corn, of which coyotes are fond.

XIV · COYOTE'S NAME
IN TWO TONGUES

SPANISH ZEAL FOR CHRISTIANITY in the New World burned to ashes most of the records of pre-Conquest civilizations, but parchments saved from the sacerdotal fires show the coyote as a frequent hieroglyphic symbol. His figure in varying forms represents, for instance, the ancient town of Coyoacan, a suburb of Mexico City. The name probably means Place-of-the-Coyote-Cult. There certainly was such a cult. The Aztecs had a god called Coyotlinauatl, to honor whom they dressed in coyote skins and held fiestas. They believed in another being called Tezcatlipoca, who was supposed to be able to transform himself into a coyote.* Thus transformed, Tezcatlipoca often placed himself on the road in front of travelers to warn them of robbers or some other danger ahead.[1] There was nothing benevolent about Huehuecoyotl (Old Coyote), another important figure in the Aztec pantheon; he was a backbiter and mischief-

* Nagualism, a cult formerly common among the natives of southern Mexico and parts of Central America, was based on the belief that some human beings have power to transform themselves into animal shapes. It is a form of the werewolf idea. For exposition of it, see *The Magic and Mysteries of Mexico*, by Lewis Spence.

maker. Coyolxauhqui, appropriately for any being bearing the name of the chief native bayer-at-the-moon, was Moon Goddess.

Anglo-American policy towards the aborigines of the New World was to push back and kill off. "The only good Indian is a dead Indian," the saying went – and pious English-speaking settlers from the Atlantic to the Pacific always wanted to make all Indians good. Any white man who married an Indian woman, with or without benefit of clergy, was stigmatized "squaw man." Spanish policy towards the aborigines was to baptize, peonize

Figures of the coyote in Aztec codices.

and cross-breed. Indians who came under the domination of priests and hidalgos were accurately termed *reducidos*. These contrasting attitudes towards Indians were extended to other native things. The English tended to give any new species of fauna or flora the name of whatever in the Old World it resembled, calling "robin," for example, a bird that is not a robin at all, even if it does have a reddish breast. The Spaniards accepted native names for plants and animals to the extent that the English accepted native names for streams. In mixing their blood with that of the indigenes, they absorbed indigenous nomenclature as well as the lore of native life.

They immediately adopted the Aztec *coyotl*, in time changing the final *l* to *e*. While many flamed to destroy Aztec paganism, a few wrote to illumine what was being destroyed. For centuries after the Spanish became familiar with the coyote and with the animal's impression on native minds, their accounts of it were, aside from physical descriptions, little more than collections of

[254]

native credulities.* The first printed description of the coyote is in a Latin work by Francisco Hernández, published at Rome in 1651. In a chapter entitled "Concerning the Coyotl, or Indian Fox," Hernández wrote:

"The coyotl, which certain people think to be the Spanish fox, others the Adipus, and which others regard as a distinct species, is an animal unknown to the Old World, with a wolf-like head, lively large pale eyes, small sharp ears, a long, dark, and not very thick muzzle, sinewy legs with thick crooked

Aztec Symbols of Coyoacan

nails, and a very thick tail. Its bite is harmful. In short, it approaches in appearance our own fox, to the genus of which it will probably be compared. It is midway between this and the wolf in size, being twice as large as our fox, and smaller than a wolf. It is said to attack and kill not only sheep and similar animals but also stags and sometimes even men. It is covered with long hair, dark and light mixed with one another. It is a keen hunter, like the fox in its ways.

* Clavijero's description of the coyote has been quoted in Chapter II; his coyote-sheep tale, which he accepted as fact, is in Chapter XIII.

"It is a persevering revenger of injuries and, remembering prey once snatched from it, if it recognizes the thief days afterward it will give chase. Sometimes it will even attack a pack of its own breed and if possible bite and kill them. And it may avenge an injury and exact a penalty from some troublesome man by finding out his dwelling place with great perseverance and care and killing some of his domestic animals. But it is grateful to those who do well by it and commonly signifies its good-will by sharing a bit of prey. Looking to its medical value, they say that the pain of extracted teeth may be allayed with the tail of a coyotl. The animal inhabits many regions in New Spain, particularly those tending toward cold and chill climate. Its food consists of weaker animals, maize and other kinds of corn, and sugar cane whenever it finds some. It is captured with traps and snares, and killed with the arrow." [2]

Friar Bernardino de Sahagún began composing his *General History of Affairs in New Spain* about 1560. Guardians against daylight in human minds considered his work dangerous, however, and it was not printed until 1830. Sahagún was more specific than Hernández in treating of the coyote's gratefulness "to those who do well by it." He wrote:

"The animal of this country called coyotl is very sagacious in waylaying. When he wishes to attack, he first casts his breath over the victim to infect and stupefy it. Diabolical, indeed, is the creature. A recent happening is worthy of note.

"A traveler on a road saw a coyotl, which motioned him with a forepaw to approach. The traveler was frightened of such conduct but went on. Upon nearing the animal, he saw a snake wrapped tightly about its neck, the snake's head in the coyotl's armpit. Within himself the traveler said, 'Which of these two should I aid?' He decided to aid the coyotl. He picked up a stick and began to strike the snake, which unwound itself, fell to the ground, and fled into the weeds.

"The coyotl fled also, but in a short while encountered the

[256]

traveler in a corn field. In his mouth he carried two chickens by the necks, and these he laid at the feet of his rescuer, making motions with his mouth that he should accept them. Then he followed behind the traveler until he arrived at his own house. Two days later the coyotl brought him another chicken, a cock." [3]

As has been said, Anglo-American discoverers of the coyote named it "prairie wolf." By 1830 English-speakers were dropping this name and adopting the Mexican. Their spellings of it, like those of Shakespeare's name, took a long time to settle down. Anglicized approaches to the now accepted form included chiota, cayotah, cojote, cuiota, collote, ciote, caygotte, cayeute, cayoti, cayote, coyoto, cuyota, koyott, kiote, kiyot. Perhaps there is no single right way for English-speakers to pronounce the word. Like morals, correctness of pronunciation often depends upon latitude or longitude. Historical pronunciation accents all three syllables of the word — co-yo-te. Coy-o-te, often abbreviated orally into ky-oht, does well enough.

The names of certain human characters and beasts are deeply imbedded in the popular speech of every land — Doctor Guillotine, "doomed through long centuries to wander, as it were, a disconsolate ghost, on the wrong side of Styx and Lethe, his name like to outlive Caesar's"; Washington, on ten thousand maps; dog, in attachments to other words, ranging from a hole in the ground to a star. No other animal of North America has by name so penetrated the American-English and Mexican-Spanish languages as the coyote.[4] Standing alone, singular and plural, prefixed and suffixed, Coyote is one of the commonest place names of Mexico and the Southwest.[5] Coyotepec (Hill of the Coyotes) and Coyotitan (Among Coyotes) of Aztec antiquity are duplicated by Coyote Hill and Coyotesville in California and by unnumbered Los Coyotes ranches from the Gulf of Mexico to the Pacific. In folk sayings and in other homely applications of the coyote's name and nature to human character and occupations, as well as to things, modern Mexican speech is bountiful. The coyote's domination of endless folk tales and superstitions has added to the name some shadings too elusive for definition or translation.

A *coyotera* is not only a pack of coyotes and a trap for catching coyotes but a group of people shouting together. *Coyotomate*, tomato of the coyote, used as a deadener of pain, owes its name to ancient belief that the coyote has power to stupefy victims with its breath. Other medicinal plants are named after the animal. A desert gourd, common to the Southwest as well as to Mexico, called coyote melon is said to be eaten by coyotes. Turkey mullein (of the family Euphorbiaceae) is also called coyote weed. On the West Coast *tabaco del coyote* grows wild. Coyote prickly pear (*Opuntia imbricata*) is another name for "candles of the coyote." The beautiful-leafed *coyotillo* plant (*Karwinskia humboldtiana*) makes up for lack of thorns by containing an ingredient poisonous to goats, which sometimes eat it; coyotes delight in and thrive on its berries. Often *coyote* is used as a synonym for *native*, and is applied to Indians and *mestizos* (mixed-bloods) as readily as to plants.

In Mexican popular speech, *coyote* means: a pettifogger, a thief, any kind of shyster or go-between, a curbstone broker, a fixer who has "pull" to sell, an oil or mining scout with "practical experience" in selling leases, also the respectable Minister of Mines, a drink of mixed beer and brandy. As Lumholtz puts it, "The regard that the Indians have for their Mexican masters is shown in the name by which they refer to them — coyotes." [6]

On the border, a smuggler-over of aliens is called a *coyote enganchista*. In the interior of Texas a certain kind of agent — sometimes a Mexican, oftener a jackleg American lawyer — who hangs around courthouses and charges ignorant Mexicans outrageous fees for getting a notary public's certification and performing other such small services is called a *coyote*. In New Mexico, the name, among other meanings, denotes a half-breed —

a mixture of Anglo and Hispano bloods or of Caucasian and Indian — who is loyal to neither line. Mexicans call a "wolf" among women *un coyote;* they call bastard children *coyotitos.* Without aspersion they call also the last child in a family a *coyotito.** In the folklore of ignorance — and not all folklore by any means springs from ignorance — the coyote is a cross between lobo and fox.

"Whoever has chickens must watch for coyotes" is a Mexican saying often applied to the owner of property as well as to the

The Gods of Pleasure, from Aztec codices.

mother of a fair damsel. Another saying, "The coyote won't get another chicken from me," asserts more aptitude for learning from experience than human history demonstrates. In folk tales of Mexico the rabbit, the fox and other creatures are continually escaping the coyote by calling upon him to hold up a rock that is about to fall down and bring the world crushing upon everybody. An example of this tale is given in its place. It explains the devastating saying, "You are like the coyote pushing against the rock."

Not all connotations of *coyote* are sinister. A shrewd man may be called *muy coyote* without necessarily implying that he is

* "When my sister Susie was born, an old Mexican woman on our ranch in Nueces County, Texas, said to my mother, '*Madama,* this is *la coyota;* this is the last one.' I heard the old woman tell someone else that the baby had a sign, a white ring around its mouth, that made her know it would be the *coyota.* Since my mother was past forty-three years old and Susie was her ninth baby, the prophecy was not wild. It may be that coyote used in this sense is a corruption of the word *cuota* (coo-ó-tah), which means *quota.* The last-born fills the quota for the family." — Ruth Dodson, Mathis, Texas.

crooked. Mexican people to whom the Spanish Conquest is still an event of yesterday and who still burn against Spanish oppression remember a pre-Cortez prince who was poet and philosopher as well as wise ruler and was called Nezahualcoyotl (Famished-for-Truth). The noble fame of Lobo and Coyote of the Chichimecs in leading resistance against Spanish conquest of their mountain homeland, north of Mexico City, yet lives. Among English-speakers, however, to call a man a "coyote" is

"A little animal that they call Jilotl."
From an Aztec codex.

to insult him, though he will purr at being called "foxy." At the same time, to "out-coyote" another means little more than to outsmart, to excel at the tricker's own game.

The mountain ridge called "hogback" by English-speakers is in the Sierra Madre "spine of the coyote." *Juego del Coyote* is a kind of checkerboard game, sometimes played by country Mexicans on marked-off ground, between "chickens" on one side and "coyotes" on the other. City Mexicans who have never seen a coyote speak familiarly of the coyote color. Of the many colors of Spanish horses, the bayo coyote (dun with dark stripe down the back), once ridden by range men from Guatemala to the Plains of Alberta, was considered the most hardy and enduring. "The *bayo coyote* will die before he gives up." The tireless trot of Indians is a coyote trot. Hidden rock basins of water — *tinajas* — are called "coyote wells." In mining lingo of early California, derived from the Mexicans, "coyote holes" and "coyote diggings" were small drift tunnels and shafts; "to coyote" was to dig or mine in a small way; a "coyote blast" was a chamber blast. Nowadays in the Southwest, "coyoting around" may mean mooching and tinhorn cheating, but oftener means drifting loosely from one place or occupation to another, without anchor or responsibility.

Mexican people of country background make endless similitudes to the coyote. "With one bottle of beer he will sing like a coyote," I have heard. A delightful correspondent gives this example: "Often Manuel walks past my house with hands clasped behind him, followed by his wife, stepping in his very tracks, it seems. If any of the five daughters is along, one or more of them always carrying a baby, they string out behind the old man and the old woman. If the 'coyote' of the family, a boy about seven years old, walks, he steps almost abreast of Manuel, sometimes holding to his father's clasped hands. He is an *hombrecito* — a little man — and, big or little, the Mexican man always has the place of respect. One day María, who tends to liberate herself from certain ancient customs, was looking out the window with me at the long cortege. 'Regard them,' she said, 'walking like coyotes, one right behind the other. Why don't they *igualar* themselves?' "

To have "coyote sense" is to have a sense of direction that guides one independently of all landmarks, stars, winds and other externally sensible aids. Here a man is; a spot of earth ten miles away that a saddle blanket would cover is his destination;

there are no trails; it is as dark as the inside of a cow. The man goes as directly as the lay of the land permits, the compass of his consciousness keeping true to the goal. As an old vaquero tried to explain, "Something in my body tells me." That "something" is the "coyote sense." More than any other animal, the vaquero people say, the coyote is *muy de campo. Campo* includes every-thing country — wilderness, desert, prairie, brush, cactus, moun-tain, fields. An *hombre de campo* is frontiersman, woodsman, plainsman, mountaineer, scout, trailer, one who can read all the signs of nature, find any seep of canyon water that a bee can find, in the cold cover his back with his belly, in hunger out-wolf the wolf. All his senses are sharp, all his instincts alive. The true *hombre de campo* is *muy coyote*, for, beyond all other creatures, the coyote himself is *de campo*. The saying goes: *El indio y el coyote nunca se pierden*. (No Indian or coyote ever gets lost.)

Pima Indian symbol of a coyote track.

XV · HERO–GOD, TRICKSTER AND TRICKED

THE TRIBAL GODS of the American Indians are many. They differ from each other as distinctly as the tribes themselves differ. Most of them, as George Bird Grinnell says about Old Man of the Blackfeet, are "a curious mixture of opposite attributes," both nebulous and concrete. The nobler and more advanced tribes people the spirit world with nobler and more beautiful beings. Essentially, the Indian's religion resides in a personal relationship to nature — a relationship that is profoundly spiritual.

For the Indians of the Plains, every plant and animal had not only its place but its right to exist in the all-enveloping harmony — the buzzard, the bull nettle and the gnat as well as the buffalo, the chokecherries and the cricket. The Dakotas set a high food value on hog peanuts (*Falcata comosa*), called also ground beans. Gathering them is tedious business for human beings, but apparently not for meadow mice. They scoop out cellars and therein store ground beans by the peck. In the old days, the Dakotas took freely from these stores, but never all, and they left bits of suet and corn to pay for what they took. It would be wicked, they said, to leave their fellow-mortals to starve. To this day, the Dakotas like to go out alone and sit near the storehouses of the bean mice and meditate.[1]

Just as the teachings of Jesus are far more spiritual than the creation myth related in the Book of Genesis, the Indian's relationship to nature is far more spiritual than his myths representing the origins of man and other earthly phenomena. One of the legendary characters of the Zuñi grew up, in the beautiful words of Frank Hamilton Cushing,[2] "kindly, yet grave, with a look of endless contentment on his face and anger forever gone out of his heart." Individuals of those tribes that had arrived at conceptions of the dignity of human life lived in constant consciousness of a Brooding Spirit, a Mysterious Power, enveloping the world. They saw visions and heard voices. They were mystics. When they prayed, they prayed for life — rain for corn, game to feed the people; they prayed for manly powers and for harmony with the beautiful world of nature. They never prayed for property and more property to satisfy greed. Prayer is what a person desires, not merely what he announces.

Geography determined that far-separated tribes should incorporate diverse animals into their respective myths. East of the Mississippi, from Hudson Bay to the Gulf, on the authority of James Mooney, the cottontail rabbit was "the hero-god, trickster, and wonder-worker of all the tribes."[3] Before the Cherokees and kindred peoples were driven over the Trail of Tears from their homes in the Southern states, they had transmitted to the Negro many traditional stories of this "trickster and wonder-worker"; the Negro made them his own and in time transmitted them to Joel Chandler Harris, who transmuted them into the classic of Uncle Remus's Br'er Rabbit. Anciently the Blackfeet were a timber people from the cold regions of Lesser

Slave Lake, where they associated with timber wolves. Later they moved down as far south as the Yellowstone and came to know the prairie wolf. Then, to this animal they transferred meanings that the big wolf had had for them. Their prayer in hours of direst need was the "coyote prayer song." Fear of coyote power, as much as sympathy, protected the animal from many Indians. The Apaches yet believe that to chase a coyote will bring harm.

To many tribes within its range, the coyote stood — and yet stands totteringly — as a god, more significant for cunning than for morals. No assemblies, diets, councils, convocations, consistories, conventicles, conferences, synods, courts both clerical and profane, vaticanal decrees, cardinalic proclamations, princely declarations, lay promulgations, secular acclamations, pontifical pontifications, bishopful announcements, archbishopical explications, ex cathedra pronouncements, hierarchal significavits, sacred damnations, sacerdotal dogmas, ukases, inquisitions, excommunications, legislated laudations, crusading children, mob oustings of heterodoxies, emperors of holy empires, anointed conquerors, and armies dedicated to celestial signs ever categorized coyote theogony or molded coyote theology into a creed. In some of the myths, Coyote and Coyote-Man are two different characters pitted against each other. First Creator, Old Man, Old Man Coyote, Chief Coyote — the name of the mythological figure varies with tribes.

He came first, next man. When good men die, their spirits go to a good place; when bad men die, their spirits go back into coyotes. Coyotes have other spirits in them also. After Coyote procreated earth and man, he naturally had to assume some responsibilities. Coyote brought salmon up the Klamath River. The wild buffalo had sharp eyes that kept hunters from approaching; Coyote threw dust into them and kicked the animal's head down near the ground, and then the animal was so dull-sighted that hunters could creep up near and kill. With a cun-

[265]

ning hardly suggestive of Prometheus, Coyote stole fire and brought it to man. He introduced Death also, for if everybody lived there would not be corn enough for all. Coyote taught the Sioux how the kidneys, back-gut and liver of a buffalo are not only good to eat but are a tonic against sickness. After he had made the pintail grouse, he instructed that bird not to dance its beautiful dances of springtime courtship in secluded places, but in the open, near trails, so that the Absarokes could see and imitate them. The Apaches say that in pre-human times Coyote created "a path" in which man is doomed to follow — a path of gluttony, lying, theft, adultery and other wrongdoings. "Coyote did first" what man does now.[4] "We are still following the coyote." He taught Geronimo, as he had taught many an Apache warrior before him, how to make himself invisible. Geronimo's strongest medicine was the coyote ceremony. Stephen Powers summed up the matter for certain California tribes: "Nature was the Indian's god, the only god he knew; the coyote was his minister."

The Tribes of California was written by Stephen Powers[5] after he had "waded too many rivers and climbed too many mountains to abate one jot of my opinions for any carpet-knight who wields a compiling pen in the office." He ranks below the superb James Mooney and the supreme Frank Hamilton Cushing as interpreter of the Indian's whole life and as narrator of Indian tales, but with them he stands apart from numerous scholarly authors who in ponderous tome after ponderous tome issued by the Smithsonian and other institutions have, while recording folklore, all too often extracted the folk out of it.

Ironic himself, he called forth irony in tribal tales. His chemistry mixed with the chemistry of the tribesmen. He found in the California fables "an element of practical humor and slyness lacking in the Atlantic Indian legends." The aborigines against the Pacific had naturally not heard of the miraculous way in which heaven-sent gulls ate up a plague of black crickets and thereby saved the first crop raised by the Latter-day Saints at Great Salt Lake — where gulls have lived since the glaciers melted. These aborigines saw nothing miraculous in the way coyotes ate up grasshoppers about to consume their crops. The event gave them no assurance whatsoever of a corner on God's attentions.

I think I could turn and live with the animals.
[And Walt Whitman might have been satisfied with red Indians.]
They do not sweat and whine about their condition,
They do not lie awake in the dark and weep for their sins,
They do not make me sick discussing their duty to God
[And reminding God over megaphones to be dutiful to them].

"Man is created in the image of God," mocked Mark Twain. "Who said so? Man." Mark Twain felt himself an original nihilist when he said this. Uncounted generations before him, the Miwoks of California had said the same thing.[6]

After Coyote had finished working on the world and made all the inferior creatures, he called them together to counsel on the creation of Man. They sat down in an open space in the forest. On Coyote's right sat the grizzly bear, next the black bear, and so on according to rank until the circle was complete, with the little mouse against Coyote's left.

The panther was the first to speak. Man, he declared, should be created with a voice that could make everybody tremble, and he should have mightily fanged claws.

The grizzly said it would be ridiculous to have Man squalling like a panther, often frightening away prey. Man should have prodigious strength; he should be able to move about silently, but swiftly when necessary, and to knock his prey senseless with the first blow.

The buck said that Man could never look proud unless a magnificent set of antlers crowned his head. He thought it absurd for any animal to cry out. He would pay less attention to

[267]

Man's throat than to his eyes and ears. He should have ears as delicate and sensitive as the spider's web, eyes bright like the stars.

The mountain ram protested that he could see no sense in the buck's style of antlers, branching out so as to get caught in thickets. If Man had two heavy down-curving horns, they would balance his head like a pair of heavy stones and enable him to butt over any opponent.

When it came Coyote's turn to speak, he declared that he could hardly keep awake listening to such a pack of egotistic nonsense. All that any speaker wanted was to make Man a mere imitation of himself. If this was the idea, why not pick out any cub of the lot and just call it Man? And nobody had even suggested a mind. As for himself, he knew he was not the best-formed animal that could be made. It was well enough to have a voice. The buffalo bull had the strongest in the land, and he was utterly stupid. The shape of the grizzly bear's legs and feet, which enabled him to stand erect and reach out, was certainly desirable for Man. The grizzly was also happy in having no tail, for he had learned from his own experience that that organ was only a harbor for fleas. The buck's eyes and ears were pretty good, perhaps better than his own. Then there was the fish to think of. He was naked and could keep cool in the summer and be free from fleas the year round. Man should be hairless, except for a patch to protect his brains. His claws ought to be long and flexible like the eagle's, so that he could grasp things. Yet, after all the separate gifts were added together, the animals must acknowledge that nobody but himself had the necessary wit to supply Man. He would be obliged, therefore, to make Man like himself in cunning and adaptability.

Here the beaver broke out, "But what about the tail? Give Man one broad and flat so that he can carry sand and mud on it."

The owl wondered that nobody had suggested giving Man

wings. How could this new creature excel all others without being able to fly?

The mole said that with wings Man would be certain to bump his head against the sky. If he had eyes and wings both, he would get his eyes burned out by flying too near the sun. Without either, he could burrow in the cool, soft earth, and be happy.

Last of all, the little mouse squeaked out that Man should have whiskers for feelers.

So the animals went on disagreeing, and the council turned into a general row. Coyote lost his patience, flew at the beaver and nipped a piece out of his cheek. The owl jumped on Coyote's head and commenced lifting his scalp, and there was a high time all around. Finally, Coyote ordered everybody to go ahead and model Man according to his own ideas. So each grabbed a piece of clay and began modeling a figure into the exact image of himself.

Only Coyote varied. He began by making Man standing up, with arms to reach with and hands to grasp with, just as he had described in the council. It was so late when they set to work that they could not finish by daylight. The debating had tired them, anyway. They all lay down and fell asleep. But cunning Coyote stayed awake, very wide awake, and worked on. When he saw that the last of the other animals was sound asleep, he went around and discharged water on all their models and so spoiled them. The Morning Star was dimming when he finished his model. He breathed life into it and cried his cry of joy, as he still does at this time of day, and woke up everybody to look at his masterpiece — Man.

Again, according to the Karoks,[7] also of California, the world and the creatures thereof were made by a being they call Kareya. Kareya ordered Man to arm all the animals and say how they should prey on each other. Man called upon them to assemble. Coyote planned to arrive at the meeting first and get first choice of whatever was to be given out. He overreached himself and got there last, only to find that all the gifts had been given away and that he was left the weakest of all animals. Man took pity on him and prayed to Kareya for him. And Kareya gave him cunning, ten times more than he already had, "so that he was cunning above all the animals of the wood. This Coyote became a friend to Man and to his children after him."

The Tonkawas pantomimed their debt to wolf-kind. In describing their rites, R. B. Marcy [8] does not specify whether the wolf actors were coyotes or lobos. According to the prevailing mythology of the Southwest, they would be coyotes.

About fifty warriors, all dressed in wolfskins from head to feet, made their entrance upon all fours in single file, and passed around the lodge, howling, growling and making other demonstrations peculiar to wolves. After continuing these actions for some time, they began to put down their noses and sniff the earth in every direction, until at length one of them suddenly stopped, uttered a shrill bark and commenced scratching the ground. The others immediately gathered around, all scratching up the earth with their hands, imitating wolf motions.

In a few minutes, they uncovered a genuine live Tonkawa, who had been buried for the performance. They ran around him, smelling of him in wolf style and examining him with the greatest delight and curiosity. Then the Tonkawa addressed them as follows: "You have taken me from the spirit land where I was contented and happy, and brought me into this world where I am a stranger. I know not what I shall do for food and clothing. It is better you should place me back where you found me; otherwise I shall freeze or starve."

After deliberation the council of wolves declined returning him to the spirit land. They advised him to gain his living as the wolves do, to go out into the wilderness and hunt and kill. They then placed a bow and arrows in his hands, and told him that with these he must furnish himself food and clothing. He might wander about from place to place like the wolves, and, like them, must never build a house or cultivate the soil.

To be known as wolf or coyote people was regarded by Indians in general as recognition of admirable stealth and ingenuity. The Pawnees, it is said, won their sobriquet of "Wolf Indians" from their cunning in lifting horses from other tribes.[9] Two divisions of the Apaches were called Coyoteros, the name a reproach as used by Anglo-Americans and a compliment as taken by themselves.[10] According to Charles F. Lummis, however, to call a Pueblo Indian of New Mexico "coyote" is to taunt him with being a coward.

In the long run, despite benefactions to man, Coyote's reputation among the tribesmen is based on a cleverness that is generally anything but philanthropic. Walking along one evening by a grinding stone, Coyote saw corn balls coming in and out of it. He snatched at one and had his nose pinioned against the grinder. Nighthawks were hunting in the air overhead. "Brothers," he called, "this corn ball grinder was saying bad things about you, and when I went to strike him, he caught me by the nose." "What did the grinder say?" a nighthawk asked. "He said that nighthawks lay their eggs on the ground because they are too lazy to make nests. He said that nighthawks have pug heads and dwarf noses." The birds were angry. They swept upward and then zoomed down with all their might against the corn grinder and split it in two. "First Creator got free. A man who is full of tricks can do many things."[11]

According to Frank B. Linderman, who lived long and intimately with Plains Indians, if one spoke of Old-Man-Coyote to a group of old-time Crows, every one of them would smile. They held him in no reverence. To him the Almighty had entrusted much of the work of creation, and it was he — not the Almighty — who made what appear to be many mistakes among earthly things.

Whatever his mythological attributes, Coyote never evolved into an unrelieved sacred cow. A sense of humor in the Indian

[271]

as well as in the coyote would prevent any such absurdity. In tribal lore, Coyote assumes three characters. As mythological creator, he is revered. As cunning trickster, often exercising magical power, he is admired. As dupe of all the other animals, the master trickster in reverse, utterly fallen from his original estate, he is mocked. The Indian laughs endlessly at the dupe; he never laughs at the revered being. Coyote is the single name for these opposites in character. Instead of confusing the meaning of one thing under two names, the Indian distinguishes nicely — within himself at least — between two things with one name.

As Indians of the Southwest advance towards mundane values, the coyote as seen in the light of common day becomes more real than Coyote-Creator or Coyote-Trickster. He is the coyote that kills sheep and wears a money-fetching pelt of his own. How fleece this third form without violating the first? Though the Navajo is not yet willing to trade his gods for the white man's, he has associated with the white man long enough to take from him "the pate of a politician, . . . one that would circumvent God." In 1931, the Biological Survey reported that the Navajo Indians with their hundreds of thousands of sheep were the heaviest of all New Mexican losers to coyotes, but that they generally refused to kill or touch one and said little about their losses, suffering them "in a spirit of religious tolerance." [12] In 1937, Charles Newcomb, post trader at Baca, New Mexico, who had then been among the Navajos for thirty years, told me that many educated tribesmen were casting aside all beliefs that hinder property interests. That same year, an Associated Press dispatch, dated May 1 and credited to Window Rock, Arizona, read in effect as follows, journalistic bombast and other insincerity omitted:

"Navajo traders outfigured their medicine men last winter to the tune of $25,000. Thousands of pelts, each representing a potential ghost to haunt some reservation hogan, went to market. Navajos believe that the spirits of departed tribesmen dwell in coyotes and that the person who skins one will release a spirit and be haunted by it. But they are willing for white traders to take the chance of being haunted. They bring the whole coyote carcass to the traders and let them do the skinning." Now, any tribesman can absolve himself from having killed or skinned any number of coyotes by producing some crude figurines representing that animal and going through a little ceremony.

Many coyote stories are of fairy tale nature, giving fanciful explanations of the animal's physical characteristics. Such tales abound about all the animals. To illustrate, Coyote's color was originally a bright green, but he wanted to be blue like the blue-bird. The bluebird told him he could get the color by bathing in a magic lake. He got it and was traveling along very happy until he went to watching his shadow to see if it were blue. He fell over a stone and rolled in dirt and when he got up his color was earth-dull.

Coyote is out-tricked far oftener than he justifies his claim to cleverness — and he seldom deserves better than he gets. He reveals himself a shameless fellow without mercy or morals, libidinous, greedy, vain, lying, ungrateful and utterly stupid. In view of his reputation for craftiness, stupidity is his crowning sin and shame. The stories are entirely outside the realm of moral values. They exist to deride the Master of Trickery.

Yet, after all, he is a likable rascal. To get the point of his de-basements, one must remember his successes. A story out of Alsae mythology, in the state of Washington, goes thus.[18] One time during a snowstorm, Coyote took refuge inside a hollow cedar tree. The snow blew into the hollow, and Coyote called out to the tree to change its hollow to the opposite side. The tree obeyed, but the wind shifted and the snow still blew in. Coyote kept ordering changes until the tree simply closed up, and then when the snowstorm was over it refused to open. There Coyote was, locked up as tight as the kernel in a mountain hickory nut.

But the woodpecker bored a hole for him. He was so impatient, however, that when the hole was big enough for the woodpecker to look in, Coyote grabbed his head. He was terribly impatient. The hole was so small that he could not crawl through it. The only way for him to get out was to disassemble the parts of his body and put them out one at a time. When he was all outside and assembled again, he was missing an eye that had been picked up by a raven.

One-eyed and very hungry, he started hunting for something to eat. By now the snow was all melted and it was the time of grasshoppers. He found many grasshoppers. They tasted good. Still, he wanted something bigger that would require two good eyes to outwatch. He gathered some nice big fat grasshoppers to take to a house he spied a little way off. He went in and found an old woman alone and without any meat. He gave her the grasshoppers to eat. She liked them.

"Whence didst thou obtain them?" she asked greedily.

"Oh, there are many right out there on the prairie," he said.

"Is that so? Then I shall be able to gather them close by. I can't go far, you know."

"No," Coyote said, "thou wilt not be able to catch any. Only people who are one-eyed like me can catch them. Yet, as you are alone and in need, I will take one of thy eyes off thee."

Then he took out one of her eyes and put it into his empty socket and ran away. After that he had two eyes just as he had had before his experience in the hollow cedar tree.

In the mythology of the Kiowa Indians of the Plains, Sinti is a long-legged giant, always hungry, never to be trusted, inseparable from his club, and habitually playing tricks on other people. He seems to be a kind of development out of Coyote himself.[14]

One day Sinti was out walking, club over his shoulder, looking for something to eat. He was unusually hungry, for he had tricked the animals so often that most of them had learned to keep a good distance away from him. At last he came to a prairie dog town. It was in a valley, under a hill. He stalked up to where the prairie dogs were scampering about their mounds. They were not much afraid of him, though each one stood ready to dart into his hole. They were so little, one of them hardly a mouthful for the giant, that Sinti had never thought it worth while to bother them. But this morning he was very, very hungry.

"Doggies, nephews," he called out — Sinti always called everybody "nephew" — "wouldn't you like to learn a new dance?"

"Yes, yes," barked the whole town of prairie dogs, "that would be very nice."

"All right then," said Sinti, "I'll sing the song and show you how to dance. First, all of you form in a circle around me and stand on your hind legs."

The prairie dogs all obeyed.

"Now," said Sinti, "notice how I sing with my eyes shut and hit the ground with my club, one, two, three, and every time I hit it I stamp, first with one foot and then with the other. You are to shut your eyes and sing after me and stamp your feet the same way."

The prairie dogs all shut their eyes, their hearts beating in their throats with eagerness to sing. Sinti began beating time with his big club like a rattle, stamping his feet upon the ground, and singing:

> Doggies, doggies, whisk your tails,
> Whisk your tails, whisk your tails,
> Just the way I say.

The prairie dogs liked the song very much and sang it very well, but the pound of the big club made the ground vibrate around the holes and frightened them. Some of them kept flinching and dodging at every lick, ready to run. Sinti stopped a minute.

"Don't be frightened, nephews," he said. "That's just the way the dance goes. Shut your eyes very tight, and sing very high, and stamp very hard, and you'll keep the circle perfect."

Kiowa Indian drawing of Sinti and prairie dogs.

So the eager prairie dogs shut their eyes tighter, and Sinti again went to pounding and stamping and singing:

> Doggies, doggies, whisk your tails,
> Whisk your tails, whisk your tails,
> Just the way I say.

And now every time he stamped his foot, he brought his club down on the head of a prairie dog. It would squeak, but all the other prairie dogs were singing so loud and stamping so hard that they couldn't hear the squeak. They were so obedient and so interested in keeping their eyes shut that they had no idea what Sinti was doing until one fat dog began to get short of breath and think that the dance was lasting a very long time. He peeped out of one eye, just as Sinti's club was rising to come down on him, and saw all his companions stretched out dead on the ground with their paws up. He made one long jump and dashed for his

[276]

hole, with Sinti after him. But he got there safe and dived in —
and so there are still prairie dogs in the world.

Sinti looked into the hole and said to himself, "That little fat
dog would have had the sweetest marrow of all, but I guess I
can make a meal from the others." He walked back to where the
prairie dogs were all lying in a circle and put them in a pile. Then
he walked over to a hollow on one side of the hill where some
bushes and low trees grew and gathered a lot of wood. He was
going to roast the prairie dogs in their skins, Kiowa fashion.

He made a fire and put two prairie dogs on a forked green
stick to hold over it. When they were well done, he put them
to one side and roasted two more. The roasting meat smelled
delicious. He was cooking the last two prairie dogs when he saw
a coyote come limping up. The coyote held one paw up from
the ground and was hopping on three feet. He looked very lean
and hungry.

"Please give me a little something to eat," he said to Sinti.

"Get out," Sinti answered gruffly. "Go run and catch your
own meat."

"I can't," said the coyote. "My leg is broken and I can't run
fast enough to catch a snake that's full of rabbit."

"Very well, then," said Sinti with a sneer, "we'll race for these
roasted prairie dogs. We'll run to that hill over yonder, go
around it and run back here, and the one that gets here first eats
the meat." Sinti was well pleased with his mockery.

"But I'm lame so that I can't run and you know it," said the
coyote, "and you have such long legs, too."

"Oh, well," said Sinti, "I'll tie stones on my ankles and that
will make us even."

The coyote acted grateful. Sinti tied two big stones on each
of his big ankles and away he started, the coyote limping painfully behind. "Come on, hurry up!" Sinti called back.

He reached the hill and started around it. Just before he made
a turn that would put him out of sight, he looked back and saw

[277]

the coyote still painfully hopping along, not more than half-way to the hill. He laughed and went on. The stones were heavy, and he just walked, lifting each foot up easily. He circled the hill, came in sight of the prairie dog town again, and sat down to rest. A little blue smoke was still coming up from the fire; the smell of roasted prairie dog made his mouth water.

"I'll not piddle with that lame coyote any longer," he said to himself. "I wonder how far behind he is anyway." He looked behind him, heard a pebble hit the grass and saw the coyote streaking by like a jack rabbit. Not lame, this deceiver! Before Sinti could untie the stones from his ankles, the coyote was at the feast. By the time Sinti got there, nothing was left but the bones. Halfway across the empty prairie dog town, the coyote barked back, "Thank you."

The name for coyote among the Salishan tribes of the Pacific Northwest is *Sin-ka-líp*, which means *Imitator*. More than anything else, Coyote's incurable propensity for trying to imitate other people and intruding upon their private affairs makes him an utter fool. He watches a dragonfly skimming the water and nothing will do him but to swim in dragonfly style. His drowning is only temporary. His eye is so delighted with the orange-rose flash under the wings of flying flickers that he is beside himself with desire to have bright under-arms. Absurdly and ignominiously, he tries to imitate the badger, the beaver, the goat, the prairie chicken, the kingfisher, the bumblebees, the chickadees — everybody he comes across. One time he tied corn-husks to his tail so as to have a rattle like Rattlesnake. Offended at being mocked, Rattlesnake said to him, "I was born that way. You were not." When he tried to ape Grizzly, Grizzly said, "This is my way, not your way. You cannot do what I can, and I do not make a fool of myself trying to imitate others." But Coyote never learns. He remains Sin-ka-líp.[15]

Out of multiplied hundreds, including variant forms, of Sin-ka-líp stories, three in Frank Hamilton Cushing's *Zuñi Folk Tales* seem to me more charming and better told than all others. They are "How the Coyote Danced with the Blackbirds," "The Coyote and the Ravens Who Raced Their Eyes," and "The Coyote and the Locust." With permission of the publisher, the first is here included: [16]

HOW THE COYOTE DANCED WITH THE BLACKBIRDS

One autumn day in the times of the ancients, a large council of Blackbirds were gathered, fluttering and chattering, on the smooth, rocky slopes of Gorge Mountain, northwest of Zuñi. They had congregated, as they always congregate in the season of harvests, to play and be gay before flying to the Land of Everlasting Summer to pass the winter.

On this particular morning they were making a great noise and having a grand dance, and this was the way of it: They would gather in one vast flock, somewhat orderly in its disposition, on the sloping face of the mountain — the older birds in front, the younger ones behind — and down the slope, chirping and fluttering, they would hop, hop, hop, singing:

Blackbirds, Blackbirds, dance away, O, dance away, O!
Blackbirds, Blackbirds, dance away, O, dance away, O!
Down the Mountain of the Gorges, Blackbirds,
Dance away, O!
Dance away, O!

Then, spreading their wings, with many a flutter, flurry, and scurry — *keh keh — keh keh — keh keh — keh keh* — they would fly away into the air, swirling off in a dense, black flock, circling far upward and onward. Finally, after wheeling about and darting down, they would dip themselves in the broad spring which flows out at the foot of the mountain, and return to their dancing place on the rocky slopes.

Coyote, out hunting, saw them and was enraptured.

[279]

"You beautiful creatures!" he exclaimed. "You graceful dancers! Delight of my senses! How do you do that, anyway? Couldn't I join in your dance — the first part of it, at least?"

"Why, certainly," said all the Blackbirds. "We are quite willing," the masters of the ceremony said.

"Well," said Coyote, "I can get on the slope of the rocks and I can sing the song with you; but I suppose that when you leap off into the air I shall have to sit there patting the rock with my tail and singing while you have the fun of it."

"It may be," said an old Blackbird, "that we can fit you out so you can fly with us."

"Is it possible?" cried Coyote. "By the Blessed Immortals, if I were able to circle off into the air like you fellows, I'd be the biggest Coyote in the world!"

"I think it will be easy," resumed the old Blackbird. "My children," said he to his people, "you are many, and many are your wing-feathers. Contribute each one of you a feather to our friend."

Thereupon the Blackbirds, each one of them, plucked a feather from his wing. Unfortunately they all plucked feathers from the wings on the same side.

"Are you sure, my friend," continued the old Blackbird, "that you are willing to go through the operation of having these feathers planted in your skin? If so, I think we can fit you out."

"Willing? — why, of course I am willing." And Coyote held up one of his arms, and, sitting down, steadied himself with his tail. Then the Blackbirds thrust in the feathers all along the rear of his forelegs and down the sides of his back, where wings ought to be. It hurt, and Coyote twitched his mustache considerably; but he said nothing. When it was done, he asked, "Am I ready now?"

"Yes," said the Blackbirds; "we think you'll do."

So they formed themselves again on the upper part of the slope, sang their songs, and hopped along down with many a

flutter, flurry, and scurry — *keh keh, keh keh, keh keh* — and away they flew off into the air.

Coyote, somewhat startled, got out of time, yet followed bravely, making heavy flops; but, as I have said, the wings he was supplied with were composed of feathers all plucked from one side, and therefore he spun down slantwise and brought up with a whack, which nearly knocked the breath out of him, against the side of the mountain. He picked himself up, and shook himself, and cried out: "Hold! Hold! Hold on there!" to the fast-disappearing Blackbirds. "You've left me behind!"

When the birds returned they explained: "Your wings are not quite thick enough, friend; and, besides, even a young Blackbird, when he is first learning to fly, does just this sort of thing that you have been doing — makes bad work of it."

"Sit down again," said the old Blackbird. And he called out to the rest: "Get feathers from your other sides also, and be careful to select a few strong feathers from the tips of the wings, for by means of these we cleave the air, guide our movements, and sustain our flight."

So the Blackbirds all did as they were bidden, and after the new feathers were planted, each one plucked out a tail-feather, and the most skillful of the Blackbirds inserted these feathers into the tip of Coyote's tail. The operation made him wince and yip occasionally; but he stood it bravely and reared his head proudly, thinking all the while: "What a splendid Coyote I shall be! Did ever anyone hear of a Coyote flying?"

The procession formed again. Down the slope they went, hoppity-hop, hoppity-hop, singing their song, and away they flew into the air, Coyote in their midst. Far off and high they circled and circled, Coyote cutting more eager pranks than any of the rest. Finally they returned, dipped themselves again into the spring, and settled on the slopes of the rocks.

"There, now," cried out Coyote, with a flutter of his feathery tail, "I can fly as well as the rest of you."

"Indeed, you do well!" exclaimed the Blackbirds. "Shall we try it again?"

"Oh, yes! Oh, yes! I'm a little winded," cried Coyote, "but this is the best fun I ever had."

The Blackbirds, however, were not satisfied with their companion. They found him less sedate than a dancer ought to be, and his irregular cuttings-up in the air were not to their taste. So the old ones whispered to one another: "This fellow is a fool, and we must pluck him when he gets into the air. We'll fly so far this time that he will get a little tired out and cry to us for assistance."

The procession formed, and hoppity-hop, hoppity-hop, down the mountain slope they went, and with many a flutter and flurry flew off into the air. Coyote, unable to restrain himself, even took the lead. On and on and on they flew, Blackbirds and Coyote, and up and up and up, and they circled round and round, until Coyote found himself missing a wing stroke occasionally and falling out of line. Then he cried out, "Help, friends, help!"

"All right!" cried the Blackbirds. "Catch hold of his wings; hold him up!" cried the old ones. The Blackbirds flew at him, and every time they caught hold of him (the old fool all the time thinking they were helping) they plucked out a feather, until at last the feathers had become so thin that he began to fall. He fell and fell and fell; flop, flop, flop, he went through the air, the few feathers left in his forelegs and sides and the tip of his tail just saving him from being utterly crushed as he hit the ground. He lost his senses completely, and lay there as if dead for a long time. When he awoke, he shook his head sadly, and, with a crestfallen countenance and tail dragging between his legs, betook himself to his home over the mountains.

The agony of that fall had been so great and the heat of his exertions so excessive, that the feathers left in his forelegs and tail-tip were all shriveled up into little black fringes of hair. His descendants were many.

Therefore you will often meet coyotes to this day who have little black fringes along the rear of their forelegs, and the tips of their tails are often black. Thus it was in the days of the ancients.

*   *   *

I have searched far trying to find representations of the coyote in pictographs and petroglyphs left by Indians over the West. Their pictures, painted on and pecked into rocks, show various animals, but, in so far as I have found, not one unmistakable coyote. There may be such; if so, the occurrence is rare. Why should not the tribesmen on whose minds the coyote made such a powerful impact picture him along with bears, snakes, birds, panthers, deer, antelopes, buffaloes and other animals? The most interesting speculation comes in a letter from Mr. Frank Beckwith, archaeologist, who lives at Delta, Utah.

In Paiute belief, man's great spirit-protector is Shenobe. Often this Shenobe manifests himself to a person in the form of an animal, at other times in the form of a human being. The manifestation is always to warn, protect, benefit man. Any animal that Shenobe assumes the form of becomes the guardian spirit of the person who sees it. He must never harm it or eat of its flesh. The animal may be a coyote. A coyote thus animated by Shenobe is cunning and sagacious beyond belief — more so than other animals that Shenobe enters. It bears a charmed life — impervious to bullet, arrow or other harm.

Opposed to Shenobe is the bad principle. A witch, wizard, magician representing evil can assume the same animal shapes that Shenobe assumes, the coyote included. Whatever the shape, it is there to lead men to harm, even destruction.

There are various ways of pronouncing — and, for outsiders, of spelling — Shenobe: Shenauv, Shenaub, Shinavav, and so on.

[285]

Ever so slight a change in vowel or inflection, and Shenobe becomes the Paiute word for coyote. Shenauv the god glides into *shanavi* the coyote. The coyote animated by Shenobe is never foolish; apart from Shenobe, the coyote is a fool — the object of obscene jokes and the butt of ridicule.

Suppose a man, a good man, should go to the rocks and there picture the coyote as his own guardian animal. Every man has his envier or enemy. The person hostile to the portrayer of the coyote could accuse him of witchcraft, using the picture as evidence. It might be hard for the artist to prove reverence instead of witchcraft. Picturing the clown-coyote might be interpreted as irreverence for the coyote of sacred myth.

Paiute duality and taboos represent attitudes in other tribes. The absence of the coyote from Indian art expresses negatively the animal's subtle and complex position in the aboriginal mind. From what I can learn, the Casas Grandes pot of which I have spoken, badger head sculptured on one side and coyote head on the other, is unique.

XVI · GOOD MEDICINE

ASIDE FROM "those shadowy recollections" of him as Creator, the coyote has meant Good Medicine to the Indian from British Columbia to southern Mexico. He has, always it seems, been a kind of revealer of good things, both material and spiritual — a being of mystery above the plane of medicine bags and talismans. "Thees man was gone now half-year, un he deed not know where he find hees people," a Crow Indian relates in Frederic Remington's *Sundown Leflare*. "Then he was see coyote runnin' 'head, un he was say 'good medicine.' He foller after leetle wolf. He was find two buffalo what was kiell by lightnin'. . . . He was give coyote some meat, un nex' day he was run on some Absaroke. They tell him where hees people was. Thees was show how good coyote was."

In 1871, White Bull of the Sioux Indians was caught far from camp, hunting alone, by blizzard following blizzard. He managed to get among some box elders along a creek, dig a hole through the snow into a shelter made by the bank and build a little fire. He was desperately hungry and all but freezing. While he was eating snow, a coyote came and sat on the other side of the fire.

"I have had nothing to eat during two days of ice," White Bull thought. "I will kill him."

Then he thought again, "Perhaps this coyote has come to tell me something." He said, "Friend, I came to this place and am having a hard time. I wish only what is good."

The coyote said nothing. Still, he seemed a friend there, a courage-maker. White Bull stood up to get more wood for the fire. The coyote moved to one side to let him pass. Outside in the driving snow White Bull glimpsed the form of his trembling horse under the trees. "Stay where you are, friend," he called out. "We shall both endure."

The day passed. Often White Bull replenished the fire. He sat so close to the coyote that he could have reached his hand out and touched it. Neither said anything by words to the other. The night passed. About dawn coyotes out on the hills began to bark. The coyote by the fire grew restless. He looked at White Bull, whined a little and trotted away. The wind had fallen. White Bull found his horse still alive. He mounted and rode towards camp, on Powder River. Not far from it he met a man, who clapped his hand over his mouth in astonishment. "Your folks are mourning you as dead," he said. "Three search parties have come back." He was alive because the coyote had given him heart.[1]

To a Kiowa warrior there was something unusual, but nothing unnatural, about having his wound licked by a coyote. After being besieged by Mexicans at Hueco Tanks in west Texas, a band of Kiowas undertook flight. One of them, Koñate by name, was so severely wounded that his comrades finally had to leave him near a spring. As the day died and night advanced, his life seemed to ebb away. He was in a kind of coma when he was aroused by a long howl in the distance; then came other howls from around him; they were repeated nearer. Koñate was sure that the gathering coyotes had scented his blood and were only waiting for him to die before feasting. Now he heard soft steps in the grass, close to his ear. The stepper came to his side and licked his wound. Then it lay down quietly beside him. He was so soothed that he fell asleep. When he awoke, the coyote was still beside him. It licked his wound again. He felt stronger, and very thirsty. He wriggled to the water and drank. Now the coyote told him — not in a vision, but as a companion, face to face — that he must endure and that he would get back to his people. That day six Comanches, friends of the Kiowas, came to the spring. They took him to a camp of his own tribesmen. At the next sun dance he made public thanksgiving to the coyote for his rescue. In the Calendar History of the tribe the year was 1839.[2]

The story of "Wolf Brother,"[3] as told by Chief Buffalo Child Long Lance, a mixed-blood of strange and tragic character, is not a coyote story. However, it expresses the relationship between Indian and wolf kind. Anyone who reads the book will understand how the author of it, in the prime of manhood, dispatched himself from "this harsh world" in which manufacturers of ammunition also manufacture popular attitudes towards nature.

Eagle Plume and his wife had no children. He often thought of adding to his lodge another wife who might bear him a child; but he could love but one woman. He liked to hunt alone. While we were camped in the northern Rockies that winter, he would go out by himself and remain for days, returning laden with pelts.

It was late winter and the snow was deep when early one morning he set out into wild country to the north. That evening as he was making his way down a mountain draw, a big timber wolf came out of the bush and howled at him. It watched him make camp; then it went quietly away.

"Go now, my brother," said Eagle Plume. "Tomorrow I will follow for that thick fur."

The next morning, running on his snowshoes, a large round ball in his muzzle-loader, Eagle Plume went on the trail of the wolf. Its tracks were bigger than any wolf tracks Eagle Plume had ever seen. They led him far across a valley and into a heavily forested range of low-lying mountains. Nothing, not even the fresh cross-trails of caribou, swerved the wolf from its course. It did not act like a hunted thing evading its pursuer.

The late afternoon sun was making long shadows when Eagle Plume sighted the big wolf on a naked ridge. For some hours light snow had been falling. Now the wind was rising in fits, making little swirling gusts of snowdrift on the white surface of the land. The new snow made the going heavy for Eagle Plume, and the wolf was now sinking to its belly with each step. Eagle Plume knew that if it kept to the open country, he, with the superiority of his snowshoes, could wear it down. He lost sight of it for a while; then he saw it again, and after the sun, with its sinister attendants of two false suns, touched the rim of the mountains to the west, the wolf remained in plain view. It seemed to be floundering in distress. The wind continued to rise until the driving, stinging snow enveloped the whole landscape. A blizzard was coming up, and the wolf was seeking harborage. The blurred outline of a pine grove stood like an island straight ahead. With wood and shelter in sight, a blizzard had no terrors for a hunter like Eagle Plume. He hurried to overtake the wolf before it escaped into the pines or became lost in the darkness.

But the storm gathered in strength and violence, and while Eagle Plume struggled against it he lost sight and track of the wolf. He rested briefly and then began to skirt the lee side of the pines for a suitable place to make fire. Suddenly he became aware that the wolf was watching him from a snowbank to one side. Turning cautiously, he leveled the long, cold barrel of his gun straight between a pair of gray eyes. They looked calmly at

him like two pieces of gray flint. He pulled the trigger. There was a flash in the nipple, but no explosion. The priming had been dampened by the snow.

With his teeth, he pulled the wooden stopper of his powder horn and poured dry powder into the pan, keeping his eyes on the steady gaze of the wolf, which made no move. As he deftly reloaded and primed his gun, he spoke softly to the wolf in the manner of the Indian, saying:

"Oh, my brother, I will not keep you waiting in the cold and snow. I am preparing the messenger I will send you. Have patience for just a little while."

The wolf made one leap — and vanished. Darkness and the howling blizzard made useless any further effort to capture this remarkable pelt. Eagle Plume now laid aside his gun, unloosened the axe at his belt and began cutting down dead spruce for a fire. Then he made himself a shelter of bushes.

During a slight pause in his labor, his ear caught a strange sound. When, listening intently, he caught it a second time, there was no mistaking what it was. It was the wail of a child. Throwing down his axe and wrapping his blanket about his head and body, he hurried blindly in the direction whence the wail had come. As he jogged along, his ears alert to hold the wailing sound above that of the screeching wind, one of his snowshoes caught in something and he fell. As he got up and reached down to pick up his blanket, his hand touched the object that had tripped him. He kneeled to look. It was a dead Indian woman.

Still the wailing continued. He walked around and around trying to locate it. It seemed to come from the air, not from the ground. From point to point he walked and stopped and listened. Finally he walked up to a tree, and there, hanging above reach of prowling animals, he saw a moss bag containing a baby a few months old. Snug in its native cradle, packed with dry moss and rabbit skins, it had suffered none from the cold.

He built a great fire and slept that night with the foundling wrapped in his arms. In the morning he snared a rabbit, and, slitting its throat, pressed the warm blood into the mouth of the hungry infant. With saplings he fashioned a rough sleigh. And so he came back to our camp in the valley, dragging the unknown dead woman behind him and, underneath his capote, carrying the child in its moss bag.

When the people of the camp came out to meet him, he handed the baby to his wife and said: "Here is our child; we will no longer have need for a strange woman in our lodge." She took it, and in after years old people told that the fires of maternity kindled in her at the touch of the infant, and that milk for its sustenance flowed from her breasts.

That night as Eagle Plume told his story to others around the campfire, a big wolf cried its deep-throated howl from a high butte overlooking camp.

"*Mokuyi* — It is he, the wolf!" cried Eagle Plume. Then raising his hand, he declared: "I shall never kill another. They are my brothers!"

And on the instant he turned to the child and christened him *Mokuyi-Oskon*, Wolf Brother. He became a great chief. His name is graven on a stone shaft that commemorates the termination of intertribal wars in the Northwest.

Every tribe recognizes a kind of *orenda, wyakin,* magic power, which not only accounts for many wonders in nature but is exercised by animals towards the spiritually sympathetic. Severe fasting and other preparations are necessary for an individual who would experience this magic power.* In the Southwest the coyote has, of all animals, the strongest power. How he

* In Mary Austin's delightful *One-Smoke Stories*, a Paiute gets from the Coyote, merely by giving him some sweet roots, a song "to warm the hearts of the tribe and stir up their thoughts within them." However, because he did not use it right, "the Father of Song-Making" came in the night and took the song back.

exercises it can be learned from the autobiography of a Papago woman.[4]

"My husband was a Coyote-Meeter. That is, when he had his medicine-man's dreams, it was our comrade, Coyote, who came to him and sang him songs. It began when he went with the other men to the ocean to get salt. . . . Running along alone, my husband saw a dead coyote in the sand. He stopped. That coyote rose up and said, 'Do you want to see something?' 'Yes.' My husband died right there and the coyote took him away. The leader with the other men knew that he must have 'met something.' 'Let him alone,' he said to the others. Next morning my husband awoke and found himself lying by that dead coyote. . . .

"Once when I was at cactus camp, I was sick. We did not have a medicine-man; my husband and his brothers were far away. I lay there and my head spun round, and I was hot and cold. Then, out of the desert, a furry, gray coyote came trotting to me. He blew on me as the medicine-man blows and I felt cool. I began to sing:

> Coyote, my comrade,
> Hither ran.
> To the end of his tail
> A cloud was tied.

I felt that cool, beautiful cloud, and I saw how funny Coyote looked, waving it over me and running away. I got well."

In order to convey the impact that the coyote has made on the mind of his public, I find it necessary to quote again and again the Zuñi Indians through Frank Hamilton Cushing. For five years, with great sympathy and intellectual alertness, this genius lived among the Zuñis in Arizona. About and from "these delightful people" he wrote four books informed by deep humanistic values. In his opinion, the "barbaric civilization" of the Zuñis had transcended that of any other tribe north of Mexico and was developing to rival the civilizations of the Aztecs and

Incas when it was "stunned by the culverin of the Spaniard." [5] Still childlike in its freshness, Zuñi imagination had passed beyond mere childishness. It had peopled the Unknown of Time and Space with beings far more spiritual and symbolical than the miracle-performing Coyote-Man. The coyote, nevertheless, remained an important character in Zuñi tradition. Tales — delightful by any standard, as Cushing relates them — heap upon the coyote derision made charming by good nature. At the same time, the deriders, always on easy terms with him, credit the coyote with teaching their people the all-important technique of the hunt.

A very long time ago, as Cushing set down the tribal history [6] — and as I abbreviate him, without quotation marks — a young man who was as voracious as a buzzard, as slow in apprehension as a horned toad, and so bunglesome that he had never killed a single deer, decided to go hunting. He took his dead uncle's bow and arrows from his grandmother's house, in which he lived, and set out alone.

After a while he met a ragged-skinned old coyote, who barked and yelped at him. The young man did not shoot or say, "How you smell, you corn-eating sage-louse," or anything like that. He just kept on until at the base of some cliffs he saw rabbit tracks in the thin snow. He followed them into a thicket, lost them amid some bigger tracks that he could not read, and suddenly saw a pair of coyote pups * sneak into a hole under the rocks. Immediately, the old coyote was there in front of him, sitting on his tail and grinning.

"How is it with you, bungler?" he finally said.

"Hey," said the youth, "did you speak?"

---

* The time of snow is not, in southern zones, the time of year for pups, though in the far North it is. Anyway, unlike a Hollywood story of an impossibility that means nothing and violates life, an Indian story of an impossibility that means something and expresses life does not have to have all the surface details accurate.

"Well, yes," said Coyote. "Why didn't you shoot at me and call me names this morning?"

"I — I don't know," stammered the youth.

"You might at least have killed my cubs. Why didn't you?"

"Why should I kill them?"

"Why, indeed?" said Coyote. "Only your brother beasts never stop to think of that. Do you know me?"

"No, not at all," said the young man.

"Well, I know you very well. You are a good sort of fellow even if you are a bungler. Come along to my house and I'll tell you something you need to know."

Coyote ran back behind a rock, reappeared with an enormous load of jack rabbits over his back, and led the way to the hole in which the two pups had disappeared.

"Step in, my friend," he said.

"Where?" asked the young man.

"Why, into my house. Don't you see the door?"

"I see a hole no bigger than one of my thighs," said the young man, putting a foot into it.

There was a rumble of the earth, and an ample passageway existed with a fine door at the end of it.

"Old woman, are you there?" Coyote shouted.

The door opened, and Coyote's wife, standing in it, said, "Come in." They stepped into a fine room, the "furlings," as Coyote called his youngsters, cowering in a corner. He stretched himself, shook himself, gave a jump, and *rip* — a fine little old man stood before the astonished youth. He hung his skin on an antler, placed a sitting block for his guest, and produced a gourd of tobacco and some shucks. "Fill and smoke," he said.

Meanwhile the little old coyote-woman was bringing out the stew and other food. The young man thought he had never smelled a richer broth. He ate so freely that he made the furlings forget their fear. "Thanks, thank you," he said when he was full.

"Be satisfied," the little old coyote-woman rejoined. She laid fresh wood on the fire.

Then the coyote-being turned to business. "I knew you," he said, "by the smell of your uncle's sweat on the bow you carry. I taught him to hunt. Nobody has ever taught you to hunt or how to gain the favors of my brothers and myself. We are the masters of prey throughout the six regions of the world of daylight. I will teach you, but first you must bring prayer-plumes, both for our use and for your use when you slay a deer."

As the young man was preparing to go, the coyote-being gave him half the rabbits he had brought in. "They will put your old grandmother into a good humor," he said. When the young man was outside the door, the earth rumbled, and again there was only a hole under the rocks.

For three days the young man made prayer-plumes, many of them. On the fourth day he set out to meet his instructor. Soon he saw him. The ragged-skinned old coyote led the way to the den. The earth rumbled, the fine door opened, and they were inside the fine room. This time other coyotes were there. Politely, they all jumped out of their skins and hung them up. The young man laid the prayer-plumes on the floor. Giving one each to his brothers, the Master Coyote put the others away.

"It is time for you to hunt," he said to his kinsmen. They jumped back into their skins and were gone, each with his prayer-plume.

"You wonder why I offered them nothing to eat," the Master Coyote said to the young man. "Now for your lesson. First of all, the thinner the stomach, the lighter the foot. A hungry hunter scents game against the wind. Never eat in the morning.

"Again, whenever you take a beast's body, give something in return. How can a man expect so much without paying something? Offer the creature you have slain, also his kind, prayer-plumes. Now, let's go for a hunt."

On the level bottom of the very first valley they came into, they struck fresh deer trails in the melting snow.

"It is your business to look at this track," said Coyote. "See, it was made by the leader. You can tell that by the way it is chipped into by the footprints of those that followed him. We will track this particular trail for a while, together. See now; the holes this leader's feet made in the snow are a little melted at the edges. This shows he has been gone some time; by and by, they will be sharper and less melted. Then you must step as though you were walking on grass-stalks and wished not to break them, for the deer will perchance be listening behind some bunch of bushes or knoll in the valley.

"I may leave you at any time, and when I do, mind not to call out, for that would be worse than stepping noisily. You must keep cautiously following the trail until you come to grass straws not yet straightened up in the bottom of the tracks where the snow is most melted. Then sit down and sing like this:

> Deer, deer!
> Thy footprints I see,
> I, following, come;
> Sacred favor for thee
> I bring as I run.
> Yea! Yea!

"If the deer hears your music, he will be charmed by it and hesitate. That will give me time to run around to the head of the valley before he gets there. Deer going home travel in canyons as men do in pathways. After you have followed the trail a little farther, sing again. I, meanwhile, will station myself where a ravine branches out from the main canyon, and there wait. When the deer sees you coming, he will be frightened and run swiftly up the valley. But there I shall be before him; there you will be coming after. To get away from us both, he will scud away into the side-canyon. Then you stop and sing again. I will skip around to head him off once more. You sing a fourth time, and hurry after.

"When he sees me again, he will turn about and lower his head to meet you. Then draw your arrow to the tip and stand ready. Just as he is about to charge past you, I will run up behind and nip his heels. He will turn sharply to see what it is, and, his side being toward you, quick! stick him hard with the arrow a little back of where the gray hair changes color behind the shoulder! If you strike there, he will fall; if you miss, you will fall, for he will see that you are a bungler — do you hear? — and run right through you as though you did not exist. Should he fall, quickly go to him, throw your arms around him, put your lips close to his, breathe in his breath, and say, 'Thanks, my father. This day have I drunken your sacred wind of life.'

"Do you understand all now?" asked Coyote, looking up at the young man.

"Yes," said the youth, "I have heard. The words of my father lodge in my heart."

The hunt followed very much as it had been anticipated by Coyote; the deer heard the singing, hesitated, was frightened, was headed once, twice, by Coyote, and in the end received the arrow into his heart. Nor did the youth forget to breathe in his last sacred breath of life and repeat the prayer of thanks. He planted the prayer-plume so that other deer would come to the place and not flee the land.

Coyote, as he watched, was almost beside himself with joy. "Thou art no bungler," he cried, "but a skillful hunter. This day thou hast entered a new trail of life, and the Beings of Game are thy friends forever. Receiving flesh wherewith to add unto thy own flesh, thou hast remembered to confer in return that which giveth new life to the spirits of slain creatures. Hereafter thou shalt hunt alone, remembering always to favor us masters of prey as well as the prey."

Then Coyote taught the young man how to skin and dress the

deer, how to wrap it in its own hide for carrying. With one word of warning he left. "Beware," he said, "of a sorcerer who, jealous of thy powers, will assume my disguise and try to destroy you. Beware of the wizard-coyote, like me, yet unlike me."

The young man became the greatest of all hunters of his people. To households without hunters he freely supplied meat. He remembered always to ask pardon of any animal whose life he took.* When he hung a deer up, he left the entrails and blood on the ground for his best friends, the coyotes. He was received into the councils of sage men. He won as wife the most beautiful and the most skillful in womanly crafts of all the daughters of the tribe. There were men jealous of him, and a sorcerer in the guise of a coyote did overpower him, but old Coyote overpowered the evil one and restored the young man. The two parted for the last time. In saying farewell, old Coyote spoke words that lodged in the young man's heart.

"My child," he said, "be thou happy many days and winters, throughout which thou wilt be a father to thy people. But an evening will come when I or one of my wandering kind will howl in the trail over which thou returnest from the chase. Then tell thy people to make thy grave-plumes, and when they are done, thou wilt take them and, living, go thy way to the Lake of the Dead."

---

* This widespread custom among American Indians simply signified their reverence for life. "What God hath cleansed, *that* call not thou common."

XVII · TALES OF DON COYOTE

Dedicated to the memory of gay, puckish Raymond
Everitt, my publisher and loved friend, who wanted me
to write a book of children's stories about Don Coyote.
This would have been it — without the learning.

SIR REYNARD AND DON COYOTE

TO THE SPANIARDS with their picaresque tradition — a
tradition in which a heartless, truthless, moral-less, cynical,
supremely crafty trickster is the recurring hero of both national
literature and folk dreams — the trickster coyote of Indian tradition that they found in America was like a letter from home. For
centuries Lazarillo de Tormés has in Spanish literature epito-
mized the character. As a folk creation of undated antiquity,
Pedro de Urdemales still lies outlandishly, cheats egregiously,
steals incontinently and performs incredible tricks on incredibly
credulous mortals wherever Spanish is spoken. Cervantes wrote
a play about him. Muleteers in the Andes, vaqueros on the mesas
of Mexico, and gauchos on the Argentine pampas who never
heard of Cervantes go on entertaining each other with preposter-

[302]

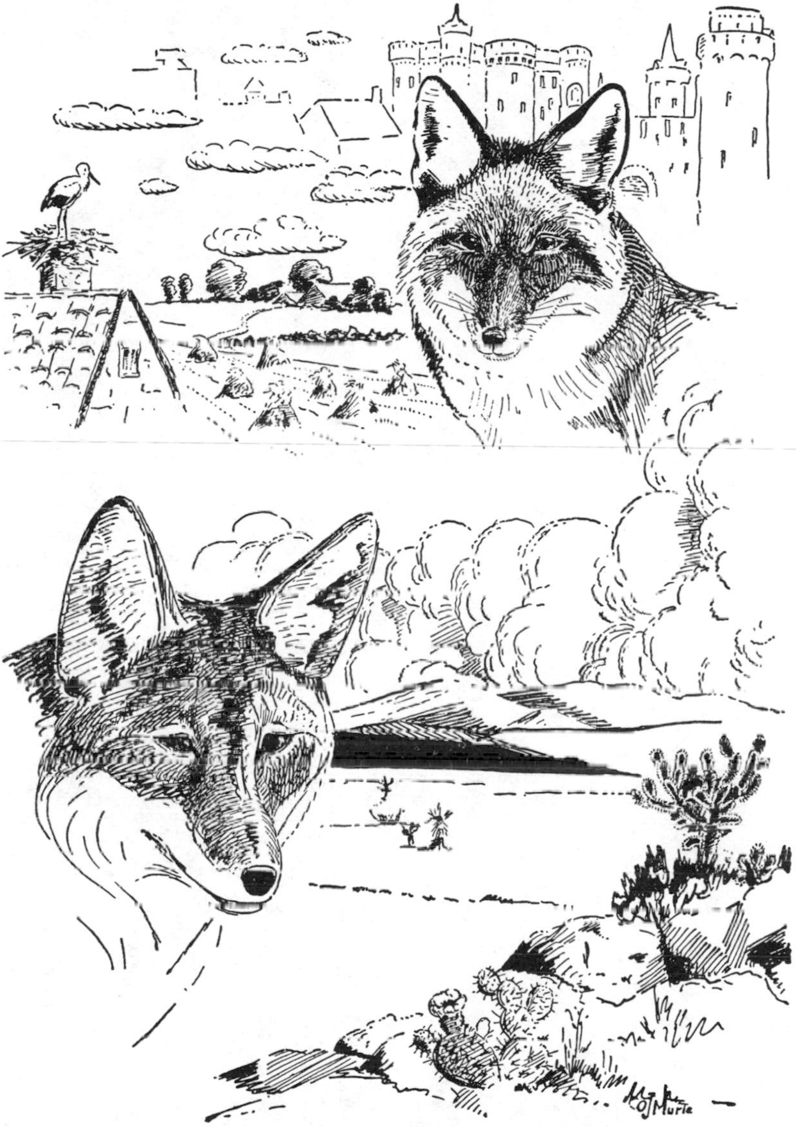
OJMurie

ous tales in which he is the hero. Scholars pile up treatises on his ubiquitous vitality.[1] Another could be written showing the interpenetration in Mexico of Pedro de Urdemales and the coyote-trickster of Indian folklore.

The *mestizo* Mexican is a blend of Spaniard and Indian, predominantly Indian. The coyote that figures in countless Mexican tales is a blend of Spanish and Indian cultures, predominantly Indian. This coyote is, however, more naturalistic and less mythological than the original. The *campesino* has the Indian's knowledge of nature. In the manner of all unskeptical people of the soil, he ascribes to animals powers and intuitions beyond his own. Moving hardly faster than his wood-bearing burro, his goats browsing on the mountains, or his wind-swayed snare for quail in the valley, he has ample time to see. On a cold day, his blanket around him, he will stand all morning against a sun-warmed adobe wall and watch the patient buzzards float into specks across the empty sky. On a summer afternoon he will shift with the shadow of a cottonwood tree, attending, apparently, only the dipping of swallows over a pool of water. In this passiveness, more idle than wise, fancies and racial memories drift through his brain. What he actually knows about the coyote, which is much, and what he has heard and imagined about the animal, which is more, are inextricably blended. Telling a tale of fancy, he will make the coyote very real; coming down to facts of natural history, he will make the coyote fanciful. Without irreverence, he asserts that the coyote is, "next to God, the smartest person on earth." In prodigal narratives illustrative of this smartness, he blends folklore and fact so indiscriminately that a scientist who is nothing more than a scientist rejects all — a mental procedure as unreasonable as accepting all.

But the Mexican, following Indian tradition, delights most in telling tales in which this "smartest animal on earth, next to God," shows himself utterly stupid and is duped by every other creature in the animal kingdom. The Mexican tales have more point

[305]

than the Indian originals; most purely Indian tales end in the un-focused way that snow melts on the ground. Furthermore, the Mexican tales are often infused with a certain Spanish satire and sophistication. Yet they are seldom told by the fair-skinned *gachupines*, the proud *hidalgos* (sons of somebody), the *Señor* attorneys and the *Señor* engineers of the city. The Mexicans who tell them are *los de abajo* — the underdogs. It is no fun to have the smart and the well-advantaged succeed. The fun lies in hav-ing the cunning smart-aleck victimized by his own victims and his own overreaching. The sympathies of the underdogs are al-ways with the helpless. Their heroes are the heroes of the humble Uncle Remus folk. Even such helpless creatures as crickets and frogs when pitted against the master of circumvention force him out the little end of the horn.

This is not a book about the nature of folklore or about the folk who tell it. It is about coyotes, but to understand the thing seen, one must understand the eyes that see it. The Mexican underdog, despite his credulity, understands his own eyes pretty well, and this understanding comes from the Spanish rather than from the Indian in him. A little tale I heard in New Mexico will somewhat explain the eyes through which we shall be looking. No "pure quill" Indian ever looked into himself with such ironic objectivity.

One time a burro driver was beating the whey out of his son Francisco when a friend appeared.

"But, *compadre*," the friend exclaimed, "why are you thus without mercy lashing our Francisco?"

"I'll tell you," replied the burro driver. "Here I have been making plans for the time when I am rich. I will have a cow. She will give so much milk that we will have all we can drink and all the cheese we can eat. Besides that, we will have cheese to sell. We will have money to throw at the birds. One thing I will buy will be a blue bowl. It will be a beautiful bowl, as blue as the sky, with little painted figures on it coming up to the rim so that they can look over inside at the beautiful white milk.

"And here, *compadre,* I have been telling my sons how the beautiful blue bowl full of milk will be set on the board with Francisco on one side of it and Juanito on the other side of it. Francisco can drink out of his side of the blue bowl and Juanito can drink out of his side. But listen! This burro of a Francisco says he will not drink out of the blue bowl with his brother. Now, *compadre,* you comprehend with what reason I beat him."

A Mexican proverb, which is probably Spanish, says that what comes out of the water goes into the water. Fables brought over by the Spaniards found the New World environment as congenial as Spanish horses and cattle found them. Reynard the Fox as chief protagonist in the fables did not survive — by name. Coyote took Reynard's place, sometimes only in name, sometimes in nature as well. The "Coyote" that one meets in Arabian Nights stories told in a pueblo on the Rio Grande is only a substituted name and bears little relation to the coyote who argued with the horned frog and got paid back for swallowing him. Scholars cannot be arbitrary on plot origins. If the science of comparative folklore has discovered anything, it is that the situations in most folk tales are common to all continents and races. European influences on tales of the American Indians are discernible not so much in plot as in emphasis on conduct. Despite interchanges and substitutions, American Coyote and European Reynard remain, as characters, as distinct from each other as Navajo hunter and British banker, or as Mexican ranchero and French diplomatist.

In the European tradition, Reynard is a dissembler who "can blow with all winds and paint his own mischief in false colors." He is adept ever in twisting the true cause the wrong way. Above all, he is an inventor, fertile in imagination and adroit in fancy, making fools of both impotent innocents and conniving potentates. He plays tricks on Bruin the bear, on Tibert the cat, on the ram, on the lordly Chanticleer, on Isegrim the wolf. He dresses like a monk to lay paw on rabbit; he plays dead in order to get the rook's head within reach of his jaws. With fawning and flattery, he wraps King Lion and Queen Lioness around his little finger. His duplicities are made to satirize priests and monks. His crimes and extrications cast ridicule not only upon the social institutions of Mediaeval Europe but upon the weaknesses of mankind of all time. His brazen self-assurance is magnificent. "Let no sorrow affright you," he says to his dear nephew Greybeard, the badger. "Let us be cheerful and pleasant together, for though the King and all the court would swear my death, yet will I be exalted above them all. Well may they prate and jangle, and tire themselves with their counsels; but without the help of my wit and policy, neither can the court nor commonwealth have any long continuance." Etymologically, the name Reynard means "Strong in Counsel." Reynard the Fox lives up to that name.[2]

What the artist Aesop, towards six centuries before Christ, created in those fables — some of them about the fox — that bear his name and what he took from folk tradition cannot be determined. Certainly, Reynard the Fox was a folk character tens of centuries before Chaucer, La Fontaine and Goethe breathed their geniuses into him — and left him more of a folk character than ever. Satire and "similitudes of men" inform the whole Reynard tradition.

Irony often sharpens the original Coyote stories, but Coyote's deceptions are never directed toward the Medicine Man and other social institutions. Priests and palm-readers have never been satirists in any society. Indian society was at once too unsophisticated and too dominated by religious taboos and ceremonials to produce satire. Had a Voltaire appeared, he would have been unable to survive tribal inquisitions. Native Indian stories are as uncritical of the affairs of men as are the tall tales of twentieth-century America — tales without either the charm of simplicity or the wit of urbanity.

The dry appraisal of life characteristic of the Spanish genius was infused into the mixed-bloods of New Spain. In time it came to be reflected in many Mexican stories about Coyote. Now for the stories themselves.

REPAYING GOOD WITH EVIL

ONE AUGUST DAY in the year 1936 I was at a small ranch leased by my brother in the Brush Country about fifty miles north of the Rio Grande. There were two men besides myself: a coyote trapper working for the government, and a vaquero named Mariano. Mariano lived by himself but had an ancient Ford car, his *cucaracha*, in which he occasionally drove to town. On this particular morning his saddle horse came up missing; not a horse could be caught, and the "cockroach" did "not wish to go." As Mariano said, it was "Sunday with us." I watched the panting paisanos water at the tank; I pumped the trapper for all the coyote lore he knew; then I begged Mariano to tell me a coyote story. This is what he told.

One time a rattlesnake got caught under a rock so that he could not move. A duck came walking along, and the rattlesnake called out, "Brother Duck, please shove this rock so that I can free myself."

"With all pleasure," said the duck, and he shoved the rock with his strong breast.

As soon as the rattlesnake was free, he said: "I have been held prisoner a long time and am hungry. I will eat you." He was in front of the duck and ready to strike, and the duck was without power to run.

"No," said the duck, "that would not be just."

"Why not just?" asked the rattlesnake.

"I have done you a good deed, and like a Christian you should do as you would be done by," the duck said.

"But do you not know," responded the rattlesnake, "that a good deed is repaid with evil?"

[309]

"No, I do not know that," the duck said. "Let us find a judge."

"The truth is so well known that I agree to leave the matter to a judge," said the rattlesnake.

So the two started off, the rattlesnake keeping close to the duck. Before they had gone very far they came upon a venerable burro.

"Here is a sage being," the rattlesnake said. "Ask him if a good deed is not repaid with an evil one."

The duck put the question to the burro.

"Yes," replied the burro, "a good deed is always repaid with an evil one. Behold me. For a lifetime, I worked for my master. I worked when I had nothing to eat. I worked whether it was hot or cold, wet or dry. I worked without complaint, always steadily, even if not swiftly. With reason I was trusted. What is the result? Now that I am old and weak and my back is one great sore from packsaddles, my master has turned me out to starve. In the end, nothing but evil is paid for good."

"One judge is not enough," said the duck. "Let us consult another."

"I accept," said the rattlesnake. "You will see."

The two went on. Soon they came upon an ox. He was lying down chewing his cud, but from the way his bones stuck out it was plain that he had little to eat.

"There is a calm and just judge," said the rattlesnake. "State the case to him."

The duck asked the ox the same question he had asked the burro.

"We judge by what we know," replied the ox. "Look at me. For many years I pulled my master's plow and his cart and the sled on which water was hauled to his cabin. It was work, work, work. I was tired at times, but I was always patient and I always pulled when the word was given. Now what is the result? I no longer have strength. My legs tremble with my own weight. So

I have been turned out to graze, but not that I may have rest and be free. Oh, no. My master thinks that this skeleton will gain a little flesh. Then he will butcher me to make jerky out of my flesh and soup out of my bones. A good deed is repaid with an evil deed. That is my judgment."

"These judges are prejudiced," said the duck. "I appeal the case to that coyote I see coming yonder. Get between me and him and ask him the question."

"I am willing to give you the benefit of the wise," the rattlesnake replied. The coyote came near, and the rattlesnake stated the case to him.

The coyote scratched his ear. "Before I render a decision," he said, "I will have to be shown exactly in what position you were when the duck freed you."

This answer pleased the duck, and the rattlesnake was willing to demonstrate. So all three went back to the rock that had been on the rattlesnake's back.

"Now lie down and allow me to place the rock just as it was before the duck rolled it off you," the coyote said.

The rattlesnake placed himself in position and the coyote pushed the rock on top of him.

"Is that how you were?" asked the coyote.

"Exactly thus," responded the rattlesnake.

"Then stay that way," the coyote laughed. "If good is repaid with evil, this time the evil brings good to the duck."

"Think you," concluded Mariano, "that in this world a good is repaid with an evil?"

"Perhaps yes, perhaps no," I replied.

"Yes, it seems to me," Mariano concluded. "Only rarely do those who raise themselves high do so by straight means."

Sometimes, as the tale varies, the coyote frees the serpent, is about to be rewarded with death and then is rescued by a clever judge. As Riley Aiken [8] tells it, after the coyote had beguiled the false serpent back under the rock from which "a wise man" had freed him, the wise man said:

"It isn't right to leave him to die this way."

"It's his own affair," said the coyote, "but you will not deny that I saved your life."

"Why deny?" the man said. "I proclaim my debt. Listen, Brother Coyote, I own a ranch near here. Beginning tomorrow, you come at eight o'clock every morning. The dog will be tied up and there'll be a fat hen in a sack for you. Every morning, remember."

"Good!" the coyote cried out. "That is repaying good with good."

Never did any other coyote find life so easy. Every morning at eight o'clock this coyote met the man. Always the hen that the man turned out of the sack was fat. Before long, however, the coyote complained that his appetite was bad and that he must have a *traguito* before eating. So the man rationed a drink of *mezcal* to go with the chicken. Then, within a few days, the coyote complained that the *mezcal* had increased his appetite so much that one hen would not satisfy it. The man added another hen to the daily allowance. Next he had to increase the *traguito* to a whole bottle of *mezcal*.

The man was not happy with these growing demands. From the first his dog had been against giving chickens to a coyote. Every morning he growled at being tied up. "It was right," the man told him, "to reward my rescuer with a chicken each morning, but now he extorts. He has become a bandit. He is repaying good with evil."

"Tomorrow," the dog growled, "your coyote friend will demand three hens a day. Just watch."

"That would indeed be too much," the man said. "What do you advise?"

"Put me in the sack, instead of the third hen," the dog said. "I'll settle the account."

Two days later the coyote announced that he was not getting enough to live on. "When I was a whelp," he said, "my mother called me Never-Full and my father called me Empty-Belly. In paying good for good you must satisfy my nature."

"Brother Coyote," the man answered, "you seem to have forgotten how contented you were in the beginning with one hen a day. That was our contract, and you said that thus good is repaid with good."

"Time changes all," the coyote responded. "You still owe me for your life. As long as you live, that will be your debt. Now I require three bottles of *mezcal* and three hens every morning."

"Very well," the man said. "*Mañana.*"

The next morning at eight o'clock the man came out to meet the coyote with three sacks and three bottles.

The coyote drank a bottle. "*Ay carray!*" he shouted. "Toss me out a hen."

The man untied a sack and out scuttled the hen. The coyote devoured her, feathers and all. He drank another bottle. "*Ay qué carray!*" he shouted. "Toss me out a hen."

The man untied another sack, and the coyote devoured his second hen. "My appetite grows with age and wisdom," he said. "Another bottle."

He drank the *mezcal* with entire gusto. "*Ah qué carray!*" he shouted. "Now for the sweet thing that comes last."

The man untied the third sack, and the dog rushed out. He was raging. The poor coyote was too drunk to fight and too stuffed to run. Just before the dog's fangs sank into his throat he called out, "Call off your dog. It is not right to repay good with evil."

"Perhaps it is not right," the man answered, "but *es la costumbre.*"

In William Caxton's *The Historye of Reynart the Foxe*, which he translated from the Dutch and printed in 1481, a man unsnares a serpent on oath to do him "none harme ne hurte," but as soon as he is free the serpent announces that "the nede of hungre may cause a man to breke his othe." Called upon to judge between the two, Reynard induces the serpent to demonstrate how the snare held him and thus, with much philosophy on "free will," saves the man. A serpent large enough to devour a person does not belong to Europe any more than to North America; it belongs to Asia. Joseph Jacobs, in his *The Most Delectable History of Reynard the Fox*, traced the tale back to India. As related by Sahagún,* it seems to be native to Mexico; this earliest known American form of it entails no debate on morals. Philosophizing over whether good is repaid with evil or with good was undoubtedly an European importation. In the character of Coyote, however, the Mexicans had a practiced actor ready and eager to take the leading role in the drama.

"Tell us some moral thing," the Canterbury pilgrims demanded of the licentious Pardoner. The Spanish "moral thing" whetted Mexican appetite for more. As the tale proliferated from repeated tellers and tellings, another question, it would seem, evolved: Which is more coyote-natured, Man or Coyote? The tale as told by a ranchero of Coahuila proceeds from the rescue of man by coyote from rattlesnake as follows.

"Señor Coyote," the man said after the rattlesnake was back under the rock, "you have done me the greatest favor that one person can do another. You have given me my life. Come with me to my house and accept a sack of chickens."

They walked until they arrived at the chaparral near the man's house.

"You must wait here," the man said, "while I go for the sack of chickens. I have two very fierce dogs and a wife no less fierce."

So the coyote waited in the thicket while the man went directly to the hen house. There he selected five of the largest and

* Quoted on page 256.

fattest hens and put them in a sack. He was moving as quietly as he could, but his wife heard the chickens squawking and cackling and rushed to them. She saw the sack. She knew every one of her hens by name.

"You have taken the five fattest and largest," she said to her husband. "*Por Dios*, why?"

He explained how the coyote had saved his life from the snake of false philosophy. "One good deed calls for another," he said, "and as a small reward I wish to present my savior with these hens."

The woman was furious. "You are stupid," she said, "to consider giving our best hens to a coyote. In truth, it would be stupid to give him even the runt of the flock."

Leaving the hens in the sack, the husband tried to quiet her. He asked for a cup of coffee, and went into the house with her. While he was drinking the coffee, she stole back to the hen house, took the five hens out of the sack, and put into it the two fierce dogs. Returning, she said nothing more on the subject, and in a little while the man went outside, picked up the sack, and carried it by a trail through the bushes to the coyote.

"Well, *compadre* Coyote," he said, "excuse my delay, but I have brought you here the five finest hens of our little ranch. It is a small reward for saving my life, but I try thus to repay good with good. Do you wish that I turn them loose one at a time or all at once?"

"All at once," replied the coyote — "the banquet of my life."

The man opened the sack, and out leaped the fierce dogs. They were chewing on the coyote before he could take his mind off the banquet. He managed to break away, however, and as he ran from the thicket, he howled out to the man:

"No more proof is necessary. Now I know that in this life good is repaid with evil."

MORAL THINGS

IT WAS NOT "some moral thing" that I expected from Feliz. He had ridden with Pancho Villa, and as he guided me into the wide and waterless Bolsón de Mapimí of northern Mexico, I rode a chunky brown horse out of a mare that Villa had given him. Probably the mare did not cost Villa much. The brown horse was "of the race that endures." Once Feliz pointed to a low mountain a day's ride distant and said that there he and other Villistas watered their horses by feeding them prickly pear from which the thorns were singed off in a cave, so that the smoke would not make a sign to the enemy.

This was one of the stories he told in the desert night.

One time a poor coyote tortured with mange was wandering over the mesa when he met a lion.

"What are you doing, Brother Coyote?" asked the lion.

"Why, Brother Lion," answered the coyote, "I am failing to find my life. My legs are so weak I can't run a cottontail rabbit down. My eyes water so that I can't see a grasshopper at my feet. My nose has grown so feeble that it cannot smell out even a billy goat across the road."

"But, Brother Coyote," said the lion, "your way of getting a living is shameful. The goats and chickens you are accustomed to steal belong to poor people. If you will come with me and follow my manner of living, you will not injure the poor. I fatten on big game belonging to the rich. I see a band of horses or a herd of cattle owned by some rich rancher and I raid them. I'd be ashamed to bother the chickens and goats of poor folk. Come on and I'll show you how to be noble in your killing."

So the coyote went with the lion, and they came to the edge of a lake. Trails led into it from the grassy range far away, and beside one of these trails a leafy tree was growing.

"Look out yonder, Brother Coyote," said the lion. "Do you see those cattle approaching?"

"Yes, Brother Lion."

"Well, now, you hide yourself and watch me."

The coyote sneaked into some underbrush. He watched the lion climb into the tree and stretch himself out on a limb overhanging the trail. Within a short time the cattle came stringing underneath on their way to water. The lion leaped upon a fat heifer, dug his claws into her loins, and with his powerful jaws fixed his fangs into her neck just back of the head. She bellowed and pitched and tried to throw him off, but the harder she struggled, the deeper the lion dug in. He broke her neck and feasted on the fattest parts of her carcass. Then, belly full and heart contented, he licked his thankful chops and told the coyote to help himself.

While the lion ate, the coyote had been circling him in a trot. Now he bolted for the carcass, and began gorging as he had not gorged in months. That very day he began to fatten.

The lion adopted him and kept killing enough for two. Within a very short time the coyote was fat and sleek and strong. The fleas had left him, and fresh, clean fur covered spots that had been mangy.

Then the lion said: "Brother Coyote, I am going into a far country. I go alone. You are now strong. You have learned how to kill. Remember to let goats and chickens and such property of poor people alone and to prey only on stock belonging to the rich ranchers. *Adiós.*"

"Good-bye, Brother Lion," the coyote cried. "You have taught me the ways of noble hunters. I will follow your example."

The lion went away. The coyote remained full of confidence. Before long he began to get hungry. He saw some cattle coming to water. He noted that they would pass under a tree that had a low limb overhanging the trail. With a great deal of trouble he crawled out on the limb, eager to try his skill.

The first animal that came underneath was a fat bull. The coyote jumped on it. But his claws would not hold and dig into the bull's back. He could not fasten his jaws on the thick neck. With one pitch and two bellows, the bull threw him off. Then the bull gored him and bellowed louder. The other cattle came at the smell of blood and gored him more. His meat was chopped fine enough for chile con carne.

"This is to teach that every man had better stick to what he can do, and not make a dead coyote out of himself by presuming to do what is foreign to his nature."

"To give *atole* [corn meal gruel] with the finger" is to deceive with false promises. At a camp on a very old mule trail — the *camino real*, or royal road, of the Sierra Madre — over which many millions in silver bars from the Batopilas Mines used to be transported, a peon in sandals told this fable. He had no idea that it was an adaptation from Aesop, coyote and heron taking the place of fox and crane.

One time a coyote who lived by a lake invited a heron to eat dinner with him. Taking care not to come within grasp of the coyote, the heron accepted the invitation. When his long legs brought him up to the *ramada* — brush-covered shed — in front of the coyote's house, he saw the white cloth already upon the table. Then the coyote's *señora* came out and sprinkled *pinole* (sweetened meal of parched corn) upon the white cloth. The heron was very fond of *pinole*, and the coyote bowed to him and said, "My friend, come and let us dine."

But with his long bill the heron could pick up only one little particle of the ground corn at a time, and when he swallowed that his throat could hardly feel it, it was so little.

"Eat, eat, my friend," the coyote kept saying, and with his

broad tongue he would lap the cloth clean. His wife sprinkled more *pinole* and thus dinner went on. After a while the heron thanked him and flew away.

A few days later he saw the coyote at the lake "Señor Coyote, he said, "you seem fond of fish."

"I am very fond of fish," the coyote said.

Then the heron invited him to a fish dinner at his house the next day. When the coyote trotted up, he saw the table already spread in the open. It was covered with a white cloth. The heron's *señora* was setting long-necked bottles containing little fishes on the table. At the smell of them the coyote wiggled his tail with joy.

"Come, Señor Coyote, and let us eat," the heron said.

Both sat down and the coyote put his mouth to a bottle. The smell was all he could get out. His tongue could not get down deep enough through the mouth of the bottle to lick olive oil off the little fishes. He watched the heron putting his long bill into his bottle and pulling out the fishes with entire ease. As soon as the heron emptied one bottle, his wife gave him another, and she would give Señor Coyote a fresh bottle also. He was too proud to admit that he could not do what the heron could do, and he would not ask for a plate into which to empty the fish.

"Won't you have some more?" the heron asked.

"No, I thank you, Señor Heron," the coyote said. "Now I must go."

That night he made up a new song to sing to the stars. This song said. "It's a poor host who does not think of his guest."

The coyote and the crow, as the folk in Mexico tell, have had many talks, many experiences with each other in which the crow often shows more discernment than the coyote. But not always. One time a crow out hunting for food met a prowling coyote not far from her nest.

"Oh, Brother Coyote," the crow said, "I am compelled to

hunt a long way off from my nest in order to get food for my darling, beautiful little nestlings. Yet I fear to leave them alone. I wonder if you would be willing to keep watch against preying animals while I am gone?"

"Certainly, certainly, Sister Crow," replied the coyote with all sympathy. "Only show me where they are, so that my eyes will not leave them."

"Yes, indeed," answered the mother crow. "Come this way. It is not far," and she began flying low over the ground, every once in a while alighting and hopping along ahead of Brother Coyote.

"Because there are no trees in this desert country," she confided, "I had to build my nest in a low bush. There it is now. Just peep at the lovely little babies in it, but please do not get close enough to disturb them. They are such tender little mites! Look! The feathers do not yet cover their bodies!"

"I would not think of disturbing them," smiled the coyote. "I'll just stay around within watching distance. I need to stop a while and play with my fleas anyhow."

The crow flew swiftly away. She was no sooner out of sight than the coyote sneaked up to the bush, pawed the nest down and ate up the baby crows. They were so small that one of them hardly made half a swallow. He was still nosing the broken nest when "caw, caw, caw" came the cry of the returning mother, bringing a grasshopper.

When she saw the destruction, she was heart-broken. "Oh, my beautiful, helpless little darlings!" she cried. "How, O treacherous coyote, could you have the heart to kill them?"

"It did not take much heart to destroy those naked gawks," the coyote answered. "You told me they were beautiful. One good look at their ugliness told me you had made a mistake in supposing them yours. I am surprised at the way you take on."

"Oh, oh," cried the crow. "Listen, you mocker without heart: *For mothers there are no ugly children.*"

In another *cuento* a mother fox entrusts her young to Brother

Coyote. After he betrays her and eats the younglings, she cries out, "No mother ever sees her own child as other than beautiful." Thus the simple stories of rightly simple folk often end with a moral truth.

One time in the middle of summer in a very dry land a coyote's nose brought him to the edge of a deserted well. It was not very deep, but the water stood far too low for lapping. While, quivering with thirst, he panted on the rim, a goat came up. This goat was just as thirsty as the coyote. His thirst made him forget his enemy, and the thirst of the coyote made him forget all hunger. He did not forget his cunning, however.

"Brother Goat," he said, "there is no remedy except that we jump in. It is better to die in cool, sweet water than to burn of thirst on the burning ground. The water is not deep, I know. We shall not drown. Perhaps God will help us get out."

"Y-e-e-s-s," bleated the goat, "I will risk my life for a drink of water."

They both jumped into the well. As the coyote had said, the water was shallow. He lapped and lapped the water with his tongue. The goat sucked and sucked the water down his throat.

After they were full and refreshed, the coyote said, "Brother Goat, I am thinking of a way to get out of this hole. Do as I say, and all will be well."

"All right, Brother Coyote," the goat quavered, "let us have your idea."

"That is sensible, Brother Goat," the coyote complimented his fellow prisoner. "Now place your front feet up on the wall of the well as high as you can. At the same time, raise your head and throw back your horns. Then I'll jump upon your back, then gather my feet on your hard head, and next leap out. When I am safely out, I can reach down and pull you out after me."

The goat followed directions and the coyote jumped out of

[321]

the well. But when he was safe, he turned with a laugh and said, "Brother Goat, I'll have to tell you good-bye."

"You have played me false. You have tricked me."

"Friend," retorted the coyote, "if you had as much astuteness in your brains as you have hairs in your beard, you would have thought how you were going to get out before you jumped in."

In the words of the storyteller, "The lesson of this fable is that we should consider the consequences of what we are about to do before we do it."

THE COYOTE AND THE OLD DOG

HAVE NO CONFIDENCE in the man who does not know that he does not know," said Isidro. I knew that his wise saw was an introduction to something. Isidro was the soft-voiced, thin little *mesero*, or waiter, at the old Saenz Hotel in Saltillo. He had the natural dignity of all peasants native to mountains and was without one tincture of the flunkyism characteristic of servitors in machine-efficient hotels. Few gringos came to the Saenz in those days, and I was as free there from the domination of time as were the shadows and the sunshine in the portaled patio and the burros sleeping on the plaza. We always had *frijoles* (pinto beans) for dinner and we always had *nacionales* (pinto beans) for supper. It was one summer evening after all the other guests, less than a dozen, had left the never-hurried dining room that Isidro told the tale, with many a joyful laugh between us.*

One time there was an old dog wandering out in the country half-starved. He met with a coyote.

"Listen, good old dog," said the coyote, "what are you doing?"

"I am looking for something to eat," said the dog. "When I was a boy my master gave me plenty to eat, but now that I am old and cannot fight the beasts off the chickens and goats, I get nothing. I go as you see me seeking some morsel in the desert. Seldom do I find it. I starve."

"Listen, good old dog," said the coyote. "Describe to me the

---

* He had never read it or other tales he knew in a book. Like all good tales of the folk, it came from far away and long ago, no one can say whence or when. After I heard it, I found a not radically different version in *El Folklore Literario de México*, by Reubén M. Campos, Mexico, D. F., 1929, 64–67. Another version is in Manuel Gamio's monumental *La Población del Valle de Teotihuacán*, Mexico, 1922, II, 301–304. In a popular Russian tale, it is a bear that be-

fattest and plumpest chicken in the barnyard of your master, and I will do you a favor."

"The chicken that is fattest and plumpest," answered the old dog, "is a young rooster marked red and white."

"Very well, I'll see you in the morning," said the coyote, and he made his farewell.

The next morning early the mistress of the farm where the dog lived was feeding corn to the chickens. "Oh, look," she cried, "at the beautiful red and white rooster! Did anybody ever see a rooster so delightful!"

The old dog was creeping along behind the housewife, and just then the coyote jumped out from behind a prickly pear and seized the rooster in his teeth and made off toward the brush. The woman yelled and the master came out yelling, and the old dog barked and began running after the coyote as fast as he could run. He was catching up with the coyote when both disappeared in the brush.

"Ah, look at our old dog!" said the master. "Maybe he is still of some worth."

Hidden in the brush, the coyote gave the rooster to the old dog and told him to carry it back to the house. It had not been injured. So the old dog came back carrying the rooster in his teeth.

"Look! Look!" cried the mistress. "Here is our beautiful rooster restored. Not a bone in his leg is broken. Not a feather has been pulled from his handsome tail."

"The old dog is still worthy," said the master. "It is a shame that we have not fed him."

"Here," he called to a servant. "Take this money and go to the market and buy some meat to give to the poor old fellow."

---

friends the old cast-off dog, who invites him to a party at his house. They both eat and drink, but the bear drinks more. The people are singing out beyond the kitchen and he insists on singing too. When the people run in, he runs away — and there is no violence.

So the old dog had meat again as he had had when he was "a boy," and now he was living very contented.

Not long after that he was walking out in the countryside and met the coyote.

"How, how, good old dog?" asked the coyote.

"Fine, fine," answered the old dog. "When I restored the chicken, my master and mistress were so pleased that they bought me meat, and now I am living as well and as contented as I lived when I was a boy. Many thanks to you."

"That is well," said the coyote. "And, now, how will you pay your thanks?"

"Listen, Brother Coyote," said the old dog. "Two nights hence my master's son is to marry, and there is to be a great feast and dance. Already a hog, a kid, a turkey and chickens have been killed and the women are making enchiladas, tamales, mole, and other delicious dishes. Besides the bounty of food, there will be tequila, pulque, cognac, and other drink. You come. I shall be waiting for you outside the kitchen door, and while the people are having the ceremony, I shall conduct you inside."

The wedding night came and with it the coyote. The old dog led him into the kitchen. It was stuffed with foods, but the coyote ate only chicken and rice. He was craving the cognac. He drained a bottle, and then he was thirsty. To relieve his thirst he drank pulque.

"Oo-lah, friend of mine," he called out to the old dog, "I'm going to sing."

"In the Virgin's name, not here, not now," warned the old dog. "S-s-ssh. Be silent. They will hear you and kill you."

"No," the coyote persisted. "I have not fear and I have desires to sing."

With that he began his song. The people rushed in, and one man ended him with a *saca tripas.**

* Literally, "it gets guts" – a scimitar-like knife.

[325]

BROTHER COYOTE AND BROTHER CRICKET

ONE SUMMER EVENING about sundown a coyote trotting across the plain put his foot down on a tuft of grass wherein a cricket was singing "*Sereno en aquellos campos*" — "Peacefully in those fields."

The cricket jumped out and cried, "But, Brother Coyote, why are you destroying my palace?"

"I really did not know you lived here until you exposed yourself," the coyote said.

"You are crude and you insult me," the cricket said. He was ready to spring away.

"Insult you!" the coyote jeered. "Why, you dwarf, I am merely seeking my living, and now that I have you, I am going to eat you up. I had rather have a red watermelon or a fat kid, but I eat a cricket when it's handy. Maybe you will fill the hollow in one of my wisdom teeth."

"But, Brother Coyote," the cricket said, now in his soothing way, "it is not fair."

The coyote sat down on the carpet of grass. "Brother Cricket," he said, "you know that when nature offers itself, it is fair for nature to accept."

"But, Brother Coyote, you haven't given me a chance."

"Chance?" exclaimed the coyote. "Why, what sort of chance do you expect?"

"I want to fight a duel," the cricket said.

"You fight a duel with me?" And the coyote laughed.

"Yes, fight a duel with you," the cricket said. "If I win, then

my song will go on. If you win, then I'll fill the hollow in one of your respectable teeth."

The coyote looked away off across the plain, and saw a crow flying down in play at the waving tail of a striped skunk. "Well," he said, "perhaps the people need a comedy. All right, we'll have your duel, Brother Cricket."

"Thank you very much, Brother Coyote," the cricket said.

"Now I sit here trembling at the sight of your armor and weapons," the coyote said. "But go on and name your terms."

"It is agreed," said the cricket. "You go and get your army together, and I will go and get my army together. Tomorrow when the sun is straight overhead, you have your army on the prairie just above the water called the Tank of the Coons, and I will have my army in the thicket in the draw just below the tank. On the hour we shall be ready to engage in mortal combat."

"That is clear, General Cricket," said the coyote. "Until tomorrow at high noon, *adiós*."

"*Adiós*, General Coyote."

That night General Coyote went east and west, north and south, summoning in his high voice his forces to gather on the prairie above the Tank of the Coons. He summoned the lobo, the badger, the tiger of the deep canyon, the panther of the rimrock, the wildcat of the chaparral, the coon, the possum, the sharp fox, and all the other people with claws and teeth.

And in a song General Cricket summoned his forces also — the horseflies, the mosquitoes, the honey bees, the bumblebees, the yellow jackets, the black hornets, and even a colony of red ants — all the people that have stingers and can stick. He told them to gather in the thicket in the draw below the Tank of the Coons.

Long before high noon, the people of fang and claw were assembling on the prairie above the water tank. General Coyote was trotting about, looking this way and that way, smelling and listening. The sun stood straight up, and still he could not see one sign of General Cricket's army.

[329]

Finally he called the fox and ordered him to scout out the position of the enemy. With his long nose pointed ahead, his ears alert and his eyes peeled, the fox went trotting down the draw. General Coyote was watching him. When he came to the edge of the thicket, the fox flattened to the ground and began twisting into the brush. Just as he was poking his keen snout into a clump of whitebrush to see and smell more closely, General Cricket ordered a battalion of black hornets to assault him.

They did, all at once. They stuck their stingers into his ears, into the corners of his eyes, into his nostrils, into his flanks, into every spot of his body where hair is short and skin is tender. He snapped and pitched, but only for a minute. He turned seventeen somersaults on the ground, and the black hornets came thicker. Then he streaked for the tank of water. He dived to escape his assaulters, and went to the bottom.

Immediately almost he came back up and, sticking his long, long mouth out of the water, cried at the top of his voice, "General Coyote, retreat! The enemy are upon us!"

General Cricket had already ordered the yellow jackets to attack the army of giants on the prairie, and the war cries of the bumblebees were in the air.

"Retreat!" the fox shrieked again.

General Coyote tucked his tail between his legs and retreated and every soldier in the army tucked his tail and retreated also — all except the bobcat. He retreated without tucking his tail. That is how General Cricket won the duel with General Coyote.

Thus a person should avoid being vainglorious and considering himself shrewder than he is. He may be outwitted by his own vanity.

THE RACE IS NOT TO THE SWIFT

THIS *cuento*, rather inane it seems to me, recurs over and over in the published folklore of Mexico and may be heard over and over by anybody who listens for tales. I heard this version in the mountains of Chihuahua occupied by the Tarahumare Indians.

One time a coyote came up to a pool of water and acted as if he were thirsty. He was not. He wanted to catch a frog. A frog on the other side of the pool saw him and said, "Señor Coyote, I will bet you that I can outrun you in a race."

"What will you bet, Señor Frog?"

"I will bet three flies," the frog said.

"Very well," said the coyote.

"Tomorrow at this hour you be here, and we will race down the draw to that stump." The frog pointed to a stump about ninety yards away.

The coyote went off, and the frog went to two of his friends and explained his idea. He himself would start the race — and be left behind. One of them must get under a rock about midway of the course, and the other under a root of the stump. When the coyote got to the rock, the first friend must jump out just ahead of him and say, "Well, I'm still running." Then he must jump back under the rock. Just as the coyote got to the stump, the other frog must jump out and say, "Well, I've beat you." The frogs agreed.

The next day the coyote was back at the pool to run the race. He and the frog got set. The frog counted "Three," and they both jumped, but the frog soon got back into his grassy hiding place by the edge of the water. The coyote went racing forward. Just as he was reaching the midway rock, the frog waiting there jumped ahead and said, "Well, I'm still running." The coyote spurred himself and ran harder, and that frog got back into his hiding place. Just as the coyote was about to reach the stump, the frog there jumped out and called, "Well, I've beat you."

"I don't see how you did it," the coyote cried, as he wheeled and looked back to the pool. The only frog in sight was the one at the stump.

The coyote had to pay three flies.

COYOTE AND FOX *

ONE MOONLIGHT NIGHT while a fox was drinking at a water hole, a coyote stole up behind him and said, "Ah-ha, Señor Zorro, I have caught you at last, and now I'm going to eat you."

But the fox is very astute. He said, "Wait a minute, and I will show you something much more savory. Look down there in the clean water. Did you ever see such a beautiful cheese?"

"It is of truth a fine-looking cheese," the coyote said as he gazed at the reflection of the moon in the water. "How big and round it is! I'll walk right out and get it."

"No, don't walk," the fox advised. "It is under the clear water. The moon shining on it makes it look near. You will have to dive for it. Jump in with your mouth open, and when you come to it, bite hard."

The coyote opened his mouth and dived. When he got back to the bank, his jaws were full of mud, and the fox was gone.

The coyote knew that the fox seldom comes out in daytime, but the next morning he sat watching for him at the water hole. The only person who came was an old terrapin. He was thirsty and came for a drink.

"I'm hungry," the coyote said to him, "and I'm going to eat you up."

The terrapin pulled his feet and his head in and said, "You can't break my shell on a rock, but be careful not to tumble me over into the water. If you do, I'll drown."

* This is one of the *cuentos* told me by the hotel waiter named Isidro in Saltillo. The date was August 19, 1933. As the *gente* (folk) tell such tales, the endless episodes in which coyote is fooled are ascribed interchangeably to the fox, rabbit, opossum, skunk, and other creatures. Some of the episodes have been printed scores, perhaps hundreds, of times.

[333]

"All right, I'll drown you and then pull you out of your shell," the coyote said.

He tumbled the terrapin into the water, and the terrapin swam away out of sight.

The coyote went on. He did not care much for terrapin, anyhow. He wanted to get even with that fox. After a while he came to a *carrizal* — a canebrake. He was smelling all around it, and he discovered the fox curled up in there.

"This time you will not fool me," he called. "What are you doing here, anyhow?"

"I am here," the fox responded, "because I heard some people planning to bring tamales, chicken cooked in white wine, sweet bread, and other good things to the spring at the edge of the *carrizal* this very afternoon. They are having a picnic. They will put their baskets of food and bottles down in the cane to hide them and wander around a while before they eat. The baskets will be covered with white cloths embroidered with red roosters. I shall lift these cloths back and choose without molestation. Then, what feasting and drinking and joy there will be in the *carrizal!* Of course, if you eat me now, I shall not be here to enjoy the benefactions."

The coyote was all eagerness. He said, "Well, since there is to be such a fine feast, I had as well enjoy it myself. You get out of the way, and I'll wait in your place."

So the fox ran off and the coyote curled up in the fox's nest to wait. Before long he was asleep. The next thing he knew the *carrizal* was on fire and flames were popping the canes right over him. He escaped with his skin, but all his hair was singed off. He knew that the fox had set the fire. He was so angry that he trembled all over.

His hair was just beginning to grow out again when one day while looking for a rat under a big boulder he came upon the fox asleep.

"You can push against that big boulder all you want to," the coyote said, "but you won't push it over and get away. I'm hungry and it's dinner time."

"Look out, Brother Coyote!" the fox cried. "Can't you see that this boulder leans and that it is about to fall over and crush both of us?"

The coyote looked up. Against broken clouds floating in the sky, the top of the boulder did seem to be leaning.

"I'm so tired of holding it," said the fox, "that unless you help, it will fall before either of us can get away. Push! Quick!"

The coyote put his shoulder against the rock.

"That is a help," the fox said. "You are fresh and can hold on a while. I know where a little kid is staked out right behind the hill. I'll go get it and we'll both eat and have strength, and then somehow we'll get free. Just wait."

Before the coyote could say anything, the fox sprang away. The coyote pushed hard, hard against the boulder. "Hurry back with the kid," he called.

He waited and he waited and he pushed and he pushed. Finally he decided that the fox had betrayed him and was not coming back at all. "Maybe," he groaned to himself, "if I jump straight to one side, the falling boulder won't catch anything but the hairs at the end of my tail."

He gave the longest leap he could make, ran a distance, then stopped and looked back. Of course, the boulder was still standing. Fires of anger were blinding his eyes. Only his nose told him where to go.

One day he was trailing a mole under a *palma* – a kind of yucca – when he looked up and saw the fox eating the wild dates. They were ripe.

"Here now, you traitor!" he called to the fox. "You fooled me once and you fooled me thrice, but you're not going to get away this time. You can climb and I can't, but this happens to be a leaning *palma*, and in one more minute you are going to feel my teeth in your throat."

[335]

"Very well," said the fox, "if there is no remedy, then there is none. But you like chicken better than you like the flesh of an old he-fox, don't you?"

"I admit that," said the coyote, "but I'm going to eat you just the same."

"Just look at those black chickens," said the fox, pointing towards a gathering of buzzards on the ground. "From up here I can see that they are eating a dead coachwhip snake. They are not watching, just filling themselves."

"Since you have shown the chickens to me," said the coyote, "I'll eat one of them before I eat you."

"All right," the fox said. "Keep in the broomweeds. Meanwhile, I'll not move a hair so as not to scare the black chickens."

The coyote was crawling on his belly towards the buzzards. He did not see the fox come down and run off. When he got close to the buzzards, he gave a jump, but they were too far away and all flew.

For many days after this the coyote could not find the fox. One evening he came upon a skunk at a beehive. The skunk was wiggling a stick through the hole and saying, "Read, read, read."

"What are you playing with those bees for?" the coyote asked.

"They are not bees at all," the skunk responded. "I am a schoolmaster, this is our schoolhouse, and these are my pupils. I must keep them studying."

"I am looking for the fox," said the coyote. "Have you seen him?"

"Yes, he passed here about an hour ago," the skunk said. "If you will take care of my school, I will go bring him back."

"I will take care of your school," the coyote said, "but don't tell him that I am here."

"Certainly not," said the skunk, "but you must keep this stick in the hole and keep telling the pupils to read."

The skunk gave the coyote the stick and the coyote went to wiggling it and calling out, "Read, read, read."

Waving his tail, the skunk paced away. He had not seen the fox, but he knew what a deceiver the coyote is and had made up the story to escape him. For a long time the coyote kept wiggling the stick and calling out, "Read, read, read."

He got bored. "That skunk is not coming back," he said to himself. Then he yelled out to the pupils, "Don't read any more. That's enough," and he pulled out the stick and threw it away. As soon as the stick came out of the hole, the bees buzzed out. They flew into the coyote. He ran and he rolled. He rolled and he ran. By the time he got rid of them, his nose was so swollen from stings that he had to breathe through his mouth and his eyelids were so sealed together that he butted into a barrel cactus.

But he got well. He made a new song for himself, and he sang it to the owls. It said: "The fox has played his last trick."

The fox heard him and said nothing. One day while the fox was stalking around a hole into which he had seen two rattlesnakes enter, the coyote came upon him. The fox was listening to the rattlesnakes shake their bells. They never want anybody bothering around them.

"Tell the earth good-bye," the coyote called out before the fox had smelled him. "You have fooled me with the moon, you have fooled me with the *carrizal*, you have fooled me with the boulder, you have fooled me with your black chickens, and you have even taught the skunk to fool me. With reason you have been hiding from me. Now I wonder at your being such a fool as to play around a hole out in plain view of everybody that passes."

"You are mistaken," said the fox. "That hole is my oven. I am sorry that you have found it."

"Your oven, my fleas!" said the coyote.

"Yes, my oven. I am cooking *chicharrones*.* Listen and you

* Cracklings. For some reason, *chicharrones*, like the *cucaracha* (cockroach), are in themselves funny to Mexicans.

[337]

can hear them frying. In a minute you'll be smelling them. I imagine they would be more to your taste than my tough hide."

"*Chicharrones*, did you say?" The coyote was licking his tongue out. "I believe I can smell them," he said.

"Yes, *chicharrones*," the fox went on. "I was just going to step over to my house and get some fresh light bread to eat with them."

"Where is your house?" the coyote asked.

"Right at the root of that red madroña tree where the little cañon comes out of rocks on yonder mountainside," the fox responded. He pointed to a madroña tree in plain sight.

"Very well," the coyote said. "And how do you happen to have fresh light bread in your house?"

"I stole it from the wife of the agrarian in the valley," the fox responded.

The coyote was fonder of *chicharrones* with fresh light bread than of any other food he had ever tasted. His lips were trembling. "See here," he said, "you are probably lying, but I see now where your house is, and I will be watching until you return with the fresh light bread. If you don't bring it, there will not be enough rocks in the mountains to hide you."

The fox trotted away towards the madroña tree on the mountainside, and the coyote put his paws on the ground in front of the "oven" and pointed his ears to listen better to the frying of the *chicharrones*. Presently he got up to smell better and poked his nose into the hole.

When he did, one of the rattlesnakes bit him. The coyote gave one long cry of pain and lay down, but he got well.

Not long after this he saw a rabbit in a valley. The rabbit saw him too and began running through the bushes. The coyote took after him. Around and around they ran. The rabbit could not get out of sight of the coyote, and the coyote could not quite get his teeth into the rabbit. Finally, the rabbit ran into a little hole. While the coyote was smelling of it, he saw the fox coming along, keeping close to some trees.

"Brother Fox," he called, "come over here."

"What is it, Brother Coyote?"

"I have a rabbit shut up in a hole, but I can't get to him. You are slimmer than I am. Squirm down and get him out and I'll give you half of him to eat."

"All right," and the fox began to investigate the hole.

"I am terribly hot and thirsty from running," said the coyote. "With your permission, while you are getting the rabbit out, I am going to step down to the creek for a drink."

"Certainly, Brother Coyote," said the fox. "I will await you."

Then while the coyote was gone, the fox made a quick dash down the hole, caught the rabbit with his teeth, pulled him out, and right there devoured him, bones, blood, hair, and all without leaving one tuft of cotton to tell the story. When the coyote returned, the fox was sitting by the hole, very disconsolate looking.

"Where is our rabbit?" asked the coyote.

"He gave me the slip and got away after all," sighed the fox.

"You are a poor hunter," said the coyote.

"Excuse me, please," said the fox. "Some day I will show you what a fine feast I can provide."

The two parted. That night the fox paid one of his visits to a farmer's hen yard. He had been stealing chickens for a long time, and the farmer had determined to end the thief. He had picked out a delicious pullet, staked her close to the corral and put a trap right by her.

About dark the fox came along, saw the pullet ready for plucking, licked his tongue out and then said to himself: "Something is wrong here. That pullet is a bait, and there is bound to be a trap laid by her."

He turned around and went the other way. Before he had traveled far he met the coyote.

"*Buenas tardes*, Friend Fox," the coyote said.

"Good evening, Brother Coyote," the fox responded. "How are you?"

"Dying of hunger — always hungry," the coyote answered. "I have postponed my little meal off you for the last time."

"How glad I am that we have met," said the fox. "I have had shame ever since I let that rabbit get away. Now I am going to tell you a secret. Of late I have been living off a farmer's chickens. I ate one only a little while ago. Then I caught another and tied her for you. When you see her plumpness and taste the pillow of fat on her back, you will forgive everything, and we shall be as good friends as ever. I was looking for you. Come on."

The coyote followed, very eager for chicken. When they got close to the pullet, the fox said, "There is my little gift. Go up and receive it."

The coyote rushed towards the pullet and just as he got to her he put his foot in a strong trap. With a laugh the fox trotted away.

The next morning the farmer came. "Ah, ha, you scoundrel coyote," he said, "you have been stealing my chickens and now you are caught. It won't take me long to put an end to you."

"Wait, wait," cried the coyote. "I did not eat any of your chickens. It was the fox, and he fooled me into getting caught by the trap set for him."

"Whoever has the stolen goods confesses himself the thief," answered the farmer.

At the end of this story my friend Isidro said, "I went in one end of the canyon and came out the other."

WHY THE COYOTE DOES NOT EAT PEOPLE

ONE TIME [4] the coyote went to see God our Father to ask if He would give coyotes license to eat His children.

God our Father said to him, "Yes, I will give you license if you will fast for a certain time."

Then after the coyote had gone away, God our Father called the *tlacuache* — the opossum — to consult with him on how the coyote might be enticed to break his fast. "You go," He said to the *tlacuache*, "and meet the coyote in a maguey plantation and ask him if he would not like to drink a little *aguamiel*." *

So the *tlacuache* went. On his way he passed through pines, and he gathered some resin and put it in his pouch. He waited at the magueys, and in time the coyote came along. They saluted each other, and then the *tlacuache* said, "How are you getting along, Coyotito †?"

"Well, I thank you."

"Come on and let's drink a little *aguamiel*," the *tlacuache* said.

"No, I cannot do that," responded the coyote. "I am fasting so that God our Father will give me license to eat His children. If I break the fast, He will deny the license."

"Oh," said the *tlacuache*, "this *aguamiel*, you know, is not food and it is not liquor. It is no more than pure water with a little drop of sweet in it."

"No," said the coyote, "not even *aguamiel*, for God will see me, and then He won't give me license to eat His children."

* Just before the stalk of a maguey plant starts to shoot up, it is cut out. The bowl thus left in the plant collects sap intended by nature for the great stalk. This sap, or unfermented juice, is called *aguamiel* (honey-water); it is extracted periodically and fermented into pulque or distilled into *mezcal*.
† The diminutive is a form of endearment — "Dear Little Coyote."

"But God won't see you here in the magueys," the *tlacuache* went on, "and He won't find out anything about the matter. After we have drunk, I will clean your mouth as clean as a whitened deer antler. Come, Coyotito, for just one little smell."

The coyote followed, and the *tlacuache* took the covering off the bowl of a big maguey. "Just a lap, Coyotito," he said.

The coyote squatted down in front of the bowl and smelled. Then he stood up and lapped the *aguamiel*. "It is very savory," he said. "Now you drink."

After the *tlacuache* had drunk, he said, "Now Coyotito, I am going to clean your mouth."

The coyote opened his mouth so wide that his eyes were closed. The *tlacuache* reached into his pouch and pulled out the resin he had gathered at the pines. Then he stuck his little hands into the coyote's mouth and filled the spaces between his teeth with the resin. It had the savor of *aguamiel* in it.

The two struck out across the country. At noon the coyote said, "It is time for me to meet God our Father."

The *tlacuache* went to his house and the coyote went on until he came to where God was waiting.

"Have you been fasting?" God asked.

"Yes, Sir," the coyote responded.

"Let's see if you have," God said. "Open your mouth."

And the coyote opened his mouth. The resin, savored with *aguamiel*, was between his teeth. God smelled of it and saw it also.

God said, "You have not kept my commandment. You have been to the *aguamiel* in the magueys. Now you cannot have license to eat my children. Only small animals such as lambs, kids, pigs, chickens, rabbits, rats and birds may you eat. These you have license to take wherever you find them, but you will not enter the homes of people or touch my children."

Then the coyote turned and went away crying. He still cries every night for what he lost.

COYOTE BETWEEN TWO SHEEP

As Señor Coyote was going down the road, he met two sheep.[5] "Aha," he said, "I see that I am not going to remain hungry long."

"But, Brother Coyote, what do you mean?" one of the sheep asked.

"I mean," said the coyote, "to invite one of you kinsmen to be my dinner."

"Which one?" the other sheep asked.

"The one that has the best meat," the coyote answered, and he felt for the fat on each of their tails.

"Do not try to eat me," said the first sheep, "I am too lean."

"Do not try to eat me," said the second sheep, "I am too tough."

"Will it take the kidney fat from both of you to make a respectable dinner?" the coyote asked.

"No, no," the sheep said in one voice.

"Then I'll tell you what we'll do," the coyote said. He looked very wise. "I will draw a line here across the road. There, see." And he scratched a plain line in the dirt across the road. "Now, Nephew Lean Sheep, you go down the road about fifty paces to that mesquite bush with the pink just showing on its beans. Now, Uncle Tough Sheep, you go up the road about fifty paces to that all-thorn bush in which the butcher-bird has her nest. You understand?"

"Yes, yes," Lean Sheep and Tough Sheep bleated together.

"Very well," Señor Coyote went on. "You will be at your stations, each looking this way and ready to run. I will count *one, two, three*. When I say 'three,' each of you starts running towards the line here. I will be standing to one side of the road looking right down the line. The sheep that crosses the line first I will slap on the back and at the same time cry out 'First.' To the second sheep I will tell a secret."

The coyote was immensely pleased with his plan. He knew that the separated sheep would not dare run off.

"Nephew Lean Sheep," he cried, "get to your mesquite. Uncle Tough Sheep, get to your all-thorn bush."

The two obeyed.

"Are you ready?" he called.

"Yes, yes, Brother Coyote," the sheep answered.

"One, two, three," the coyote counted. He stood at the edge of the road facing down the line. He looked to the right and Nephew Lean Sheep was coming. He looked to the left and Uncle Tough Sheep was coming. After that he did not take his eyes from the mark. He put one paw up ready to tag the lead racer. Then he put it down. "No," he said to himself low, "they are going to butt into each other exactly at my nose."

His laughter at the joke ended when the sheep rammed into his sides at the same time. Before he got his breath back, Nephew Lean Sheep and Uncle Tough Sheep were two specks side by side close to their master's house.

COYOTE MEETS THE TAR BABY

THE FOLK MIND is beyond any one individual's comprehension. In vitality and fecundity, in creative originality, in variety, and also in repetitive monotony, it is cosmic. For thousands of years, upon dispersed continents, the cumulative folk mind had spun the tales now inseparable from the name of Uncle Remus before a final artist gave them final form. No other story of the Uncle Remus cycle is so well known or is so often reread and retold as "The Wonderful Tar Baby Story." Joel Chandler Harris published it in 1880. In 1888, the great English scholar Joseph Jacobs brought to light a version from India at least fifteen hundred, perhaps two thousand, years old, in which a human being, not an animal, is caught by a sticky figure. Before the end of 1930, Professor Aurelio M. Espinosa, of Stanford University, had amassed a hundred and sixty versions of the story from Asia, Africa, Europe, Spanish and Portuguese America, the Cape Verde Islands, the Philippines, Dutch Guiana, Indian reservations in the United States, and elsewhere. By processes of scholarly speculation he originates the story in India, has it travel thence to Europe and Africa and transmits it to America through the Spanish.[6]

Whatever the origin and whatever the travels of the tale, it is, with the coyote as one of the characters, as much at home in Mexico and among Indians of the West as in India or among Uncle Remus's own people. In the idle days of the 1930's, a Mexican by the usual name of Juan used to work sometimes in our yard at Austin and at other times to visit with me. One summer day while we sat in the shade he took almost an hour tell-

[345]

ing of what passed between Brother Rabbit and Brother Coyote before a monkey made of wax brought the episodes to a climax. Occupation with something else prevented my reducing the tale to writing while the details were all fresh in memory. They did not differ materially from what has been told in print over and over; the originality lay in the telling. The tale I am going to tell now begins with an episode related by Feliz, the guide of Pancho Villa experience whom I have already introduced as teller of the coyote-lion morality; the remainder is an amalgam from Juan and certain printed sources.[7]

One morning a coyote came upon a rabbit.

"Now," he said, "I have you and I am going to eat you."

"All right, Brother Coyote," said the rabbit, "but I have an engagement. If you will just let me meet my obligation, I'll come back and you may eat me. I simply have to see an individual, and also I'd like to dress up before traveling down your red lane."

The coyote agreed and the rabbit loped off.

He came to a muddy water hole in which a dun mare had bogged and was dead. He saw that buzzards and wild animals had eaten all of her but the hide. He saw, too, the dead mare's long black mane. He gnawed off some of the hairs and began plaiting them into his little short tail.

All this took him a long time and the coyote meanwhile was growing very impatient. "That rabbit," he said, "has fooled me. I should not have let him go. I'll trail him down."

So, sniffing and smelling, the coyote took out after the rabbit and before long scented the dead mare. When he got to the bog hole, he saw the rabbit plaiting the mane into his tail.

"Ah, you deceiver," he said, "I have you now."

"Yes," replied the rabbit, "I thought you would come here, and if you did not come, I was going to return at once. I have tended to my business and now I am dressing up as I told you I wanted to dress."

"Well, are you ready?" asked the coyote.

"Yes, Brother Coyote, I am about ready, but you should dress up also. I am a tailor and will help you. Just look at this mare hide. See how soft it is. If it pleases you, I will fit it over your body and legs. Then you can rush through thorns and catch the fat rats scurrying over the prickly pears. See, too, how the dun hide and black trimmings match your complexion."

The coyote was delighted with the idea, and he went to tearing off hide to make the suit. The rabbit draped it over his body and around his legs. Then the rabbit chewed off some catclaw thorns and pinned the hide in place.

"Now come out here in the sunshine," he said.

The coyote hobbled into the sunshine.

"You must remain standing," the rabbit said. "If you don't, the hide won't dry to fit you. You must not lie down and you must not walk. Now we are both dressed up. While your new suit is drying, I shall tell my wife and children good-bye. Then I'll be ready to go any place you please."

"All right," said the coyote, "but be sure to return before sundown."

It was now after midday. The hot sun began to dry the mare's hide on the coyote. He became tired of standing still, but he remembered his tailor's directions and he stood, resting one foot and then another. Finally, he became so weary that he decided to crawl into the shade and lie down, even if the fit of the suit was spoiled. He started to the shade, but the hide was so stiff he could barely move.

There he was when a wild bull and six sharp-horned cows came to the mud hole to drink. He tried to run, but could not. They smelled him and with a bellow rushed up and tossed him with their horns until the thorn fastenings came loose. He was too stiff to run, but he dodged into low chaparral and then sneaked away. He was not singing a love song. He had an idea where that rabbit could be found.

[347]

The next evening he went to a garden kept by an old man and an old woman. It grew beans and chile, and the plants were just up, the way rabbits like them. The old man and the old woman had set a snare.

The dew was making all smells fresh when the coyote came to the garden by moonlight, and he smelled the rabbit before he saw him. He need not have been so cautious. There the rabbit was in the snare, pulling so hard that his eyes stuck out even farther than usual.

"Why, Brother Rabbit," the coyote said, "it can't be that you have decided to hang yourself?"

"I should say not, Brother Coyote," the rabbit replied. "There is a chance to everything. It happened that when I came here a little before dusk, the kind-hearted old man and the kind-hearted old woman who plant fresh vegetables for us every spring saw me. 'He is the very man,' the old woman said to her husband. Then before I knew it, he had roped me. I thought sure they were going to kill me, but, imagine, I am 'the very man' to whom they want to marry their daughter. They left me tied here and are coming back with her right away. I thought at first that I was lucky, but I have decided that she will be too big to be my wife. When you came up I was trying to break away and run off."

"Ah, Brother Rabbit," the coyote said, "this being the case, I will not eat you as I was intending. That girl will not be too big for me. Here, I'll pull the loop from around your neck and get in it myself and take your place. You scoot."

The exchange was made. Soon the coyote heard the old man asking the old woman just where the snare had been placed.

"Why, look what's in it!" the old woman said. With that the old man whacked down with his stick; the coyote gave a desperate leap, broke the snare and ran off.

"That deceiver will be back here just the same tomorrow

evening," the coyote said to himself. "Then he won't be here any more."

But the old woman had her plan too. She knew a muleteer down the road who always had more beans and chile in his garden than anybody else. She went to him and asked him how he kept the rabbits out. He told her to make a monkey out of wax and put it in the middle of the garden. She got some chicle gum and made an image exactly like a little monkey and put it in the garden.

That night, sure enough, the rabbit came again. He saw the little monkey there in the middle of the garden and he walked up to him and said, "What are you doing here?"

The image said nothing.

"You have no business in our garden, and if you don't explain I'm going to slap you," the rabbit said.

The image said nothing.

"Take that," and the rabbit struck the image with his right hand. It stuck.

"Loose my hand or I'll box your ears with my other," the rabbit said.

The image did not move.

"Another time," and the rabbit banged with his left hand. It stuck.

"Look here, little monkey, you'd better turn my hands loose right now or I'll show you how I can kick."

The image did not move. The rabbit kicked once, twice, and both feet were stuck.

"Little monkey," he said, "you'd better turn loose now, or you'll learn how my head can butt a hole through your stomach."

The image said nothing.

"Hold your breath," the rabbit cried. He butted, and his head was stuck as fast as his hands and feet.

The old man and the old woman heard him. They came with

a sack and the old man jerked the rabbit off the wax monkey and put him into the sack.

"Old woman," he said, "this is the fattest rabbit I ever felt. Quick, let's boil him and have a feast."

"Good, with a little garlic," she said. "Tie the sack and leave him here, while we make the fire and put water in the pot."

He tied the sack, and both rushed to make the fire and put on the pot. Now the coyote came. His nose told him what his eyes did not see.

"Oh, Brother Rabbit," he said, "this is a peculiar way in which you await your destiny."

"Peculiar, yes, Brother Coyote," the rabbit answered. "The kind-hearted old man and the kind-hearted old woman are even kinder than I expected. Raise your nose. What do you smell?"

"I smell garlic."

"Raise your ears. What do you hear?"

"I hear a big spoon stirring in an iron pot."

"Raise your eyes. What do you see?"

"I see the flicker of a fire in the kitchen."

"Exactly," said the rabbit. "The pot is to boil soup in. The garlic is seasoning the meat. I came along just as the old man and the old woman were getting everything ready. They insisted that I share the soup with them. They made me promise not to run away, and then they put me inside the sack so they would be sure to have me for company."

"Well, this is hospitality," said the coyote.

"Brother Coyote," the rabbit said, "if you will promise never to molest me again, I will let you share the soup. You will get acquainted with these kind-hearted people and there will be soup for you whenever you want it."

"It is a trade, Brother Rabbit."

The coyote untied the sack, the rabbit got out and scooted away and the coyote took his place.

There he was lying when the old man came for the rabbit. He

picked up the sack. "How heavy he has grown!" he said. He carried the sack to the kitchen.

"The water is ready for the meat," the old woman said.

"He will skin easier if we scald him first," the old man said, and doused the sack into the pot.

The coyote leaped out of the sack and out of the water at the same time. He still had his hair, and he went crying into the brush.

"I went in one end of the canyon and came out the other."

NOTES

The publishers of T. E. Lawrence's Revolt in the Desert queried him on his inconsistent spellings of the name of a she camel as Jedha on one page and Jedhah on another. He replied: "She was a splendid beast."

I · THE FATHER OF SONG-MAKING

[1] Wallace, Ernest, "Some Explanatory Origins in Comanche Folklore," *West Texas Historical Association Year Book*, Abilene, Texas, 1947, XXIII, 65–66.

[2] Forde, C. Daryll, *Ethnology of the Yuma Indians*, University of California Press, Berkeley, California, 1931, 250.

[3] Haile, Father Berard, *Origin Legend of the Navajo Flintway*, University of Chicago Press, Chicago, 1943, 101.

[4] Coolidge, Dane and Mary Roberts, *The Last of the Seris*, 188, 199. Published by E. P. Dutton and Company, New York, 1939, and quoted with permission.

[5] This version was given to me by my friend Joe Roach, of Laredo, Texas, in the time of ripe corn in 1933. He knew it from his own childhood. Somehow the Englished words do not say the same thing as the Spanish:

THE LEADER: *"Al maiz morado."*
THE MATE: *"Para qué?"*
THE LEADER: *"A hacer atole."*
THE MATE: *"Con que lo meneas?"*
THE LEADER: *"Con la cola, con la cola."*
THE MATE: *"No es de hueso, no es de hueso."*
THE LEADER: *"Sí, es de hueso, sí, es de hueso."*

[6] DeSmet, P. J., *Letters and Sketches*, Philadelphia, 1843, 122–123.

[7] Russell, Osborne, *Journal of a Trapper*, . . . *1834–1843*, Boise, Idaho, 1921, 131. See also Washington Irving's account of Buckeye, a Delaware Indian, in Chapter 40 of *The Adventures of Captain Bonneville*.

[8] Alter, J. Cecil, *James Bridger*, Salt Lake City, 1925, 449. See also page 421.

[353]

[9] Grinnell, George Bird, *Blackfoot Lodge Tales*, published by Charles Scribner's Sons, New York, 1913, 261; "Wolves and Wolf Nature," in *Trail and Camp-Fire*, The Book of the Boone and Crockett Club, edited by George Bird Grinnell and Theodore Roosevelt, New York, 1897, 152–153.

[10] Schultz, James Willard, *My Life as an Indian*, Houghton Mifflin Company, Boston, 1935, 268.

[11] Coolidge, Dane and Mary Roberts, *The Last of the Seris*, E. P. Dutton and Company, New York, 1939, 189.

[12] Gilfillan, Archer B., *Sheep*, published by Little, Brown and Company, Boston, 1929, 169–170.

[13] Webb, W. E., *Buffalo Land*, Philadelphia, 1873, 230.

[14] Baylor, Frances Courtenay, *Juan and Juanita* (first published in 1886), Houghton Mifflin Company, Boston, 1915, 67–68.

[15] Drannan, Captain William F., *Chief of Scouts, As Pilot to Emigrant and Government Trains, Across the Plains of the Wild West of Fifty Years Ago*, Thomas W. Jackson Publishing Company, Chicago, 1910, 111–112, 123–124.

[16] Coe, Urling C., *Frontier Doctor*, published by The Macmillan Company, New York, 1939, 32–36. Used by permission.

[17] *Fore and Aft; or, Leaves from the Life of an Old Sailor*, by "Webfoot," Boston, 1871, 301.

[18] The end of the story of "The Young Hunter," as told by Frank Hamilton Cushing, in *Zuñi Breadstuff*, Museum of the American Indian, Heye Foundation, New York, 1920, 515.

[19] Seton, Ernest Thompson, *Lives of Game Animals*, Doubleday, Doran & Company, Garden City, N. Y., 1929, Vol. I, Pt. II, 416–417.

[20] Sterling, George, from "Father Coyote" in *Beyond the Breakers and Other Poems*, A. M. Robertson, San Francisco, 1914.

II · *ADAPTATION*

[1] *History of the Expedition under the Command of Lewis and Clark*, edited by Elliott Coues, New York, 1893, I, 297.

[2] Thomas Say's Notes in *Account of an Expedition from Pittsburgh to the Rocky Mountains, . . . under the Command of Maj. S. H. Long*, London, 1823, I, 153–155.

[3] *History of Mexico*, by Clavijero, translated by Charles Cullen, London, 1787, II, 282; also, I, 42–43.

[4] Ruxton, George Frederick, *Life in the Far West*, New York,

1849; citation from edition of 1924 (Macmillan, New York) under title of *In the Old West*, 118. Lieutenant Abert, in Emory, W. H., *Notes on a Military Reconnaissance from Fort Leavenworth, in Missouri, to San Diego, in California*, Ex. Doc. No. 41, Washington, 1848, 402. Houzeau, Jean Charles, *Études sur les facultés mentales des animaux*, 1872, II, 463 (cited by Kropotkin, *Mutual Aid;* I have been unable to consult Houzeau myself). Emory, W. H., *Report on the United States and Mexican Boundary Survey*, Washington, 1857, 1859, II, page 16 in Baird's "Mammals of the Border." Audubon, John J., and Bachman, John, *Quadrupeds of America*, New York, 1852, II, 153–154. Vivian, A. Pendarves, *Wanderings in the Western Land*, London, 1879, 172.

⁵ Cox, Ross, *Adventures on the Columbia River*, two volumes, London, 1831. Citation is from reprint by the California State Library, San Francisco, 1941, I, 40.

⁶ *Journal of Rudolph Friederich Kurz*, translated by Myrtis Jarrell and edited by J. N. B. Hewitt, Smithsonian Institution, Bureau of American Ethnology, Washington, 1937, 298. Kurz went west in 1847.

⁷ Gregg, Josiah, *Commerce of the Prairies* (1844), XX, 274, in *Early Western Travels*, edited by Thwaites (1904–1907).

⁸ Hastings, Lansford Warren, *The Emigrant Guide to Oregon and California*, Cincinnati, 1857; page 98 in 1929 reprint by Princeton University Press, Princeton, New Jersey.

⁹ Grinnell, George Bird, *Blackfoot Lodge Tales*, New York, 1892, 240–241. "The stakes for the stockade were placed at an angle of about forty-five degrees a few inches apart, all pointing towards the center of the circle. At one place, dirt was piled up against the stakes from the outside, and the wolves climbing up on this, jumped down into the enclosure, but were unable to jump out."

¹⁰ Parkman, Francis, *The Oregon Trail*, first published in 1847; Henry Holt and Company, New York, 1918, 318, 321, 347, 348–349.

¹¹ Powers, Stephen, *The Tribes of California*, in *Contributions to North American Ethnology*, Vol. III, U. S. Department of the Interior, Washington, 1877, 379.

¹² Burton, Richard F., *The City of the Saints*, London, 1861, 219, 233.

[13] Almirall, Leon V., *Canines and Coyotes*, The Caxton Printers, Caldwell, Idaho, 1941, 41 and *passim*.

[14] Evarts, Hal G., "The Spread of the Coyote," in *Saturday Evening Post*, December 15, 1925, 44.

[15] Bailey, Vernon, *Mammals of New Mexico*, Washington, D. C., 1931, 315.

[16] Young, Stanley P., *Sketches of American Wildlife*, The Montreal Press, Baltimore, Maryland, 1946, 5–6.

[17] Letter to J. Frank Dobie from Clifford C. Presnall, Fish and Wildlife Service, U. S. Department of the Interior, Chicago, Illinois, January 24, 1947.

[18] Lantz, David E., *Coyotes in Their Economic Relations*, U. S. Department of Agriculture, Biological Survey, Bulletin No. 20, Washington, D. C., 1905, 8.

[19] Letter by Victor A. Croley, San Diego, California, in *Country Gentleman*, January 1948, 6.

[20] Borell, Adrey E., and Bryant, Monroe D., *Mammals of the Big Bend Area of Texas*, University of California Press, Berkeley, California, 1942, 18.

[21] Goldman, E. A., "The Coyote as Archpredator," in *Journal of Mammalogy*, Vol. 11 (1930), 325–335.

[22] Ligon, J. Stokley, *History and Management of Merriam's Wild Turkey*, New Mexico Game and Fish Commission, Santa Fe, New Mexico, 1946, 44–45, 70–71.

[23] Lehman, V. W., and Fuller, W. G., "Don Coyote, Arch Enemy of Nesting Bobwhites," in *Texas Game and Wildlife*, Austin, Texas, I (1943), 9ff. *California Fish and Game*, XVII, 283–284.

[24] Burt, William H., *The Mammals of Michigan*, The University of Michigan Press, Ann Arbor, Michigan, 1946, 161. Cahalane, Victor H., *Mammals of North America*, The Macmillan Company, New York, 1947, 254.

[25] Murie, Adolph, *Ecology of the Coyote of the Yellowstone: Fauna Series No. 4*, U. S. Department of the Interior, National Parks Service, Washington, D. C., 1940, 146–148.

III · *TAKING ADVANTAGE OF THE SITUATION*

[1] Williams, O. W., *Historic Review of Animal Life in Pecos County*, undated, privately printed pamphlet (taken from articles

published in the *Fort Stockton Pioneer*, Fort Stockton, Texas, in 1908), 65.

[2] Bailey, Vernon, *North American Fauna No. 25*, U. S. Department of Agriculture, Biological Survey, Washington, D. C., 1905, 184. See Ernest Thompson Seton, *Lives of Game Animals*, Garden City, New York, 1929, Vol. II, Part I, 292.

[3] Grey Owl, *The Men of the Last Frontier*, New York, 1932, 16–17, 89.

[4] Price, Con, *Memories of Old Montana*, The Highland Press, Hollywood, California, 1945, 53. Shoemaker, T., "Kiote," in *The Outlook*, Vol. 101, July 27, 1912, 680.

[5] Warren, Edward Royal, *The Mammals of Colorado*, University of Oklahoma Press, Norman, Oklahoma, 1942, 98–99. Note by Weldon B. Robinson and Maynard W. Cummings in *Journal of Mammalogy*, Vol. 28 (1947), 64. Louis Martin, trapper, Marathon, Texas, told me that he had seen a badger following a coyote more than once. Ernest Thompson Seton, *Lives of Game Animals*, Vol. II, Part I, 302–303, reports an instance.

[6] Sperry, Charles C., *Food Habits of the Coyote*, Wildlife Research Bulletin 4, Washington, D. C., 1941, 43.

[7] Murie, Adolph, *Ecology of the Coyote of the Yellowstone*, U. S. Government Printing Office, Washington, D. C., 1940, 121–122.

[8] Russell, Andrew G. A., "Can Animals Think?" in *Natural History*, December 1946, LV, 478–479.

[9] Murie, *op. cit.*, 140–141.

[10] *Report* of the Chief of the Biological Survey, U. S. Department of the Interior, 1931, 28.

[11] Joseph Grinnell, Joseph S. Dixon and Jean M. Linsdale, *Fur-Bearing Mammals of California*, University of California Press, Berkeley, California, 1937, II, 520. Quoted by permission of the publishers.

[12] See *Journal of Mammalogy*, Vol. 16, 229, for instance of a coyote being killed by a lion it was following.

[13] Robertson, Thomas A., *A Southwestern Utopia*, The Ward Ritchie Press, Los Angeles, California, 1947, 215–216.

[14] See Young, Stanley P., *Sketches of American Wildlife*, Baltimore, Maryland, 1946, 56–57, mainly a résumé from Clavijero.

[15] Murie, Adolph, *op. cit.* (as in Note 7), 33–35, 142.

[16] This is a relationship that we should know more about, and will know when the coyote of the Brush Country has been studied as thoroughly as the coyote of the Yellowstone. A privately printed book in fiction form, *The Two Conspiracies*, by C. L. Patterson (The Christopher Publishing House, Boston, 1928), gives, along with other nature lore from southern Texas, a circumstantial description of the caracara-coyote-rabbit operations, pages 25–27.

[17] Alcorn, J. R., "On the Decoying of Coyotes," *Journal of Mammalogy*, Vol. 27 (1946), 122–126.

IV · CO–OPERATION

[1] Wise, Lieutenant, *Los Gringos*, New York, 1857, 59.

[2] Mills, Enos, *Watched by Wild Animals*, Houghton Mifflin Company, Boston, 1932, 85–86.

[3] Kropotkin, P., *Mutual Aid*, Alfred A. Knopf, New York, 1916, 51.

[4] Bob Beverly sent a condensed form of this account to *Reader's Digest*, which was editorialized into conventional language and published by that magazine, July 1944, 111.

[5] Skinner, M. P., *The Yellowstone Nature Book*, published by A. C. McClurg & Company, Chicago, 1924, 107–108.

[6] Marcy, R. B., *Thirty Years of Army Life on the Border*, New York, 1866, 145, 349–352. Bartlett, John Russell, *Personal Narrative of Explorations and Incidents . . . connected with the United States and Mexican Boundary Commission*, New York, 1854, II, 557–558. Merriam, Hart, "The Prairie Dog of the Great Plains," in *Yearbook of the U. S. Department of Agriculture*, 1901, 260–261. Bailey, Vernon, *Mammals of New Mexico*, North American Fauna No. 53, U. S. Department of Agriculture, Biological Survey, Washington, D. C., 1931, 124.

[7] Grinnell, George Bird, "Wolves and Wolf Nature," in *Trail and Camp-Fire*, The Book of the Boone and Crockett Club, edited by George Bird Grinnell and Theodore Roosevelt, New York, 1897, 200–201. Vernon Bailey, *Mammals of New Mexico*, 313–314, describes other coyote procedures in a dog town.

[8] Sperry, Charles C., *Food Habits of the Coyote*, Wildlife Research Bulletin 4, U. S. Department of the Interior, Washington, D. C., 1941, 9–11.

[9] Holden, W. C., *Rollie Burns*, Dallas, Texas, 1932, 116. Another good account of strategy on an antelope is in Grinnell, Dixon and Linsdale, *Fur-Bearing Mammals of California*, II, 521.

[10] Grinnell, George Bird, as cited in Note 7 above, 191–197.

[11] See Sperry as cited in Note 8 above, 39; Adolph Murie, *Ecology of the Coyote of the Yellowstone*, U. S. Department of the Interior, Washington, D. C., 1940, 100–101.

[12] For an extraordinarily detailed account of the behavior of both deer and coyotes see "A Deer-Coyote Episode," by Victor H. Cahalane in *Journal of Mammalogy*, Vol. 28, No. 1 (1947), 36–39. See also Murie, as cited in Note 11 above, 22, 84; *California Fish and Game*, Vol. 20, 226.

[13] Grinnell, Dixon and Linsdale, *Fur-Bearing Mammals of California*, II, 503–504.

[14] Cahalane, Victor H., *Mammals of North America*, The Macmillan Company, New York, 1947, 252.

[15] Almirall, Leon V., *Canines and Coyotes*, The Caxton Printers, Caldwell, Idaho, 1941, 123.

V · CALL THOU NOTHING UNCLEAN

[1] Steele, James W., *The Sons of the Border*, Topeka, Kansas, 1873, gives (pp. 188–196) about the best early popular exposition in English of the coyote to be found. Mark Twain's noted description of the coyote in *Roughing It* is a caricature, with little knowledge and less sympathy.

[2] Strahorn, Carrie Adell, *Fifteen Thousand Miles by Stage*, New York, 1915, 328–330. George Estes, Oregon humorist, is credited with "The Rawhide Railroad" yarn.

[3] Smithwick, Noah, *The Evolution of a State*, Austin, Texas, 1900, 73–74.

[4] Williams, O. W., *Historic Review of Animal Life in Pecos County*, privately printed by Judge O. W. Williams of Fort Stockton, Texas, n. d., 35–36.

[5] See especially Olaus J. Murie, *Food Habits of the Coyote in Jackson Hole, Wyoming* (1935); Adolph Murie, *Ecology of the Coyote of the Yellowstone* (1940); Charles C. Sperry, *Food Habits of the Coyote* (1941), based on examination of 14,829 stomachs,

with an extensive bibliography to the publications of other examiners. In the *Journal of Mammalogy*, Vol. 11 (1930), 336–353, W. C. Henderson summarized, from field reports, the stomach contents of about 80,000 coyotes.

[6] Barrows, Walter B., and Schwarz, E. A., *The Common Crow of the United States*, U. S. Department of Agriculture, Washington, D. C., 1895, 70.

[7] *Journal of Mammalogy*, Vol. 17, (1936), 169–170. For further snake-eating evidence, see *Journal of Mammalogy*, 26, 33–40.

[8] "White Satan of the Desert," by Vance Hoyt, in the *Desert Magazine*, El Centro, California, March 1940, 14. Dr. Hoyt in a letter to me dated March 10, 1947, supplemented his published account.

[9] Bailey, Vernon, *Mammals of New Mexico*, Bureau of Biological Survey, Washington, D. C., 1931, 221–225. Murie, Olaus J., *Food Habits of the Coyote in Jackson Hole, Wyoming*, U. S. Department of Agriculture, Washington, D. C., 1935, 11–13. Keller, L. Floyd, "Porcupines Killed and Eaten by Coyotes," *Journal of Mammalogy*, 17, 169–170. Sperry, Charles C., *Food Habits of the Coyote*, Washington, 1941, 25.

[10] Gudger, E. W., "Does the Jaguar Use His Tail as a Lure in Fishing?" *Journal of Mammalogy*, Vol. 27 (1946), 37–49.

[11] Murie, Olaus J., *Food Habits of the Coyote in Jackson Hole, Wyoming*, 21.

[12] *Ibid.*, 22.

[13] Barnes, Claude T., *Mammals of Utah*, Bulletin of the University of Utah, Salt Lake City, *circum* 1923, 116. Barnes was a lawyer and wrote his bulletin as a "diversion."

[14] Smithwick, Noah, *The Evolution of a State*, Austin, Texas, 1900, 131, 344.

[15] Taylor, Bayard, *Eldorado*, New York, 1857, 371. Borthwick, J. D., *The Gold Hunters*, New York, 1924, 138–139.

[16] Waugh, Julia Nott, *Castroville and Henry Castro*, San Antonio, Texas, 1934, 40.

[17] Gillett, James B., *Six Years with the Texas Rangers*, Austin, Texas, 1921, 235. See also Alexander Topence, *Reminiscences*, Ogden, Utah, 1923, 26.

[18] Townshend, R. B., *A Tenderfoot in Colorado*, London, 1923, 178–183.

[19] Grey, G. F., *Seeking Fortune in America*, London, 1912, 120–121.

[20] Mathews, John Joseph, *Sundown*, published by Longmans, Green and Company, New York, 1934, 168–169. Quoted by permission of publisher and author.

VI · SCENT AND CURIOSITY

[1] Hall, E. Raymond, *Mammals of Nevada*, University of California Press, Berkeley, California, 1946, 245.

[2] Young, Stanley Paul, *The Wolf in North American History*, The Caxton Printers, Caldwell, Idaho, 1946, 40–41.

VII · TRAPPER AND TRAPPED

[1] Barker, Elliott S., *When the Dogs Barked "Treed,"* The University of New Mexico Press, Albuquerque, New Mexico, 1946, 170–171.

VIII · BIOLOGICAL

[1] Mathews, John Joseph, *Talking to the Moon*, University of Chicago Press, Chicago, 1945, 236. Quoted by permission of publisher and author.

[2] Hamlett, G. W. D., *The Reproductive Cycle of the Coyote*, Technical Bulletin No. 616, U. S. Department of Agriculture, Washington, D. C., July 1938, 12 pp.

[3] Hall, E. Raymond, *Mammals of Nevada*, University of California Press, Berkeley, California, 1946, 248.

[4] Cahalane, Victor H., *Mammals of North America*, The Macmillan Company, New York, 1947, 247.

[5] Grinnell, Dixon and Linsdale, *Fur-Bearing Mammals of California*, II, 488.

[6] Mathews, John Joseph, as cited in Note 1 above, 62–63.

[7] *The Outlook*, CXV, January-April, 1917, 568–571.

[8] *Journal of Mammalogy*, Vol. 28 (1947), 64–65.

[9] *Report* of the Chief of the Biological Survey for 1932, Washington, 1933, 13–14.

[10] Barker, Elliott S., *When the Dogs Barked "Treed,"* University

of New Mexico Press, Albuquerque, New Mexico, 1946, 173. Quoted by permission of publisher.

[11] Hornby, Harry P., *Going Around*, The Hornby Press, Uvalde, Texas, 1945, 71–72.

[12] *Yearbook of the Department of Agriculture*, 1920, 293–294. Goldman, E. A., "The Coyote — Archpredator," *Journal of Mammalogy*, Vol. 11 (1930), 329–330.

[13] "Mad Coyotes in the Brush Country," by O. W. Nolen, *The Cattleman*, Fort Worth, Texas, Vol. XXXIV, No. 5, October 1947, 34 ff.

[14] Palacio, Riva, quoted by Robelo, Cecelio A., in *Diccionario de Aztequismos*, Mexico, D. F., 1912, 107. The dog was important in civilizations of Mexico that had perished before the advent of the Spaniards. See Tozzer, A. M., and Allen, G. M., *Animal Figures in Maya Codices*, Peabody Museum, Cambridge, Massachusetts, 1910, 359–364.

[15] Hunter, Colonel George, *Reminiscences of an Old Timer*, San Francisco, 1887, 82. — "The barking of coyote dogs in the canyon assured us that we had brought the wily savages to bay."

[16] Say, Thomas, Notes, in *Account of an Expedition from Pittsburgh to the Rocky Mountains, . . . under the Command of Maj. S. H. Long*, London, 1823, I, 153–155.

[17] Wilhelm, Paul, Duke of Württemberg, *First Journey to North America*, 1822–1824, translated from the German by William G. Bek, in *South Dakota Historical Collections*, South Dakota State Historical Society, Pierre, South Dakota, 1938, XIX, 377.

[18] Audubon, John J., "The Missouri River Journal," in *Audubon and His Journals*, by Maria R. Audubon, New York, 1900, I, 520–521.

[19] Lord, J. K., *The Naturalist in Vancouver Island and British Columbia*, London, 1866, II, 218.

[20] Richardson, Sir John, *Fauna Boreali-Americana*, 1829, 73, 78, 80, cited by Darwin in *The Variation of Animals and Plants under Domestication*, New York, 1896, I, 22–23.

[21] Coues, Elliott, "The Prairie Wolf, or Coyote: *Canis Latrans*," in *American Naturalist*, Vol. 7 (1873), 385–389.

[22] Darwin, Charles, *The Variation of Animals and Plants under Domestication*, first published in 1868, Chapter I of Volume I, and *passim*.

[23] Allen, Glover M., *Dogs of the American Aborigines*, Bulletin of the Museum of Comparative Zoology at Harvard College, No. 9 in Vol. LXIII, Cambridge, Massachusetts, 1919–1920, 429–517. The work contains an extended bibliography.

[24] Stanley P. Young cites evidence of cross-breeding: "What Was the Early Indian Dog?" in *American Forests*, Vol. 49 (1943), 571 ff., and Vol. 50 (1944), 26 ff.; also in *Sketches of American Wildlife*, Baltimore, Maryland, 1946, 5; further, in *The Wolves of North America* (with E. A. Goldman), Washington, D. C., 1944, 180–186. Lee R. Dice gives a detailed instance of crossing, in "A Family of Dog-Coyote Hybrids," which did not live long enough to establish fertility, *Journal of Mammalogy*, Vol. 23 (1942), 186–192. A. S. Packard trusted absolutely reports on fertility, in "Origin of American Species of Dogs," *American Naturalist*, XIX (1885), 901. Without going into the subject of fertility, Vernon Bailey, in *Biological Survey of Texas*, 1905, 176, recorded that he had seen "several hybrids with erect ears and wolfish appearance" resulting from "not infrequent" crosses between ranch dogs and coyotes. John W. Crook of Monte Vista, Colorado, and other trappers have assured me of the proved fertility of at least some crosses.

IX · IN FIELDS OF PSYCHOLOGY AND SPORT

[1] Grinnell, George Bird, "Wolves and Wolf Nature," in *Trail and Camp-Fire*, edited by Grinnell and Roosevelt, New York, 1897, 202. See also pages 155, 183.

[2] Hoyt, Vance, "White Satan of the Desert," in the *Desert Magazine*, El Centro, California, March 1940.

[3] Grinnell, George Bird, *op. cit.*, 179.

[4] The account of this episode originally appeared in the *San Francisco Chronicle*, March 31, 1878, and was reprinted in *Frontier and Midland*, Missoula, Montana, Vol. 18, 1938, 244–246.

[5] Grinnell, *op. cit.*, 180–183.

[6] Williams, O. W., *Historic Review of Animal Life in Pecos County*, pamphlet, n. d., "Taken from the *Fort Stockton* [Texas] *Pioneer* of the Year 1908," 44–45.

[7] Mathews, John Joseph, *Talking to the Moon*, University of Chicago Press, Chicago, 1945, 185–186.

[8] Lyon, G. F., *Journal of Residence and Tour in the Republiç of Mexico in the Year 1826*, London, 1828, I, 247.
[9] Ward, H. G., *Mexico in 1827*, London, 1828, II, 533.

X · THE COYOTE COMES TO MAN

[1] Richardson, Rupert N. "A Baptist Preacher on the Old Frontier," in *West Texas Historical Association Year Book*, Abilene, Texas, IX (1935), 54.
[2] Roosevelt, Theodore, *Outdoor Pastimes of an American Hunter*, New York, 1905, 105–107.
[3] Lofberg, Lila, and Malcolmson, David, *Sierra Outpost*, published by Duell, Sloan and Pearce, New York, 1941. Permission from both publishers and authors to quote is acknowledged. Mrs. Lofberg, in addition, gave me the use of some of her diary notes.

XI · ROMA, CARLOS AND OTHER CAPTIVES

[1] A good account of a pet coyote is found in *Wild Animal Pets*, by William Lovell Finley and Irene Finley, published by Charles Scribner's Sons, New York, 1928, 59–65. Among the very best of all accounts is that of Bravo, subject of a chapter entitled "The Lonely Coyote," in *The Land of Shorter Shadows*, by Erle Stanley Gardner, published by William Morrow & Company, New York, 1948.
[2] Springer, George T., "The Tame Coyote," *Our Dumb Animals*, May 1918, 181.
[3] Whitney, J. Parker, *Reminiscences of a Sportsman*, Forest and Stream Publishing Company, New York, 1906, 273–274.
[4] Graham, Gid, *Animal Outlaws*, published by the author, Collinsville, Oklahoma, 1938, 52–57. The story of Spotted Tail is here reprinted by gracious permission of the author-publisher. His book narrates an account of another captive coyote named Idaho, who escaped and became a daring and uncatchable killer.

XII · PLAYING DEAD

[1] Evans, Will, *Border Skylines*, Dallas, Texas, 1940, 461–462.
[2] Quoted by Ernest Thompson Seton in *Lives of Game Animals*, Vol. I, Part I, 305.
[3] Adapted from *Old Man Coyote*, by Clara Kern Bayliss, T. Y. Crowell & Company, New York, 1908, 60–62.

XIII · FOLKLORE ODDITIES

[1] Ligon, J. Stokley, *History and Management of Merriam's Wild Turkey*, New Mexico Game and Fish Commission, Santa Fe, New Mexico, 1946, 44–45.

[2] Clavijero, Francisco Javier, *History of Mexico*, translated by Charles Cullen, London, 1787, I, 42–43.

[3] See Mary Austin, *The Flock*, Boston, 1906, 179–182, for an authentic account of coyote attack on sheep.

[4] Nuttall, Zelia, "A note on Ancient Mexican Folklore," in *Journal of American Folklore*, VIII, 127–128.

[5] Seton, *Lives of Game Animals*, Vol. I, Part II, 381.

[6] Williams, O. W., *Historic Review of Animal Life in Pecos County*, Fort Stockton, Texas, 46–47. This is a privately printed pamphlet made up of articles published in the *Fort Stockton Pioneer* during the year 1908.

XIV · COYOTE'S NAME IN TWO TONGUES

[1] Sahagún, Fr. Bernardino de, *Historia General de las Cosas de Nueva España*, Mexico, D. F., 1938, II, 389–390. Sahagún wrote 1560–1575, but his manuscripts were not published until 1829–1830. The Mexico edition referred to is excellent.

[2] Translation graciously made for me by Mr. Vincent L. Eaton, Assistant Chief of Rare Books Division, The Library of Congress, Washington, from pages 4–5 of *Historia Animalium et Mineralium Novae Hispaniae*, by Francisco Hernández, appended to his *Nova Plantarum, Animalium et Mineralium Mexicanorum Historia*, Rome, 1651.

[3] Sahagún, as cited in Note 1, III, 151–152.

[4] For historical treatment of the word, see Cecelio Augustín Robelo, *Diccionario de Aztequismos*, Mexico, D. F., 1912, 103–108; also, Robelo, *Nombres Geográficos Indígenas del Estado de Morelos*, Cuernavaca, Mexico, 1897. Elias Amador, *Nombres Indígenas . . . en el Estado de Zacatecas*, Zacatecas, Mexico, 1897, lists several coyote words; so does Remi Simeon in his extensive *Dictionnaire de la Langue Nahuatl ou Mexicaine*, Paris, France, 1885.

[5] Peñafiel, Antonio, *Nomenclatura Geográfica de México*, Mexico, 1897, *passim*.

[6] Lumholtz, Carl, *Unknown Mexico*, New York, 1902, II, 330.

[1] Gilmore, Melvin Randolph, *Prairie Smoke*, Bismarck, North Dakota, 1921, 17–19, 50–52.

[2] See Frank Hamilton Cushing's relation of "The Corn Priests" in *Zuñi Breadstuff*, Vol. VIII of *Indian Notes and Monographs*, Museum of the American Indian, Heye Foundation, New York, 1920, 107.

[3] Mooney, James, *Myths of the Cherokee*, in 19th Annual Report of the Bureau of American Ethnology, Washington, D. C., 1900, 233–234.

[4] Opler, Morris Edward, "The Coyote Cycle" (especially introductory paragraphs) in *Myths and Legends of the Lipan Apache Indians*, Memoirs of the American Folklore Society, New York, 1940, 106–193; "The Coyote Cycle" (introductory paragraphs especially) in *Myths and Tales of the Chiricahua Apache Indians*, Memoirs of the American Folklore Society, XXXVII, New York, 1942, 28–72; *An Apache Life-Way*, Chicago, 1941, 197, 438–439.

[5] Powers, Stephen, *The Tribes of California*, in *Contributions to North American Ethnology*, Vol. III, under editorship of J. W. Powell, U. S. Department of the Interior, Washington, D. C., 1877.

[6] *Ibid.*, 358–360. I have made numerous changes in the relation of the story.

[7] *Ibid.*, 35–37.

[8] Marcy, Colonel R. B., *Thirty Years of Army Life on the Border*, New York, 1866, 174–178. I have stripped a great deal of verbiage from the account and changed the last paragraph to express Tonkawa meaning. Marcy, taking the description from a major who got the speeches by translation, says that the wolves told the warrior to go out and "rob, kill and steal." There was no owner to rob, no landlord or government to steal from. Every man and every animal, according to Indian philosophy, had a natural right to the food and shelter provided by nature.

[9] Hamilton, W. T., *My Sixty Years on the Plains*, New York, 1906, 40.

[10] See Hodge, *Handbook of American Indians*, which is alphabetically arranged.

[11] Beckwith, Martha Warren, *Mandan and Hidatsa Tales*, Third Series, Vassar College, Poughkeepsie, New York, 1934, 292–293.

[12] Bailey, Vernon, *Mammals of New Mexico*, No. 53 in North

American Fauna Series, issued by U. S. Department of Agriculture, Bureau of Biological Survey, Washington, D. C., 1931, 319, 320.

[13] Frachtenberg, Leo J., *Alsae Texts and Myths*, Bureau of American Ethnology, Bulletin 67, Smithsonian Institution, Washington, D. C., 1920, 191–195. Alsae mythology characterizes tribal lore over Washington, Oregon and northern California.

[14] The story as told here follows the version by Major General O. O. Howard in *My Life and Experiences Among Our Hostile Indians*, published by A. D. Worthington and Company, Hartford, Connecticut, 1907, 553–556. General Howard credits it, with illustrations by a Kiowa artist, to James Mooney. Other versions of the story are told in other tribes. Mooney, in *Calendar History of the Kiowa*, does not tell the story but lists the name of the giant-trickster as Sindi. In Alice Marriott's *Winter-Telling Stories* (of the Kiowas) it is spelled Saynday.

[15] Two collections of tales that bring out this propensity especially well are *Coyote Stories*, by Mourning Dove, especially pages 7, 15–18, published by The Caxton Printers, Ltd., Caldwell, Idaho, 1934; and *Myths and Tales of the Chiricahua Apache Indians*, by Morris Edward Opler, Memoirs of the American Folk-Lore Society, Vol. XXXVII, 1942.

[16] Cushing, Frank Hamilton, *Zuñi Folk Tales*, with a Foreword by J. W. Powell and an Introduction by Mary Austin. Published by Alfred A. Knopf, New York, 1931, 237–242. Reprinted by permission.

XVI · *GOOD MEDICINE*

[1] Vestal, Stanley, *Warpath*, published by Houghton Mifflin Company, Boston, 1934, 127–130. Quoted by permission.

[2] Mooney, James, *Calendar History of the Kiowa Indians*, 17th Annual Report of the Bureau of American Ethnology, Washington, 1898, Part I, 302–305. The episode is also related in Mooney's *Myths of the Cherokee*, 19th Annual Report of the Bureau of American Ethnology, Washington, 1900, 489.

[3] Quoted with abbreviations and with permission of the copyright holders, from *Long Lance*, by Chief Buffalo Child Long Lance, published by the Cosmopolitan Book Corporation, New York, 1928, 180–188.

[4] Underhill, Ruth, *The Autobiography of a Papago Woman*,

Memoirs of the American Anthropological Association, No. 46, 1936, 7, 47, 52–53.

[5] *Zuñi Breadstuff*, by Frank Hamilton Cushing, Vol. VIII of *Indian Notes and Monographs*, Museum of the American Indian, Heye Foundation, New York, 1920, 220, 517.

[6] *Ibid.*, "The Young Hunter," 395–515. The story has many divigations and implications. I include only the parts essential to the coyote. As Cushing says, the Zuñis "work up their own experiences into folk tales."

XVII · TALES OF DON COYOTE

[1] In a doctor's thesis, yet unpublished, the University of Texas, 1945, entitled *An Interpretation of the Hispanic Folk Hero, Pedro Urdemales*, Frank Goodwyn sums up the whole tradition.

[2] This cursory analysis of Reynard is derived largely from *The Most Delectable History of Reynard the Fox*, by Joseph Jacobs, London, 1895.

[3] Riley Aiken, "A Pack Load of Mexican Tales," in *Puro Mexicano* (Publication No. XII of the Texas Folklore Society), edited by J. Frank Dobie, Austin, Texas, 1935, 4–7.

[4] Adapted from *El Folklore Literario de México*, by Rubén M. Campos, Mexico, D. F., 1929, 62–64. Another version is in *La Población del Valle de Teotihuacán*, by Manuel Gambio, Mexico, D. F., 1922, II, 304–305.

[5] My friend Dan Storm, now of Glencoe, New Mexico, heard this tale in San Luís Potosí in 1932 and gave me a transcript of it. The plot is contained in his *Picture Tales from Mexico*, Frederick A. Stokes Company, New York, 1941, 14–19.

[6] Espinosa, Aurelio M., "European Versions of the Tar-Baby Story," in *Folk-Lore*, XL (1929), 217–227; "Notes on the Origin and History of the Tar-Baby Story," *Journal of America Folklore*, Vol. 43 (1930), 129–209; "A Third European Version of the Tar-Baby Story," *ibid.*, 329–331; "New Mexican Versions of the Tar-Baby Story," *New Mexico Quarterly*, I (1931), 85–104. The long article in the *Journal of American Folklore* contains a complete bibliography.

[7] Notably *Journal of American Folklore*, Vols. 24, 25, 29, 45.

MY CREDITORS: BOOKS AND PEOPLE

In 1937 Miss Lillian Elizabeth Barclay wrote, under my supervision at the University of Texas, an outstanding Master's thesis on *The Coyote in American Literature*. The following year, the Texas Folklore Society, of which I was editor, published the major part of this thesis, along with related matter, in a volume entitled *Coyote Wisdom* * (Publications of Texas Folklore Society No. XIV, Austin, Texas, 1938.) One of the excellences of this publication is Miss Barclay's bibliography. It does not by any means list all printed folklore pertaining to the ubiquitous coyote, much less all that has been printed concerning the animal from the point of view of natural history; it is, however, the most inclusive bibliography on the coyote that has appeared. I am indebted to Miss Barclay for the use of it.

A bibliography that exhausted the subject would entail an enormous amount of clerical work on the part of one familiar with the fields of folklore and natural history and would be a book within itself. Mr. Stanley Paul Young, Senior Biologist of the U. S. Fish and Wildlife Service and co-author, with Edward A. Goldman, of *The Wolves of North America* and *The Puma: Mysterious American Cat*, has long been writing a book on the coyote; it will, no doubt, contain a bibliography strong in history and natural history like the bibliographies supplied on the other two animals.

A bibliography at the tail end of a book serves three purposes: It suggests new acquisitions to book collectors; it directs students to sources of knowledge; it advertises the author's learning to the unsophisticated and his ignorance to the learned. Many shallow authors parade in their bibliographies all the background and circumjacent reading they happen to have stumbled upon, listing, without page references, works that except in a paragraph or so barely touch on the subject under consideration. For instance, such a bibliography

* "And those that think them wise, are greatest fools." – *Old Play*

[369]

for this book might include *On a Mexican Mustang, through Texas, from the Gulf to the Rio Grande,* by Alex E. Sweet and J. Armoy Knox, Hartford, Connecticut, 1883. An eager scholar taking the hint might begin searching through this unindexed work of 672 pages and, after finding numerous irreverent and not very relevant passages on centipedes, devil's horses, wild horses, hairless dogs and other creatures, at last come to the coyote. He would on page 491 learn that two travelers in a camp one night saw their horses looking at something, which one camper said was "only a coyote," and the other said was "worse than a coyote."

The coyote is such an integral part of the West that hundreds, even thousands, of books of travel, sport and reminiscences have mentioned and frequently made particular observations on the animal. A full bibliography would necessarily include many of these books. Some of the best were written in the last century by British sportsmen with interests transcending shooting. William A. Baillie-Grohman's *Camps in the Rockies* (1882), John Mortimer Murphy's *Sporting Adventures in the Far West* (1879), and A. Pendarves Vivian's *Wanderings in the Western Land* (1879) are examples. Numerous chroniclers from abroad who were not sportsmen but were of venturesome mettle with minds that inquired into nature as well as into Indians, may be represented by Rudolph F. Kurz, whose *Journal* I have quoted. From the time of Lewis and Clark until late in the century many government scientists and military men made reports on the West that embody interesting data on both flora and fauna, not overlooking the coyote. The reports of Randolph B. Marcy, William H. Emory, John Russell Bartlett and Philip St. George Cooke are good examples. The reminiscences of nearly all plainsmen have something about the two kinds of wolves. Materials for the life histories of all the common quadrupeds of America, especially the quadrupeds of the West, lie scattered amid multitudes of unindexed books better known to dealers in rare Americana and to historians than to naturalists.

Most of the sources from which this book has been mosaicked are cited either in the text or in notes, frequently in both — and the notes are congregated so that the bibliographically hungry can skim them. I am debtor to many writings and to many non-writing individuals, both Greek and Barbarian. I wish to evaluate some of the former and at least to name some of the latter.

When I first read several years ago George Bird Grinnell's essay on "Wolves and Wolf Nature," I considered the part, less than thirty pages, dealing with the coyote the most illuminating treatment of the animal I had found. My opinion has not changed. The essay is in one of the Boone and Crockett Club books entitled *Trail and Camp-Fire*, edited by Grinnell and Theodore Roosevelt. As primary editor of five or six Boone and Crockett Club books, George Bird Grinnell assembled the most valuable miscellany of writings on American game animals that has been published in book form. Compared with him, Theodore Roosevelt seems always on the outside of the animal. Grinnell's treatment of the buffalo, in two essays and in the beautifully simple *When Buffalo Ran*, has an imaginative and spiritual quality lacking in the basic works of J. A. Allen and W. T. Hornaday on that subject. His books on the Blackfeet, Cheyennes and Pawnees express a nobility and an essential understanding of Plains Indians that few other writers have attained to. "My son," an old Pawnee said to him, "my mind is big when I look at you and talk to you." He was the leading founder of the National Audubon Society; his life (1849–1938) was full of good works. The quality, compass and volume of George Bird Grinnell's work entitle him to a higher standing as interpreter of the West than he has generally received.

I have a high respect for scientific studies on the coyote, but, considering the whole literature pertaining to the animal, I find the most revealing things — things that enlarge the reader's point of view as well as add knowledge about the animal — to be generally from non-scientific sources. Often they occur only incidentally, as in the books by James Willard Schultz on the Indians of the Northwest. Of recent books, there is in *Talking to the Moon*, by John Joseph Mathews, from whom I have quoted extensively, more comprehension of the coyote as a living creature of the earth than can be found in some of the scientific treatises that regard the coyote as nothing more than a stomach, as unanimated as a pipeline. The basis for Chapter X in this book, *Sierra Outpost*, by Lila Lofberg and David Malcolmson, is not scientific, though it is informed with scientific perspective; I have said that it embodies "the most remarkable account of coyote behavior ever published."

In general works on natural history, treatment of the coyote has received superior treatment in *Mammals of North America* by Victor H. Cahalane, *Fur-Bearing Mammals of California* by Joseph Grinnell, Joseph S. Dixon and Jean M. Linsdale, and in *Lives of Game*

[371]

Animals by Ernest Thompson Seton. One of the pleasantest essays, not without inaccuracies however, on the coyote is in Edmund C. Jaeger's *Denizens of the Desert*, Boston, 1921.

It takes all sorts of parts to make a whole. Very important parts of the whole coyote are the purely physical, the materially measurable — the realm of science proper. A masterpiece in this realm is Charles C. Sperry's *Food Habits of the Coyote*, to which I have referred again and again. Adolph Murie's *Ecology of the Coyote of the Yellowstone*, to which I have referred just as often, is less laboratorial in method and is a contribution to natural history in its most liberal aspects. A wide variety of observable aspects of the coyote has been published in the *Journal of Mammalogy*, and future volumes will probably add to knowledge on the subject. More popular in nature, *Natural History*, published by the American Museum of Natural History, is a continuing source for information.

Fictional treatments of the coyote have not generally added much to understanding. However, *The Yellow Breed*, by Hal G. Evarts (Little, Brown and Company, Boston, 1921), which is about a cross between a coyote and a lobo, contains many realities as well as enlightened sympathy concerning the coyote kind.

Now and then any searcher for facts finds fresh, firsthand observations in obscure publications, often privately printed. The two such that I have found most meaty on the coyote are (1) *Historic Review of Animal Life in Pecos County*, by O. W. Williams, which ran serially in the Fort Stockton, Texas, *Pioneer* (a weekly newspaper) in 1908 and was about thirty years later printed at Fort Stockton in pamphlet form; (2) *Under Western Skies*, by Olai Aslagasson, printed in 1923 by the Augsburg Publishing House, Minneapolis, Minnesota.

Folklore has come to be of two kinds. First, there is the folklore, mainly narrative in form, with human and humanistic values, such as Grimm's *Fairy Tales*, the saga of Deirdre as told by Synge, James Stephens and other Irish writers, and the Uncle Remus tales by Joel Chandler Harris. The other kind of folklore has left humanistic values behind and seems to be recorded for the purpose of affording scientific analysis of plot motifs and folk mores. This kind of folklore is a scientific development of modern times; it has its value, but often the human values of it are as non-apparent as vitality is in a poorly stuffed bird. In the wilderness of folklore pertaining to the coyote some tales stand out because the animal, the folk who tell about him, and the writers of their tales are all alive. The tellers, both oral and scriptory, of the good tales have art as well as vitality.

Among the tellers of Indian folk tales about the coyote I have ranked Frank Hamilton Cushing, author of *Zuñi Folk Tales* and *Zuñi Breadstuff*, first. Mary Austin considered him the only scholar in the field of the American Indian possessed of "adequate literary understanding." "He never yields," she says, "to that curious obsession of the American scholar which leads him to regard all aesthetic considerations as 'embellishments,' 'figures of speech,' 'emotional interpretations.' " In a few stories, notably in "The Coyote Song," in *One-Smoke Stories*, Mary Austin herself showed the "literary understanding" that distinguishes all effective tellers of folk tales.

"A man must carry knowledge with him, if he would bring home knowledge," Doctor Johnson said. A recorder of Indian lore who looks only for segregated anthropological and ethnological values will draw out of his sources only those values. Frank Hamilton Cushing has not been the only American ethnologist to transcend ethnology in eliciting Indian lore and transmitting it. In telling Indian coyote stories, Stephen Powers, author of *The Tribes of California*, comes second to him perhaps. Martha Warren Beckwith, in *Mandan and Hidatsa Tales;* Morris Edward Opler, in his books on the Apache Indians, and certain other scientific recorders have put life into their recordings.

Several collections of Indian coyote stories have been published. The best, it seems to me, and it is excellent, is *Old Man Coyote*, by Clara Kern Bayliss (T. Y. Crowell & Company, New York, 1908). Dan Storm's *Picture Tales from Mexico* (Frederick A. Stokes Company, New York, 1941) is composed of coyote stories, divertingly told, collected from Mexicans. Some of the best of Mexican coyote stories are in *El Folklore Literario de Mexico*, by Ruben M. Campos (Mexico, D. F., 1929). The *Journal of American Folklore*, now (1948) in its sixty-first volume, is a repository of many scores of coyote tales from both Indians and Mexicans; a majority of them have been edited by scholars who cite analogues in other collections.

And now I come to individuals who have helped me, a few by correspondence only, most of them by talk, many adding by letter something not completed in conversation. In regarding them I reflect as I have reflected many times on how kindly and gracious people generally are. The list is far from complete. It contains, for instance, none of the names of the storytellers of Mexico, some of which are embodied in the stories themselves; some tellers I knew only by their first names; others were nameless to me. Many little facts and incidents about coyotes have come to me in many places as impersonally as a cup of water.

My most important source of knowledge outside of print has been trappers, including game wardens. Without what they have contributed, the coyote in this book would be a mutilated skeleton. As observer and imparter of facts, both through interviews and through letters, Joe E. Hill, Sr., of Fort Stockton, Texas, stands out. I should like to particularize several other individuals but only record their names.

J. F. Barnes, Waco, Texas; Ed Bateman, Knox City, Texas; R. E. Bateman, Fish and Wildlife Service, Billings, Montana; Frank Beckwith, Delta, Utah; Bob Beverly, Lovington, New Mexico; George Bigford (deceased), Carrizo Springs, Texas; Don Biggers, Stephenville, Texas; Warren Bloys, Billings, Montana; Ray Brotherton, Comstock, Texas; William James Burns, Del Rio, Texas; Mrs. Ruth Lapham Butler, and her assistant, Mrs. Barbara B. McNeil, of the Ayer Collection, in the Newberry Library, Chicago; A. B. Bynum, Uvalde, Texas; E. C. Cates, Fish and Wildlife Service, Albuquerque, New Mexico; John W. Crook, Monte Vista, Colorado.

J. J. Dent, Kerrville, Texas; Fred M. Dille, Nogales, Arizona; Miss Ruth Dodson, Mathis, Texas; Vincent L. Eaton, Library of Congress, Washington, D. C., who graciously translated the Latin of Hernández (Chapter XIV); Houston Ellis, Eagle Pass, Texas; Henry Fletcher, Marfa, Texas; Ira Franks, Del Rio, Texas; H. C. (Pete) Gamison, Eagle Lake, New Mexico; John Gatlin, Fish and Wildlife Service, Albuquerque, New Mexico; John Gould, Wichita Falls, Texas; Gid Graham, Collinsville, Oklahoma; Ross Graves, Fort Davis, Texas; Don Alberto Guajardo (deceased), Piedras Negras, Coahuila, Mexico; W. S. Hall, Dripping Springs, Texas; Joe E. Hill, Sr., Fort Stockton, Texas; Vance Joseph Hoyt, West Los Angeles, California; A. L. Inman, Cliff, New Mexico; Darwin Ivy, Marfa, Texas; Asa C. Jones, Alpine, Texas; Dr. E. B. Kamback, Fish and Wildlife Service, Denver, Colorado.

C. R. Landon, District Agent (for Texas) of the Fish and Wildlife Service, San Antonio, Texas; Mrs. Edith C. Lane, El Paso, Texas; Louis H. Laney, Fish and Wildlife Service, Albuquerque, New

Mexico; Tom Lea, Sr. (deceased), El Paso, Texas; J. Stokley Ligon, Carlsbad, New Mexico; Loyd Ligon, Fort Stockton, Texas; Mrs. Lila Lofberg, Isabella, California; Mrs. Estelle McCracken, Sinton, Texas; Brownie (N. L.) McNeil, Trinity University, San Antonio, Texas; Gus McGuiness, Nueva Casas Grandes, Chihuahua, Mexico; David Malcolmson, Potomac, Illinois; J. H. Maltsberger, Cotulla, Texas; Louis Martin, Marathon, Texas; John Joseph Mathews, The Blackjacks, Pawhuska, Oklahoma; Fred Messer, Sealy Lake, Montana; J. W. Montgomery, Langtry, Texas; Miss Davis Monts, Washington, D. C.; Adolph Murie, Research Biologist, Fish and Wildlife Service, Mount McKinley, Alaska; Olaus J. Murie, Moose, Wyoming.

O. W. Nolen, Odem, Texas; Walter Perry, Missoula, Montana; Elonzo G. Pope, Fish and Wildlife Service, Lubbock, Texas; Jack Potter, Clayton, New Mexico; Con Price, Napa, California; A. Phimister Proctor, Wilton, Connecticut; Joe Roach, Laredo, Texas; Weldon B. Robinson, Denver, Colorado; C. B. Ruggles, somewhere in some mountains.

Ross Santee, Arden, Delaware; F. R. Seyffert, Cusihuiriachic, Chihuahua, Mexico; Guy Skiles, Langtry, Texas; Louis C. Slothower, Colorado Springs, Colorado; Robert Snow, Kerrville, Texas; Marcus Snyder and his son Ed, Billings, Montana; D. A. Spencer, Fish and Wildlife Service, Denver, Colorado; Al Stephenson, White Sulphur Springs, Montana; Luke Stillwell, Quemado, Texas; Charlie Stone, Fort Stockton, Texas; Dan Storm, Glencoe, New Mexico; B. F. Sylvester, Omaha, Nebraska; Miss Nina Sue Taylor, Fort Worth, Texas; Herbert Ward, Catarina, Texas; Justus C. Ward, Fish and Wildlife Service, Denver, Colorado; Guy West, Valentine, Texas; Bryan Wildenthal, San Marcos, Texas; J. R. Williams, San Marino, California; Ray Williams, Alpine, Texas; Sam Woolford, *San Antonio Light*, San Antonio, Texas; Stanley Paul Young, United States Fish and Wildlife Service, Washington, D. C.

Over a period of years numerous parts of this book have appeared in a variety of magazines: *Arizona Highways, American Mercury, Country Gentleman, Living Wilderness, Natural History, New Mexico Quarterly, New York Herald Tribune Magazine, Pacific Spectator, Saturday Evening Post, Sheep and Goat Raiser, Southern Agriculturist, Southwest Review, This Week, True, Western Sportsman;* also in the Sunday issues of these Texas newspapers:

Austin American-Statesman, Dallas Morning News, Houston Post, San Antonio Light, Valley Evening Monitor. The editors of all these publications are thanked for releasing book rights to such coyote material as they published. A lecture entitled "Animal Tales of the Southwest" that I delivered at the Lawrenceville School in New Jersey was incorporated in *A Man's Reach*, edited by Thomas H. Johnson and published by G. P. Putnam's Sons, New York, 1947. Two or three coyote tales and something of my philosophy on the traditional American attitude towards nature are contained in that lecture. Permission to use the material has been graciously granted by both Professor Johnson and the publisher.

The author of any composition in which thought and art are integrant owes debts to the moulders of the ways in which he looks at a subject as well as to the sources of his subject matter. Many of these debts, however, are too subtle, too complex and too profound for precise reckoning. Only to suggest the creditors of this category of debts, I name here the bullbats, more accurately called night-hawks, that used on spotted wings to hunt the evening air, often breaking the silence with downward zoom, over a valley in front of the ranch home where as child and youth I had time "to stand and stare." From these bullbats and from other illiterate instillers of a love of harmony this long-time listener to, and now transmitter of, the voice of the coyote owes more than is recordable. They belong to an autobiography rather than to a bibliography.

INDEX

INDEX

Russell, Osborne, 16
Ruxton, George Frederick, xi–xii, 17, 28, 34, 127, 155

Sahagún, Bernardino de, 248, 256
Salmon, 121
Sandhill cranes. See Cranes
Santee, Ross, 7n., 135, 375
Say, Thomas, 34–35, 177
Scent post, 140
Schultz, James Willard, 17, 371
Screwworms, 145
Seri Indians, 10, 20
Seton, Ernest Thompson, 30, 93–94, 163, 371
Seyffert, F. R., 234, 375
Shark-sucker fish, 84
Sheep, 40, 41, 43–47, 51, 53, 66, 83, 96, 118, 136, 138, 150, 153, 156–158, 167–168, 202n., 245–246, 249, 272; and coyote, 343–344
Sheepherder, 40, 59, 245–246
Sheepmen, 44, 171
Shenobe, 285
Shoshonies, 16
Siberian deer, musk, 143
Simpson, Sloan, 194
Sin-ka-líp (Imitator), 278
Sinti, of Kiowa mythology, 274–278
Sioux Indians, 266, 287–288
Skäta, magpie character, 211–212
Skiles, Guy, 78, 375
Skinner, M. P., naturalist, 87–88
Skunk, 17, 44, 46, 50, 52, 60, 91, 114n., 143, 149, 150; and coyote, 336–337
Slaughter, W. J., 239–240
Slothower, Louis C., 133, 375
Smell, sense of. See under Coyote
Smith, Thomas, Life of a Fox, 98n.
Smithwick, Noah, 108, 124
Snake Indians, 16
Snow, Robert, 375
Snyder, Ed, 40, 375
Snyder, Marcus, 375
Sonora, 27
Sotol, 117
South Texas Wolf Hunters Association, 191
Sowell, Bert, 127
Spanish attitudes towards Indians, 254
Spanish influence on coyote folklore, 302–308

Sparrow hawk, 21
Spencer, D. A., 375
Sperry, Charles C., 96, 372
Spider, pet, 153
Springer, George, 214
Squirrel, xi, 16, 196, 197, 198
Staked Plains, 90, 109
Standish, Melman, 143
Stell, H. G., 8n.
Stephenson, Al, trapper, 60, 325, 375
Sterling, George, 30
Stillwell, Luke, 118, 152–160, 375
Stone, Charlie, 105, 118, 375
Storm, Dan, 368, 373, 375
Straw, Nat, trapper, 136–137
Superstitions concerning coyotes, 15–19, 21, 23, 135–139, 146, 237–257 passim
Sylvester, B. F., 240, 375
Symbiosis, 60–65, 83–84

Tarahumare Indians, 331
Tarbaby and coyote, 345–351
Taylor, Nina Sue, 217–221, 375
Tayoltita, Durango, 238
Telepathy in animals, 63
Terrapin, 155–156; and coyote, 333–334. See also Tortoise
Tezcatlipoca, 253
Tillous, Barnes, 87
Tlacoyote, 59, 69. See also Badger
Toads, 154
Tonkawa Indians, 270
Tormés, Lazarillo de, 302
Tortoise, 120, 148. See also Terrapin
Townshend, R. B., 127–128
"Tracks in the sky," 79
Trail drivers, 42, 97
Trap, steel, 19n., 49, 86, 110, 123, 134–151, 156–160, 168, 210
Trappers, 132–161
Truchas Peaks, 41
Turkey, wild, xi, 16, 52, 237, 241
Turner, Jeff, 174
Turtles, sea, 121
Twain, Mark, 186

Uncle Remus, 264, 306, 345–346
Urdemales, Pedro de, 302–305
U. S. Biological Survey, 34, 43, 165, 172, 272

[385]

U. S. Fish and Wildlife Service, 34, 49n., 140, 153
Ute Indian, 126

VALLEJO, GENERAL, OF CALIFORNIA, 7
Vaqueros, Mexican, singing, 4-5, 12
Villa, Pancho, 125
Vivian, A. Pendarves, 36, 370
Vultures, 39. See also Buzzards, Zopilotes

WARD, H. G., 191
Ward, Herbert, trapper, 121, 375
Ward, Justus C., 375
Warren, Edward Royal, 65
Watermelons, 114-115, 187-188
Weasel, 86
Weather signs, 12-15, 92
Webb, W. E., 22
West, George, 50-51
West, Guy, trapper, 139, 375
Wied, Prince of, 36
Wildcat, 44, 91, 126, 136, 180, 329
Wild Horse Prairie, Arizona, 66
Wildenthal, Bryan, 375
Wilhelm, Paul, Duke of Württemberg, 177
Williams, Clayton, 105
Williams, J. R., 375

Williams, Judge O. W., 109, 187-188, 249, 372
Williams, Ray, 101, 375
Wise, Lieutenant, of Los Gringos, 85
Wolf, lobo (gray), xi-xii, 23, 32, 33, 35, 36, 38, 47, 89, 91, 136, 137, 147, 156, 172, 180-181, 182, 214, 229, 233-234, 246, 249, 265, 270-271, 289-294
Wolf Indians, 271
"Wolf mutton," 91n.
"Wolf of the plains," 33
Wolf, prairie. See Prairie wolf
Wolves, Russian, 98n.
Woodpecker, 23, 84, 274
Wood ticks, 81-82
Woolford, Sam, journalist, 98, 375
Wren, Canyon, 28
Wurzbach, Emil Frederich, 83n.

YELLOW JACKETS, 329
Yellowstone National Park, 54-55, 65, 73, 88, 194
Yosemite Indians, 146
Young, Stanley P., biologist, 136, 170n., 369, 375
Yucca, 242-245, 335
Yuma Indians, 10

Zopilotes, 121
Zuñi Indians, 9, 29, 264, 295-301